Your Employment
Standards
Questions
Answered –
**Federal and Provincial
Guidance**

Wolters Kluwer
CCH

CCH Canadian Limited
300-90 Sheppard Avenue East
Toronto Ontario
M2N 6X1
1 800 268 4522
www.cch.ca

6th Edition

DENTONS

Anneli LeGault
Andy Pushalik

Published by CCH Canadian Limited

Important Disclaimer: This publication is sold with the understanding that (1) the authors and editors are not responsible for the results of any actions taken on the basis of information in this work, nor for any errors or omissions; and (2) the publisher is not engaged in rendering legal, accounting or other professional services. The publisher, and the authors and editors, expressly disclaim all and any liability to any person, whether a purchaser of this publication or not, in respect of anything and of the consequences of anything done or omitted to be done by any such person in reliance, whether whole or partial, upon the whole or any part of the contents of this publication. If legal advice or other expert assistance is required, the services of a competent professional person should be sought.

Edited by:

David Iggulden, B.A., M.L.S.

Library and Archives Canada Cataloguing in Publication

LeGault, Anneli
Your employment standards questions answered — federal and provincial guidance–6th ed. by Anneli LeGault and Andy Pushalik.
Includes index.
ISBN 978-1-55496-597-7

1. Labour laws and legislation — Canada 2. Employee rights — Canada.
I. Pushalik, Andy II. Title.

KE3244.L43 2008   KF3455.L43 2008   344.7101   C2008-906325-2

Typeset by CCH Canadian Limited.
Printed in the United States of America.

ACKNOWLEDGEMENT

We would like to acknowledge the assistance of a number of people at Dentons Canada LLP in the preparation of this edition of the book. Summer students Aiwen Xu and Ben Iscoe and articling students Matt Maynard and Jackson Phillips provided us with research assistance on this project. Our librarian, Ian Colvin, and our research specialist, Rossina Malik, also deserve our thanks for their ongoing assistance. In addition, we acknowledge the contribution of our Montreal colleague, Marie-Noël Massicotte, who provided helpful comments on the pay equity chapter. Finally, we wish to express our gratitude to Dentons Canada LLP for its continued support in this venture.

Anneli LeGault

Andy Pushalik

PREFACE

Your Employment Standards Questions Answered — Federal and Provincial Guidance provides answers to the most commonly asked questions related to employment standards, wrongful dismissal, human rights, and workplace equity, and covers such topics as maternity and parental leave, termination of employment, hours of work and overtime, vacations, and harassment in the workplace. This book is intended for employers, human resources professionals, employees, consultants, and all those concerned with the employment relationship.

Questions related to unionization, collective bargaining, and collective agreement administration are not covered in this book, except to note where these fields have an impact on the resolution of employment law and human rights issues.

This book covers the legislation from all 14 jurisdictions in Canada: the federal government, the 10 provinces, and the three territories. While the principles underlying employment and human rights law are standard across the country, the details vary. The answers provided attempt to be as detailed as possible, while retaining clarity and brevity. Those who require more detailed information than can be provided in a publication of this type may wish to refer to the comprehensive reporting services provided by Wolters Kluwer CCH in both print and electronic formats.

Legislation in the field of employment and human rights law changes regularly. The information in this book is updated to September 1, 2013.

PENDING SASKATCHEWAN LEGISLATION

On May 2, 2012, the government of Saskatchewan issued a call for submissions in response to a consultation paper on renewal of labour legislation in the province. More than 3,800 written submissions were received by the Ministry of Labour Relations and Workplace Safety.

The purpose of the review was to modernize and simplify the Acts to ensure that they are clear, easy to use, and responsive to the needs of Saskatchewan's employers and employees. The employment standards topics under consideration included:

- application of *The Saskatchewan Employment Act*;

- employment agencies charging fees;

- variable hours of work to meet needs of both employers and employees;

- clarification of overtime provisions;

- adding new leaves of absence such as organ donation and citizenship ceremonies;

- clarification and expansion of annual leave and public holiday provisions;

- notice requirements;

- collection of employees' wages after business closure; and

- indexation of the minimum wage.

On December 4, 2012, *The Saskatchewan Employment Act* was introduced in the legislature. The new employment Act is a consolidation of 12 Acts:

- *The Assignment of Wages Act*;
- *The Building Trades Protection Act*;
- *The Construction Industry Labour Relations Act, 1992*;
- *The Employment Agencies Act*;
- *The Fire Departments Platoon Act*;
- *The Health Labour Relations Reorganization Act*;
- *The Labour-Management Dispute (Temporary Provisions) Act*;
- *The Labour Standards Act*;
- *The Occupational Health and Safety Act, 1993*;
- *The Radiation Health and Safety Act, 1985*;
- *The Trade Union Act*; and
- *The Wages Recovery Act*.

What follows below is the summary of the employment standards amendments and other sections of the new Act that have an effect on human resources.

PART II — EMPLOYMENT STANDARDS

Scope

- Maintain exemption for agriculture workers in the Act, but move all other exemptions to regulations.

Employment Agencies

- Ensure job seekers are not charged a fee by employment agencies for finding a job.
- The penalty for charging a fee is equivalent to the amount of the fee.

Hours of Work

- Overtime is to be paid after eight hours in a day and 40 hours in a week unless a modified work arrangement exists or a permit has been issued.
- Maintain the employee's ability to refuse to work more than 44 hours per week, unless agreed to by the employee.
- Two work arrangements are permitted in the legislation: (1) eight hours per day, five days per week; and (2) 10 hours per day, four days per week.

- Permits continue to be required for longer work periods without a day of rest.

- Incorporate firefighter hours of work provisions in Part II and regulations but maintain current existing provisions.

Leave Provisions

- Add five new leaves — organ donation (maximum 26 weeks); critically ill child leave (37 weeks); crime-related death (104 weeks); crime-related child disappearance (52 weeks); and leave to attend citizenship ceremonies (one day).

- Lower the qualifying period for maternity, parental and adoption leave from 20 weeks to 13 weeks.

- Waive four weeks' notice for leaves, where it is unreasonable to assume that notice can be given.

- Allow the accruing of service, to a maximum of 52 weeks, for nomination/election leave (currently exists for maternity, parental and adoption leaves).

Annual Holidays — No Change

- Maintained current three weeks per year for first nine years, and four weeks after completing 10 years of service or more with an employer.

- Allow employer to create a common date for calculating vacation entitlement as long as it does not reduce entitlements.

Public Holiday Provisions — No Change

- Maintained at 10.

- Continue to allow a public holiday to be moved if approved by the Director of Employment Standards.

Notice Provisions — No Change

- Continue the individual notice requirement which increases from one week's notice for 13 weeks to one year of service to eight weeks' notice for 10 or more years of service.

- Continue the group termination requirement in the Act with the specific requirements in regulations.

Minimum Wage

- Index the minimum wage based on a formula that gives equal weight to the annual change in the average hourly wage and the Consumer Price Index. All increases will be subject to Cabinet approval.

- Remove the Minimum Wage Board.

- Remove the ability for the Director to approve a lower minimum wage for persons with a disability.

Payment of Wages

- Allow for electronic payment of wages.

- Enable the payment of wages by other means in regulations (e.g., prepaid cards).

- Continue the requirement to provide a statement of earnings and deductions.

Collection of Wages

- New provisions to modernize wage collection include creating a legislated payment priority for wage debts owed and introduce enhanced enforcement tools to assist in recovery of outstanding wage debts.

Assignment of Wages

- Continue to restrict what an employer can deduct from an employee's wages.

Equal Pay

- Stipulate that no two people can be paid a different wage based upon a prohibited ground found in *The Saskatchewan Human Rights Code*.

Discriminatory Actions

- Continue to prohibit an employer from taking any discriminatory action against an employee for reporting an offence to a lawful authority.

- Prohibit discrimination for requesting or taking maternity, parental, adoption, nomination, and reservist leaves, or requesting modified duties or reassignment due to disability, illness or maternity.

Fines

- Increase the maximum fine from $10,000 to $50,000.

Time Banks

- Allow for the establishment of time banks for overtime hours worked on agreement of employer and employee.

The Wages Recovery Act

- Ensure employees employed under a contract of employment are paid their wages, and where this has not occurred enable the collection of wages through the processes provided for in Part II.

PART IV — APPEALS

- Create a single avenue for appeals of employment standards and occupational health and safety complaints.

- Appeals from employment standards and occupational health and safety will continue to be heard by adjudicators appointed under Part II and Part III.

- The powers and duties of the adjudicators are maintained.

- The Labour Relations Board ("LRB") will be responsible for assigning adjudicators to hearings.

- Decisions of adjudicators can be appealed to the LRB.

- Decisions of the LRB can be appealed to the Court of Appeal.

- Adjudicators are to consider mitigation when rendering a decision related to lost wages.

The new Act received Royal Assent on May 13, 2013 but is not yet in force. In the meantime, the Government of Saskatchewan has commenced a second consultation process inviting interested stakeholders to comment on the Regulations associated with the predecessor legislation.

TABLE OF CONTENTS

Page

Acknowlegement iii

Preface v

Pending Saskatchewan Legislation vii

Chapter

1   Defining and Regulating the Employment
Relationship 1

2   Minimum Age of Employment 13

3   Minimum Wages and Call-In Pay 19

4   Hours of Work and Overtime Pay 27

5   Statutory Holidays 43

6   Vacations with Pay 55

7   Leaves of Absence 71

8   Payment of Wages 119

9   Personnel Records 129

10   Termination of Employment 137

11   Wrongful Dismissal 169

12   Discrimination in Employment 181

13   Harassment at Work 201

14   Equal Pay and Pay Equity 213

15   Employment Equity 227

16   Enforcement of Employment Standards 237

Appendix 249

Topical Index 257

Chapter 1

DEFINING AND REGULATING THE EMPLOYMENT RELATIONSHIP

Page

INTRODUCTION 2

DEFINING THE EMPLOYMENT RELATIONSHIP — INTRODUCTION 2

Is There a Definition of an Employee? 3

What Should the Parties Do To Avoid Confusion and Possible Disputes? 4

Volunteers and Interns Are Not Employees Are They? 5

When in Doubt, How Would I Apply the Elements of Control, Ownership of Tools, Risk of Profit or Loss, and Integration to the Employment Relationship? 5

LABOUR JURISDICTIONS — INTRODUCTION 6

Why Is It Important To Know Which Law Applies? 6

How Do I Determine Which Law Applies to Me? 7

If the Law in a Particular Province Is Silent on a Particular Topic — For Example, Parental Leave — Do the Federal Labour Standards Provisions in the *Canada Labour Code* Apply? 7

We Have Employees in a Number of Provinces. Because It Is Easy To Administer, We Want To Establish One Set of Employment Standards for All Employees. Can We Do This? 8

How Does the Law Regulate the Employment Relationship? 8

Does Employment Law Cover All Employees? 9

What if the Employment Contract or Collective Agreement Provisions Differ from Employment Law Requirements? 10

What Happens if an Employer Sells the Business, or Merges with Another Company? Do Employees Lose the Rights That Have Been Built Up? 10

CHECKLIST FOR EMPLOYEE/INDEPENDENT CONTRACTOR STATUS 11

1

INTRODUCTION

The employment relationship can be a complex one. This chapter provides an overview of the issues and legislative requirements that define and regulate the relationship. First, it examines the definition of an employee and provides a checklist to help define an employee as opposed to an independent contractor. Second, it explains what "jurisdiction" means, examines why jurisdiction matters from a human resources ("HR") perspective, and provides guidance on how to determine which laws apply to your organization. Third, it summarizes the laws that regulate the relationship and addresses specific issues, such as which employees are covered, the effect of collective agreements, and what happens if a business is sold or amalgamated.

DEFINING THE EMPLOYMENT RELATIONSHIP — INTRODUCTION

Rather than hire additional staff, many organizations look to special skills providers on an as-needed basis. For a number of companies, this results in working relationships involving both employees and independent contractors.

Properly defining the working relationship at the outset as either employment or contractual is critical. Employer duties and obligations under employment standards legislation, such as vacation/vacation pay, notice of termination, payment of wages and overtime, maternity/parental leave, etc., arise only with respect to employees. Payments to employees are processed through the payroll department and require the accurate withholding and remittance of various statutory deductions (i.e., tax, Employment Insurance ("EI"), and Canada/Quebec Pension Plan ("CPP/QPP")). These withholdings and remittances also attract employer contributions that are a significant cost of doing business. Payments to independent contractors, on the other hand, are not considered part of payroll activity, do not attract corresponding employer contributions, and are usually handled through the accounts payable function of the organization. Many independent contractors are required to charge the Goods and Services Tax ("GST") or Harmonized Sales Tax ("HST") on the services they provide.

Failure to properly define the working relationship can be costly to the organization and may result in inconvenient and expensive audits, penalties for failure to withhold and remit, and employment standards complaints.

Q. Is There a Definition of an Employee?

A. Defining the nature of the working arrangement is not easily done. While the provincial employment standards Acts all impose various duties and obligations with respect to an employment relationship, the legislation provides little in the way of a definition of "employee". **Prince Edward Island** and **Newfoundland and Labrador** go a bit further than other jurisdictions by defining a contract of service to mean a contract (written or unwritten) in which an employer reserves the right of control and direction of the manner and method by which the employee carries out the duties to be performed under the contract. In order to determine who is an employee and who is an independent contractor, we must turn to the common law or case law which is discussed below. However, some ministries have developed detailed policies and/or tests for determining whether an individual is an employee. For an excellent and accessible example, see the British Columbia Employment Standards Branch "Interpretation Guidelines Manual" (available on the government's website at www.labour.gov.bc.ca/esb/igm/welcome.htm), which describes the control test, permanency test, specific result test, and economic reality test in detail in its definition of "employee".

The leading case on the distinction between an employee and an independent contractor remains *Wiebe Door Services Ltd. v. The Minister of National Revenue*, Federal Court of Appeal, June 18, 1986 (87 DTC 5025). This test was affirmed by the Supreme Court of Canada in 2001 in *671122 Ontario Ltd. v. Sagaz Industries Canada Inc.* (2002 CLLC ¶210-013). Wiebe Door was in the business of installing and repairing overhead doors. It carried on its business through the services of a considerable number of door installers and repairers, with the specific understanding that they would be running their own businesses, and would therefore be responsible for their own taxes and any contributions for workers' compensation, Unemployment Insurance ("UI"), and CPP. The Minister assessed Wiebe Door for UI (EI) premiums and CPP contributions in respect of these individuals. In determining that the door installers were independent contractors and not employees, the Court applied what is now known as the "fourfold test" of control, ownership of tools, chance of profit, and risk of loss, within the context of the total relationship between the parties. The Court went on to examine the "integration test" (the integration of the workers into the company's business) and noted that it was a useful test, but only if applied from the workers' perspective and not the company's perspective. As you can see, even if both parties agree to characterize a relationship as not being an employee–employer relationship, this is not determinative, and government agencies and tribunals may scrutinize the relationship to determine its true legal nature.

The Supreme Court stated that the central question is whether the person who has been engaged to perform the services is performing them as a person in business on his or her own account. In making this decision, the degree of control the "employer" has over the worker's activities will always be a factor. Other factors to consider include whether the worker provides his or her own equipment, whether the worker hires helpers, the degree of financial risk taken by the worker, the degree of responsibility for investment and management held by the worker, and the worker's opportunity for profit in the performance of the services. It is also helpful if the worker is incorporated, issues invoices, and has other clients.

Q. What Should the Parties Do To Avoid Confusion and Possible Disputes?

A. Ideally, the organization in need of services and the individual providing services share a common intention either to establish an employment relationship or a contractual relationship. The basic terms should be set out in writing and signed by both parties. This is particularly important where the parties have agreed that the individual is an independent contractor and not an employee. The contractor cannot be placed in the group health benefit plan or pension plan. Nor is the contractor paid when not providing services; specifically, the concepts of holidays, vacations, and sick leave do not apply.

The parties need to be aware, however, that simply stating that the individual is not an employee is not sufficient. In the event of a dispute (typically with the Canada Revenue Agency ("CRA") over remittances), the wording of the contract will not override the true essence of the relationship. Nor is the intent of the parties binding on the CRA, other government agencies, and tribunals.

In a case involving dancers engaged by the Royal Winnipeg Ballet, both the CRA and the Tax Court of Canada ruled that the dancers were employees. The Tax Court disregarded the uncontradicted evidence that the dancers and the Ballet shared a common understanding that the dancers were self-employed and were not employees. The dancers were registered for GST purposes and charged GST for their services. In *The Royal Winnipeg Ballet v. Canada (Minister of National Revenue)* (2006 CLLC ¶ 240-004) the Federal Court of Appeal agreed that the central question is whether the person engaged to perform the services is performing them as a person in business on his or her own account. However, in overruling the CRA and the Tax Court of Canada, it looked at the intention of the parties, found that there was no dispute between the parties as to what they believed the relationship to be, and concluded that it is wrong in principle to set aside as worthy of no weight at all the uncontradicted evidence of the parties as to their common understanding of their legal relationship, even if that evidence is not conclusive. Instead, the facts need to be examined in light of this uncontradicted evidence of intention and it needs to be determined whether the facts are consistent with the parties' understanding. Having said that, it is important to bear in mind, when entering into a relationship, that parties to a contract cannot change the legal status of that contract merely by asserting that it is something else.

More recently, the Federal Court of Appeal in *1392644 Ontario Inc., O/A Connor Homes v. MNR* (2013 FCA 85) further clarified and affirmed the role of the parties' intention. The Court set out a two-step process of inquiry to follow when determining the legal nature of the relationship:

(1) ascertain the subjective intent of each party to the relationship (for example, the written contract terms, behaviour including invoicing, registration for GST/HST, form of income tax filings); and

(2) ascertain whether the objective reality sustains the intent (this is often an application of the *Wiebe Door* and *Sagaz* tests above looked at "in light of" the parties' intent).

Bear in mind, however, that the parties' intent cannot trump the reality of the relationship as ascertained through objective facts.

Q. Volunteers and Interns Are Not Employees Are They?

A. It is correct that on rare occasions certain volunteers, student interns, and students on a *practicum* are not employees and do not need to be paid. However, such relationships should be carefully documented and generally avoided due to the legal risk involved. In general, the "volunteer" should not be performing the type of work performed by employees, and the employer should not be deriving a significant benefit from the relationship.

Q. When in Doubt, How Would I Apply the Elements of Control, Ownership of Tools, Risk of Profit or Loss, and Integration to the Employment Relationship?

A. In order to help define the employment or contractor relationship, see the checklist on page 11. The checklist uses the elements set out in the fourfold test above and can be used as a benchmark for the types of factors that would tend to indicate how the relationship would be defined.

LABOUR JURISDICTIONS — INTRODUCTION

In Canada, the power to pass laws ("jurisdiction") is divided between the federal government and the provinces and territories.

The *Constitution Act, 1867* (s. 92), gives the provinces exclusive jurisdiction regarding property and civil rights. From this stems the provincial authority to regulate the employment relationship through the passage of legislation and the establishment of minimum standards. With certain exceptions, local works and undertakings are within provincial jurisdiction.

Each province regulates working conditions for employees, industries, and occupations within its jurisdiction (within that province), principally through an employment or labour standards Act. This is what is meant by jurisdiction, a term that is used throughout this book. Additional statutes and regulations exist in all provinces, governing either particular industries or particular conditions of employment.

Under the *Constitution Act, 1867* (s. 91), the federal government has the authority to regulate and control those industries and undertakings of an interprovincial, national, or international nature, which currently include: shipping, airlines, interprovincial railways, and trucking; telecommunications; radio and television broadcasting; banking; uranium mining; grain elevators and flour and feed operations; companies whose operations have been declared for the "general advantage" of Canada or of two or more provinces; and Crown corporations such as the Canadian Broadcasting Corporation. In accordance with its authority, the federal government enacts legislation, setting minimum standards and conditions of employment for workers engaged in occupations and industries within the **federal** jurisdiction. Approximately 10% of the Canadian workforce is **federally regulated**.

The principal governing legislation for industries falling within the **federal** jurisdiction is the *Canada Labour Code* (R.S.C. 1985, c. L-2, as amended), which is supplemented by a number of regulations.

Both the **Yukon** and the **Northwest Territories** have passed their own employment standards Acts.

On April 1, 1999, the territory of **Nunavut** came into being. The federal legislation creating the new territory declared that **Northwest Territories** legislation will apply to **Nunavut** until the new territory passes its own legislation. Separate **Nunavut** employment standards legislation has not yet been passed. Therefore, those readers needing information on **Nunavut** should refer to the former *Labour Standards Act* of the **Northwest Territories**, as amended by **Nunavut**.

Q. Why Is It Important To Know Which Law Applies?

A. While employment standards laws are fairly similar across Canada, there are still differences between the federal provisions and provincial provisions and from province to province. For example, only **British Columbia** requires overtime to be paid at double time for certain hours, **Saskatchewan** uses a unique formula for calculating vacation pay, minimum vacation varies from two to four weeks, depending on the province, and Boxing Day and Family Day are statutory holidays only in a handful of jurisdictions.

Where you have employees in more than one province, it is extremely important to ensure that each employee's protections and rights with respect to such items as wages, overtime pay, holiday pay, vacations, leaves of absence, and termination are calculated based on the requirements of the province where the employee is working, and not the province where your organization has its head office.

Q. How Do I Determine Which Law Applies to Me?

A. If you are unsure about which employment standards laws apply to your situation, you should first look at the type of industry in which the organization is engaged. The activities of the organization are relevant, not whether the organization was federally or provincially incorporated. As noted above, the **federal** jurisdiction is fairly restricted and covers various types of businesses of an interprovincial, national, or international nature such as shipping, airlines, interprovincial railways and trucking, telecommunications, radio and television broadcasting, banking, uranium mining, and grain elevators. Most employers will find themselves covered by provincial legislation. Please note that the fact that a company operates in more than one province does not make it a **federally regulated** employer. Instead, the employees of each province will be regulated by the local provincial employment or labour standards Act. Therefore, a company in retail sales, for example, with employees in eight provinces, will need to be familiar with eight different pieces of employment standards legislation. Fortunately, the legislation is fairly consistent. Typical employers that fall under provincial legislation include those in retail sales, warehousing, distribution, manufacturing, food services, publishing, maintenance and repairs, construction, accounting, medicine, software development, architecture, consulting services, and real estate.

Q. If the Law in a Particular Province Is Silent on a Particular Topic — For Example, Parental Leave — Do the Federal Labour Standards Provisions in the *Canada Labour Code* Apply?

A. No. A common mistake made by employers is to assume that the labour standards provisions of the *Canada Labour Code* apply when the provincial law is silent (i.e., the legislation does not mention the issue). As noted previously, the provisions of the *Canada Labour Code* only apply to employees in **federally regulated** industries. Where provincial law is silent on a particular topic, it may mean one of a number of things:

- the employer has discretion in developing policies and procedures in that area;

- the issue has been addressed in the administrative policies of the province's employment standards division; or

- the common law (court decisions or case law) has determined the issue.

Where you have a particular question about a topic not addressed in the provincial legislation, you should contact the employment standards division for your province and/or consult an employment law lawyer.

Q. We Have Employees in a Number of Provinces. Because It Is Easy To Administer, We Want To Establish One Set of Employment Standards for All Employees. Can We Do This?

A. Yes, but only if the highest standards are used. For example, a company has employees in **British Columbia**, **New Brunswick**, and **Alberta** and wants to establish a company-wide policy for bereavement leave. **New Brunswick** requires that employees be given up to five consecutive days leave on the death of a person in a close family relationship. In **British Columbia**, employees are entitled to up to three days of leave on the death of an immediate family member. **Alberta** does not require employers to grant any bereavement leave. If a company-wide set of employment standards were established, all employees, including those in **Alberta**, would need to be granted the bereavement leave established by **New Brunswick** law. To develop a complete company policy, this exercise should be repeated for all policies governed by employment standards.

Q. How Does the Law Regulate the Employment Relationship?

A. There are a number of different types of laws governing the employment relationship:

- **Employment standards legislation:** Employment standards legislation has been passed by each of the provincial and two of the territorial governments, as well as by the federal government. Employment standards legislation sets out minimum standards for the working conditions of employees, covering issues such as minimum wages, payment of wages, employee records, hours of work and overtime, vacations with pay, maternity/parental and miscellaneous leaves, statutory holidays, and termination of employment.

- **Human rights legislation:** Human rights legislation attempts to ensure equality of treatment for groups who have historically faced discrimination. One of the areas covered by human rights legislation is the employment relationship. Human rights legislation prohibits employers from discriminating against employees or job applicants. As well, there are some statutes dealing specifically with equality issues in employment, such as pay equity and employment equity statutes.

- **Labour relations legislation:** Labour relations legislation regulates the relationship between employers and trade unions, and sets out the circumstances under which unions may be certified to represent employees, and conditions for the negotiation and administration of collective agreements between unions and employers. This book does not deal with the law relating to labour relations.

- **Common law:** Common law has evolved over the centuries, through the decisions of various courts in individual cases. The common law has developed a number of principles that directly affect the employment relationship. Where legislation has been passed on a particular topic, that legislation generally sets the minimum standards that must be met. However, there are a number of areas, such as the termination of employment, in which the common law remains important.

- **Employment contracts:** Often, employers will enter into agreements with individual employees as to the conditions that will govern the working relationship and under which it may be severed. These contracts may be formalized in writing, or they may simply be implied. These agreements are generally legally binding on employers and employees, unless they violate the applicable legislation. The employment contract may include not only the individual document signed and agreed to at the commencement of employment, but also the terms of an organization's policies to which the employee has agreed.

Q. Does Employment Law Cover All Employees?

A. Human rights legislation applies to all employees, without exception. However, employment standards legislation exempts some employees from many provisions. These exemptions vary across the country, but in most parts of the country they include managerial staff; professionals such as lawyers, professional accountants, doctors, architects, and dentists; and students training for the professions. In some parts of the country, agricultural workers are specifically exempted.

As well, employment standards legislation also contains specific exemptions for certain types of employees from particular provisions of the Act, which reflect the varying economic activities of the provinces. For example, **British Columbia** exempts hunting and fishing guides, and various employees involved in towboat or chartered boat operations, and mineral exploration from its requirements on hours of work and overtime.

A common misconception is that temporary, part-time, or casual employees are not covered by employment standards legislation. This is not the case, and they are covered by the legislation with very few narrow exceptions.

Exclusions from employment standards legislation are detailed and vary widely across the country.

Q. What if the Employment Contract or Collective Agreement Provisions Differ from Employment Law Requirements?

A. An employment contract or collective agreement will often cover many areas and issues not specifically addressed in human rights or employment standards law, in which case there is no conflict. Where the contract or agreement conflicts with human rights law, the contract or agreement will have no force or effect, as the courts have stated that workers cannot contract out of their human rights. Where provisions in the employment contract or collective agreement fall below the minimum standards set out in employment standards law, the employment standards protections will generally prevail.

The legislation in certain jurisdictions specifically addresses the interplay between union contracts and the legislated standards. For example, in **Prince Edward Island**, employees who are covered by a collective agreement are exempted from all employment standards provisions except those relating to maternity/parental, adoption, child care, compassionate care, and reservist leaves, holidays, sexual harassment, and certain payroll-related provisions. **British Columbia** provides specifically that, if a collective agreement addresses hours of work, overtime, statutory holidays, vacations, seniority retention, recall, layoff, or termination of employment, the corresponding parts of the legislation do not apply to the employees covered by the union contract.

Q. What Happens if an Employer Sells the Business, or Merges with Another Company? Do Employees Lose the Rights That Have Been Built Up?

A. Following business amalgamations and acquisitions, companies can find themselves with entire new divisions and large groups of "new" employees. HR departments charged with blending two or more organizations into one can sometimes run into difficulties sorting out the issues of employee rights and employer obligations.

With respect to employment standards, where an employer sells, buys, leases, merges, or otherwise transfers the business to another employer that retains some or all of the employees, the employment of such employees is deemed to be continuous. In other words, it is as if the employees had continued to work for the same employer with no interruption. Generally speaking, the rights of the employees with respect to vacations, vacation pay, notice of termination, or pay in lieu of notice of termination, statutory holidays, maternity/parental leave, and other miscellaneous leaves are preserved.

CHECKLIST FOR EMPLOYEE/INDEPENDENT CONTRACTOR STATUS

Factors Indicating an Independent Contractor Relationship	Factors Indicating an Employee–Employer Relationship
Control	**Control**
❐ no set hours of work	❐ company sets hours of work and vacation entitlement
❐ work/project is assigned but how work is done is not supervised	❐ company supervises what the worker does and how the work is done
❐ worker not required to report to/work on company premises	❐ worker is required to report to/work on company premises on a regular basis
❐ worker not limited to services for one company	❐ worker works exclusively for one company
❐ worker not required to perform services personally but can hire others	❐ worker required to perform services personally
Ownership of Tools	❐ worker receives training from company on how to do the work
❐ worker purchases/maintains and owns tools and equipment	**Ownership of Tools**
Chance of Profit/Risk of Loss	❐ company pays for and provides worker with most of the tools and equipment
❐ worker paid by percentage of sales or daily billing rate	**Chance of Profit/Risk of Loss**
❐ parties negotiate the fees	❐ worker paid salary or hourly wage
❐ worker not paid if services not provided or work not performed	❐ company sets wages and increases
❐ no paid vacations or paid time off	❐ worker paid even if deadlines not met or quality of work poor
❐ worker pays own expenses related to work performed, i.e., supplies, office rent	❐ worker is not required to pay expenses related to work performed
❐ no payment of benefits such as health/dental/disability insurance: worker must buy them	❐ company pays benefits such as health/dental/disability insurance
❐ no pension plan or RRSP	❐ pension plan or RRSP provided
❐ worker is incorporated	**Total Relationship**
Total Relationship	❐ no written contract indicating independent contractor relationship
❐ written contract indicating independent contractor relationship	❐ contract for indefinite period of time
❐ contract for specific project or period of time	❐ no invoices submitted
❐ invoices submitted for payment	❐ no GST (or HST) charged by worker
❐ GST (or HST) charged for work performed	❐ paid through payroll
❐ paid through accounts payable	
❐ worker has other customers	

Chapter 2

MINIMUM AGE OF EMPLOYMENT

	Page
INTRODUCTION	13
RESTRICTIONS ON THE EMPLOYMENT OF YOUNG PEOPLE	13
Are Employers Prohibited from Hiring Young People?	13
Must Young People Be Treated Differently from Adult Employees?	14
Are There Exceptions to These Rules?	14
MINIMUM AGE CHART	15
REQUIREMENTS AND RESTRICTIONS IF UNDER MINIMUM AGE CHART	16

INTRODUCTION

In recognition of the importance of ensuring that children have access to education and of protecting their health and moral development, restrictions on child labour were among the first employment laws to be enacted. The federal, provincial, and territorial governments have all established minimum age requirements for employment. Also, there are often special limitations on the employment conditions of minors that do not apply to adult workers.

RESTRICTIONS ON THE EMPLOYMENT OF YOUNG PEOPLE

Q. Are Employers Prohibited from Hiring Young People?

A. Provided that the minors have reached the minimum age of employment set by the federal, provincial, or territorial governments, employers are permitted to hire them. The employment of minors is, however, subject to age-specific restrictions. The minimum ages for the various jurisdictions and the types of requirements and restrictions for the employment of minors are set out in the charts on pages 15 to 18.

13

Q. Must Young People Be Treated Differently from Adult Employees?

A. Young employees are entitled to all of the same employment standards protections as their adult co-workers. However, most jurisdictions have also set out special protections for young employees. These include the following:

- **Work must not interfere with school for those young people who are required to attend.**

- **Work must not endanger the health and safety or moral development of the young person.**

- **Hours of work may be limited.** These limitations are to ensure that work does not interfere with attendance at school. Thus, the number of hours that a young person can work on a school day may be limited to two or three hours, while students are permitted to work longer hours on those days when school attendance is not required.

- **Work at night may be restricted.** Because of concerns about the safety of young persons left to work alone at night, the **federal** jurisdiction and most provinces and territories either severely restrict or completely prohibit young people from working late at night, from the hours of 10:00 p.m. or 11:00 p.m. until 6:00 a.m.

- **Consent of a parent or guardian, or of the Director of Employment or Labour Standards, may be required.** In some provinces, the employer must obtain the written consent of either the parent or guardian of the young person, or of the Director of Employment or Labour Standards. The requirement for consent is generally limited to those circumstances where the worker in question is under the age of 16.

Q. Are There Exceptions to These Rules?

A. Some jurisdictions specifically exclude certain types of occupations, such as acting, certain types of agricultural work, and newspaper vending, from the restrictions described above. Work by young persons in family businesses and participation in work–study programs or vocational training programs are also permitted in most provinces.

MINIMUM AGE CHART

Jurisdiction	Minimum Age
Federal	17
Alberta	15
British Columbia	15
Manitoba	16
New Brunswick	16
Newfoundland and Labrador	16
Nova Scotia	16
Ontario	14
Prince Edward Island	16
Quebec	14
Saskatchewan	14
Northwest Territories	16
Nunavut	17
Yukon Territory	17

REQUIREMENTS AND RESTRICTIONS IF UNDER MINIMUM AGE CHART

Jurisdiction	Age	Requirements and Restrictions
Federal	under 17	• prohibited from working during school hours • restrictions on the type of work and must be unlikely to endanger health and safety
Alberta	12 to 14	• parent or guardian's written consent and approval of Director of Employment Standards required • prohibited from working during normal school hours • restrictions on number of hours of work per day and on working at night
	15 to 17	• prohibited from working during normal school hours • restrictions on working at night
British Columbia	under 12	• permission of Director of Employment Standards required
	12 to 14	• parent or guardian's written consent required • prohibited from working during school hours • restrictions on number of hours of work per day and per week • employee must be under direct and immediate supervision of employee who is at least 19 years old
Manitoba	under 16	• permission of Director of Employment Standards required upon joint application from employer and parent or guardian • work cannot adversely affect the safety, health, or well-being of the child • restrictions on number of hours of work per week and on working at night

Jurisdiction	Age	Requirements and Restrictions
Manitoba (continued)	16 to 18	• prohibited from working alone at night • prohibited from working in certain industries
New Brunswick	under 14	• only with permission of the Director of Employment Standards
	under 16	• restrictions on number of hours of work per day and on working at night • prohibited from work that is unwholesome or harmful to health, welfare, or moral or physical development
Newfoundland and Labrador	under 16	• work cannot be unwholesome or harmful to the child's health or prejudicial to school attendance • restrictions on number of hours of work per day • prohibited from working during strike or lockout
Northwest Territories	under 16	• work cannot be detrimental to the health, education, or moral character of the young person • prohibited from working in certain industries • prohibited from working certain hours at night
Nova Scotia	under 14	• prohibited from work that is unwholesome, harmful to health or moral development, or prejudicial to the child's education • restrictions on number of hours of work per day and on working at night
Nunavut	under 16	• prohibited from working in certain industries
	under 17	• work cannot be detrimental to the health, education, or moral character of the young person • prohibited from working in certain industries • prohibited from working certain hours at night

Jurisdiction	Age	Requirements and Restrictions
Ontario	14	• restrictions on type of work (cannot be employed in a factory or an industrial establishment)
Prince Edward Island	under 16	• work cannot be harmful to the health and safety or moral or physical development of the young person • prohibited from working during school hours and from working at night • restrictions on the number of hours of work per day and per week
Quebec	under 14	• written consent of parent or tutor required • work cannot be detrimental to education, health, or development of the child • prohibited from working during school hours or at night
	under 16	• restrictions on working at night
Saskatchewan	14 to 16	• written consent of parent or guardian required • prohibited from working in certain industries • restrictions on number of hours of work per day and per week and at night • prohibited from working during school hours
Yukon	under 17	• prohibited from working during school hours and in certain industries

Chapter 3

MINIMUM WAGES AND CALL-IN PAY

Page

INTRODUCTION 19

MINIMUM WAGES 20

What Are the Minimum Wages in Canada? 20

Can Students Be Paid a Lower Minimum Wage? 20

I Have Heard That Inexperienced Workers Can Also Be Paid a Lower Minimum Wage. Is This True? 20

How Is Minimum Wage Calculated for Employees Who Do Not Receive Hourly Remuneration? 20

Do Tips and Gratuities Count Towards Minimum Wage? 21

Can Employers Charge Employees for Uniforms and Special Clothing? 21

What Kinds of Deductions Can Employers Make for Room and Board? 22

Are There Any Workers Who Are Not Entitled To Minimum Wage? 22

CALL-IN PAY 22

What Is Call-In Pay? 22

When Are Employees Entitled To Call-In Pay? 23

To How Much Call-In Pay Are Employees Entitled? 23

What if the Cancellation of Work Was Beyond the Control of the Employer? 23

Are Any Workers Not Entitled To Protection under Call-In Pay Legislation? 24

MINIMUM WAGE CHART 25

INTRODUCTION

Minimum wage legislation has been established in all jurisdictions for various classes of employees. Additionally, some jurisdictions provide a separate minimum wage for young or inexperienced workers and students. While the minimum standards are continually updated to reflect changing labour market and economic conditions, the legislation regarding minimum wages is the most frequently revised employment standard.

The effect on the minimum wage of additional moneys, such as tips and gratuities, and the maximum deduction for employer-supplied board and lodging is specifically considered in the legislation of most jurisdictions. Special provisions are often made for particular industries.

Finally, certain persons are excluded from the minimum wage provisions in the legislation or from the entire Act respecting employment standards itself.

MINIMUM WAGES

Q. What Are the Minimum Wages in Canada?

A. The two charts on pages 25 and 26 set out the general minimum wages across Canada. These figures, of course, do change from time to time, sometimes on an annual basis. Each April, the **Yukon** minimum wage is adjusted based on the previous year's Consumer Price Index ("CPI") for Whitehorse.

Q. Can Students Be Paid a Lower Minimum Wage?

A. A separate, lower minimum wage for students has been established only in **Ontario**. These student wages are set out in the chart on page 26.

Q. I Have Heard That Inexperienced Workers Can Also Be Paid a Lower Minimum Wage. Is This True?

A. Only **Nova Scotia** maintains a separate minimum wage for inexperienced workers. In that province the minimum wage for inexperienced workers is $9.80 per hour as of April 1, 2013. Inexperienced employees are defined as those with less than three months' experience in the work for which they are employed.

Q. How Is Minimum Wage Calculated for Employees Who Do Not Receive Hourly Remuneration?

A. Generally, the minimum wage rate applies both to employees paid by the hour and those who are salaried. In some jurisdictions, regulations set out minimum wages for specific types of employment, such as live-in domestics and agricultural workers, but for the most part it is left up to the employer to ensure that an employee who is being paid on an other than hourly basis is receiving the minimum wage. It is a good idea to double-check your jurisdiction, because a number of jurisdictions set out very specific formulas for calculating whether or not an employee is receiving at least the minimum wage rate. There are also a few minimum weekly rates and monthly rates for certain industries, like forestry (**Nova Scotia** has a monthly rate for certain logging and forestry workers). **Alberta** stipulates a weekly minimum wage (currently $397) for various sales employees. Similarly, **New Brunswick** has a minimum weekly wage for employees whose hours of work are not verifiable (currently $440). As a rule, vacation pay, overtime pay, and general holiday pay are not counted as part of an employee's wages when calculating the employee's hourly rate of pay. For more information on the minimum wage rate for a particular jurisdiction, contact your local Employment Standards office.

Q. Do Tips and Gratuities Count Towards Minimum Wage?

A. All provinces/territories except **Manitoba** and **Saskatchewan** specify that tips and gratuities do not form part of an employee's wages. As well, **British Columbia**, **Alberta**, **Ontario**, and **Quebec** set out special minimum wage rates for employees who normally receive gratuities (or serve liquor in the case of **British Columbia**, **Alberta**, and **Ontario**).

Q. Can Employers Charge Employees for Uniforms and Special Clothing?

A. This varies across the country. The **federal** jurisdiction, **Ontario**, **New Brunswick**, and the **Yukon** make no provisions regarding charges for providing, repairing, or cleaning uniforms. Other jurisdictions, such as **Alberta**, **British Columbia**, **Quebec**, the **Northwest Territories**, and **Nunavut**, protect low-wage workers by prohibiting employers from making deductions or charges for uniforms that would reduce an employee's wages below the minimum wage. **Quebec** law requires special clothing to be supplied free of charge to employees paid minimum wage, or where the clothing identifies the employee as an employee of the employer's business. **Nova Scotia** prohibits employers from deducting from the minimum wage for the purchase or laundering of a uniform, but does allow employers to charge for dry cleaning where that is necessary. **British Columbia** and **Saskatchewan** require employers to provide special clothing to employees free of charge, without any deduction from wages (except in the case of registered nurses' uniforms in **Saskatchewan**). In **British Columbia**, an employer and a majority of the affected employees may agree that the employees will be responsible for cleaning and maintaining the special clothing at the employer's cost. **Prince Edward Island** and **Newfoundland and Labrador** no longer allow deductions (although a 25% returnable deposit is allowed in **Prince Edward Island**) for uniforms that are unique to the business, identified with the business, and of no practical use after employment ends.

Q. What Kinds of Deductions Can Employers Make for Room and Board?

A. In most provinces and territories, the amount that employers can deduct for room and board is limited. Some jurisdictions place an absolute limit on the amount that may be charged for room and board, others restrict the amount by which wages may be reduced below minimum wage for charges for room and board, and some prohibit any reduction of the minimum wage. For information specific to your province or territory, contact the local Employment Standards office, as these amounts are revised frequently.

It should also be noted that, because of the special circumstances surrounding domestics and live-in care providers, many jurisdictions make special provisions for these workers.

Q. Are There Any Workers Who Are Not Entitled To Minimum Wage?

A. Yes, there are numerous individuals who are excluded from protection under the minimum wage requirements. In certain jurisdictions, professionals, such as doctors, engineers, lawyers, and architects, are excluded from minimum wage protection, as are students who are articled to such professionals. As well, in many jurisdictions, students and apprentices who are registered under provincial training Acts are also excluded. In other jurisdictions, agricultural workers do not receive protection under minimum wage laws. **British Columbia** has established minimum piecework rates for harvesting various crops, and a few jurisdictions have rules about daily rates for jobs such as household domestic staff, and piecework homeworkers.

CALL-IN PAY

Q. What Is Call-In Pay?

A. Call-in pay is the minimum payment to which employees are entitled if they are called into or report to work, but are not given the opportunity to work an entire shift or normal workday. Essentially, call-in pay protects workers from being called into work and then being sent home with no remuneration.

Q. When Are Employees Entitled To Call-In Pay?

A. In some jurisdictions, such as **Nova Scotia**, the **Northwest Territories**, **Nunavut**, and the **federal** jurisdiction, employees are only entitled to call-in pay if they are summoned to work outside of their regularly scheduled hours, only to find that little or no work is available. In these jurisdictions, the purpose of call-in pay is to provide protection to employees who are unexpectedly called into work. In **Alberta**, **British Columbia**, **Manitoba**, **Newfoundland and Labrador**, **Ontario**, **Quebec**, **Prince Edward Island**, **Saskatchewan**, and the **Yukon**, call-in pay is also available to workers whose regularly scheduled work is cancelled or truncated after they report for a normal workday, as well as to those called in unexpectedly. **New Brunswick** provides call-in pay protection for non-union workers with a wage rate of less than twice the minimum wage. See the "Hours of Work Chart" and "Overtime Pay Chart" on pages 39 and 41, respectively, for the number of hours of pay to which employees are entitled.

Q. To How Much Call-In Pay Are Employees Entitled?

A. In the **federal** jurisdiction, **Alberta**, **Manitoba**, **New Brunswick**, **Newfoundland and Labrador**, **Nova Scotia**, **Ontario**, **Prince Edward Island**, and **Quebec**, workers protected by call-in pay provisions are entitled to a minimum of three hours' pay. **Saskatchewan** requires a minimum payment of $30 for an employee required to report to work. In **Ontario**, the legislation requires three hours of pay at the minimum wage rate. The Ministry's interpretation is that the employee is entitled to the greater of three hours' pay at minimum wage or actual hours worked at the regular rate.

In the **Northwest Territories** and **Nunavut**, workers are entitled to four hours' call-in pay. In **British Columbia**, workers are entitled to two hours' call-in pay unless the employee had been scheduled to work more than eight hours, in which case, the call-in pay is four hours. In the **Yukon**, workers are entitled to two hours' call-in pay.

Q. What if the Cancellation of Work Was Beyond the Control of the Employer?

A. **British Columbia**, **Ontario**, **Quebec**, and the **Yukon** specifically provide that where work is not provided because of a fortuitous event, or circumstances beyond the control of the employer (i.e., fire, power failure, machinery breakdown, unsuitable weather), the call-in pay provisions do not apply. Other jurisdictions are silent on the issue. Some jurisdictions, such as **British Columbia** and the **Yukon**, also make exceptions for cases where an employee who reports to work is not fit to work.

Q. Are Any Workers Not Entitled To Protection under Call-In Pay Legislation?

A. Yes. In most jurisdictions, there are some employees who are not covered by employment standards legislation at all. As well, in some jurisdictions there are specific provisions or exemptions relating to call-in pay for certain types of workers. In **Alberta**, two hours of call-in pay are required for students, employees of a recreation/athletic program, or school bus drivers. In **Nova Scotia**, call-in pay is not required for emergency work performed by firefighters, police officers, hospital workers, or certain farm workers. In **Ontario**, call-in pay is not required for students, or if the employee regularly works less than three hours a day. In **Quebec**, call-in pay is not required if the work is such that it can be performed in less than three hours (i.e., school bus drivers, school crossing guards, or ushers). In **Saskatchewan**, call-in pay is not required for students, school bus drivers, school noon-hour supervisors, janitors, caretakers, or building cleaners. In the **Yukon**, call-in pay is not required if the work is such that it usually requires employees to report for periods of less than two hours.

MINIMUM WAGE CHART

	Rate*	**Effective Date**
Federal..............................	see below**	July 1, 1996
Alberta...............................	$ 9.95	September 1, 2013
British Columbia	10.25	May 1, 2012
Manitoba.............................	10.45	October 1, 2013
New Brunswick......................	10.00	April 1, 2012
Newfoundland and Labrador......	10.00	July 1, 2010
Nova Scotia	10.30	April 1, 2013
Ontario...............................	10.25	March 31, 2010
Prince Edward Island	10.00	April 1, 2012
Quebec...............................	10.15	May 1, 2013
Saskatchewan.......................	10.00	December 1, 2012
Northwest Territories	10.00	April 1, 2011
Nunavut..............................	11.00	January 1, 2011
Yukon	10.54	April 1, 2013

* The general minimum wage rate for each jurisdiction is provided in this chart. Many jurisdictions also have special minimum wage rates for certain defined classes of workers, such as construction, forestry, and those who receive tips or gratuities.

** The federal minimum wage rate is aligned with the rate in each province and territory.

Age-Based or Experience-Based Rates

	Rate	Effective Date
Federal...............................	aligned with provincial rates	July 1, 1996
Alberta................................	no special rate established	
British Columbia	no special rate established	
Manitoba...............................	no special rate established	
New Brunswick.........................	no special rate established	
Newfoundland and Labrador.........	no special rate established	
Nova Scotia (inexperienced employees (with under three months of experience))...............	$9.80	April 1, 2013
under age 16 working on a farm in work directly related to primary production of a variety of enumerated products..........................	no minimum wage	
Ontario (students under age 18, if weekly hours are not in excess of 28 or if employed during a school holiday).................................	$9.60	March 31, 2010
Prince Edward Island	no special rate established	
Quebec.................................	no special rate established	
Saskatchewan..........................	no special rate established	
Northwest Territories	no special rate established	
Nunavut................................	no special rate established	
Yukon	no special rate established	

Chapter 4

HOURS OF WORK AND OVERTIME PAY

	Page
INTRODUCTION	28
STANDARD HOURS OF WORK...	28
Are There Limits on the Number of Hours That an Employee Can Be Required To Work in a Day or in a Week?	28
Is an Employee Who Is Waiting for Work To Be Assigned Considered To Be Working for the Purpose of Calculating Hours of Work?	28
When Deciding Whether the Standard Working Hours Have Been Reached, How Is a "Week" Defined?..	29
Do Standard Hours of Work Apply to All Employees?	29
What Happens if Employees Work More Hours Than the Standard?	29
Are There Any Exceptions to the Legislated Hours of Work?........................	30
Can an Employer Get Permission from Employment Standards Officials To Exceed the Legislated Hours of Work?...	30
Can the Hours of Work Be Averaged over a Longer Period of Time?	30
Can an Employer Implement a Compressed Workweek?..............................	31
How Do Public Holidays Affect Standard Hours Calculations?	31
How Do Employees Know What Their Hours of Work Are?	32
TAKING A BREAK	32
Are Employees Entitled To a Weekly Rest Period?...................................	32
Are Employees Entitled To Meal and Rest Breaks During the Day?	33
Can Employees Be Required To Work During Their Meal Breaks?	34
Is There Any Protection for Shift Workers?..	34
Are Split Shifts Regulated?	34
DAYS OF REST..	34
OVERTIME PAY...	35
What Constitutes Overtime Work?	35
What if a Worker Is on a Shortened Workweek?......................................	35
What if a Worker's Hours of Work Vary from Week-to-Week?.......................	35
What Rate of Pay Must Be Given for Overtime Work?	35
Can Employers Force Employees To Work Overtime Hours?	36

Page

Are There Any Workers Who Are Excluded from Protection under Overtime
    Provisions? 36
Can Employers Give Time Off in Lieu of Overtime Pay? 36
HOURS OF WORK CHART 39
OVERTIME PAY CHART 41

INTRODUCTION

Governments across Canada have passed laws restricting the hours of work of employees. These laws set out standard hours of work for employees, provide for extra payment (overtime pay) for employees who work more than these standard hours, and require that employees be given rest and meal breaks. The questions and answers set out below explain these legal requirements for all parts of Canada.

STANDARD HOURS OF WORK

Q. Are There Limits on the Number of Hours That an Employee Can Be Required To Work in a Day or in a Week?

A. All jurisdictions set standard hours of work. If employees work beyond these hours, employers must pay overtime. Some simply set standard weekly hours, while others regulate hours per day as well as hours per week. However, some jurisdictions also place upper limits on the number of hours employees may be required to work in a day or a week, even if overtime pay is provided.

All of the jurisdictions that set a standard working day do so at eight hours. The standard number of hours in the week varies between 40 and 48 hours. To find the maximum working hours allowed in your workplace, please refer to the "Hours of Work Chart" found on page 39.

Q. Is an Employee Who Is Waiting for Work To Be Assigned Considered To Be Working for the Purpose of Calculating Hours of Work?

A. The provinces of **Nova Scotia**, **Ontario**, and **Quebec** directly deal with this issue in their employment standards legislation. In these provinces, a person who is at his or her place of employment and is required to wait for work to be assigned is deemed to be working. **Prince Edward Island** takes the same policy position, but the legislation is silent on this point. However, there are a number of jurisdictions that deem an employee to be working when the employee is not performing work, but is required to remain at the workplace holding himself or herself ready for a call to work.

Q. When Deciding Whether the Standard Working Hours Have Been Reached, How Is a "Week" Defined?

A. A week is a period of seven consecutive days. In **Alberta, Saskatchewan**, and the **federal** jurisdiction, the week commences at midnight on Saturday. In other parts of Canada (including **Alberta**), the employer can set the workweek to begin at any time, so long as the practice is consistent. This prevents employers from repeatedly shifting the start of the week in an attempt to minimize the hours worked over the weekly standard. In **Ontario** and **Nova Scotia**, where there is no established practice, the week runs from Sunday to Sunday. In **British Columbia**, an employer can generally establish a workweek, but a week begins on Sunday for the purpose of calculating overtime and for averaging arrangements (and compassionate care leave).

Q. Do Standard Hours of Work Apply to All Employees?

A. No, not all employees are affected by standard hours laws, because not all employees are covered by employment standards laws. Employees with professional designations are often excepted from employment standards protections with respect to hours of work and overtime. If a person is employed as an architect, lawyer, doctor, dentist, engineer, or other professional, employment standards laws may not apply.

As well, special rules about hours of work may apply to employees in certain industries, such as truck drivers and construction workers.

If you have a concern about the application of employment standards laws, contact the appropriate Employment Standards office for further information.

Q. What Happens if Employees Work More Hours Than the Standard?

A. Hours worked by employees beyond the standard hours set out by law are considered "overtime" and employers must pay employees extra for overtime hours worked. The overtime rate is usually 1.5 times the regular rate of pay received by the employee. However, in **Nova Scotia** for certain classifications exempt from the usual overtime wage, and generally in **New Brunswick** and **Newfoundland and Labrador**, the overtime rate is 1.5 times the minimum wage. (Unionized workers in **Newfoundland and Labrador** are entitled to overtime pay of 1.5 times their regular rate if the collective agreement is drafted in a stipulated manner.) For more information on overtime, refer to the "Overtime Pay Chart" at page 41.

Q. Are There Any Exceptions to the Legislated Hours of Work?

A. The **federal** government, **Alberta**, **Manitoba**, **Newfoundland and Labrador**, **Nova Scotia**, **Ontario**, **Quebec**, **Saskatchewan**, the **Northwest Territories**, and **Nunavut** allow exceptions to the legislated hours of work where there is an emergency. In the **Yukon**, in an emergency, an employer may require an employee to work overtime without the reasonable advance notice that is otherwise required. The definition of an emergency varies, but it includes such things as accidents, interruptions to the provision of essential services such as utilities, and urgent and essential work to be done to machinery, equipment, or plant in order to prevent serious interference with the functioning of the business. Generally speaking, the circumstances must be unforeseen or unpreventable, and the hours may be extended only to the extent necessary to prevent serious interference with the ordinary working of the industrial establishment.

Q. Can an Employer Get Permission from Employment Standards Officials To Exceed the Legislated Hours of Work?

A. Under **federal**, **Alberta**, **British Columbia**, **Manitoba**, **Prince Edward Island**, the **Northwest Territories**, and **Nunavut** law, employment standards officials may, when an employer applies, permit an employer to exceed the maximum hours by issuing a permit, order, or variance. In **Ontario**, an employer may apply for approval to work excess hours if a written agreement has been entered into with the employees. If approval has not been denied within 30 days, an employer may, where certain conditions are met, proceed with the excess hours work schedule, provided the employees have agreed, the employer keeps posted in the workplace a copy of the application to the Ministry of Labour, and the hours do not exceed 60 in a week. An employee may revoke his or her consent to such an agreement by giving the employer two weeks' written notice, and the employer may revoke the agreement by giving the employee reasonable notice. In certain other parts of Canada that issue permits, the employer must usually show some special circumstances, such as the seasonal or intermittent nature of the industry.

Q. Can the Hours of Work Be Averaged over a Longer Period of Time?

A. In **British Columbia**, **Manitoba**, **Ontario**, **Quebec**, **Saskatchewan**, the **Northwest Territories**, **Nunavut**, the **Yukon**, and the **federal** jurisdiction, employers are permitted to pay standard non-overtime rates by averaging out the number of hours employees work over a number of weeks. With this system, an employee could work 50 hours one week, 10 the next, and 45 the next, and still comply with a maximum 40-hour workweek because the average hours of work in each week over the three-week period is only 35, which is still well below the maximum. Averaging agreements are often limited to a specific period of time. For example, in **British Columbia** and **Ontario**, hours of work may be averaged over a period of two or more weeks, but the averaging agreement must have an expiry date and last no longer than two years for non-union employees. Employers must obtain the agreement of the employees or trade union representing the employees and/or permission from employment standards officials before they put an averaging system into place. Under **federal** legislation, the averaging agreement can run no longer than three years, except where the agreement is with a union.

Q. Can an Employer Implement a Compressed Workweek?

A. Compressed workweeks are scheduling schemes where employees work the same number of hours in a week but in fewer days, without attracting overtime pay rates. They are specifically permitted in **Alberta**, **British Columbia**, **Manitoba**, **Nova Scotia**, **Ontario**, **Saskatchewan**, the **Northwest Territories**, **Nunavut**, the **Yukon**, and the **federal** jurisdiction. Of course, in those jurisdictions such as **New Brunswick**, **Newfoundland and Labrador**, **Prince Edward Island**, and **Quebec**, which do not set standard daily hours, only weekly hours, such provisions are not necessary. Thus, compressed workweeks are permitted in all parts of Canada in some circumstances, allowing the workday to be extended past the usual eight-hour daily maximum without overtime being paid, if it means that fewer days will be worked in that week. Prior to implementing a compressed workweek, the employer (other than in **Alberta**) must obtain either permission from the Employment Standards Department and/or the agreement of the trade union that represents the employees, or, if there is no union, the agreement of a majority of the affected employees.

Proposed **Saskatchewan** legislation will permit two types of work arrangements: eight hours per day/five days per week; or 10 hours per day/four days per week.

Q. How Do Public Holidays Affect Standard Hours Calculations?

A. In many provinces and territories, when a week contains a public holiday to which an employee is entitled, the standard hours of work for that week are reduced. Thus, where the standard workweek is 40 hours and the standard workday is eight hours, the standard working hours during the week of the public holiday will be 32.

Therefore, employees subject to a 40-hour workweek will receive overtime pay only if, in the week of the public holiday, they work more than 32 hours on the days that are not a public holiday. The legislation in **Manitoba**, **Quebec**, **Saskatchewan**, the **Northwest Territories**, **Nunavut**, and the **federal** jurisdiction is quite explicit on this point.

In most jurisdictions, hours worked on public holidays should not count towards overtime entitlement given that the employee will be compensated for work on a public holiday by the higher rates of pay and/or the provision for another day off at a later date. In **Alberta**, **New Brunswick**, **Ontario**, **Saskatchewan**, the **federal** jurisdiction, the **Northwest Territories**, **Nunavut**, and the **Yukon**, hours worked on a holiday do not count when calculating overtime hours.

Q. How Do Employees Know What Their Hours of Work Are?

A. In **Alberta**, **British Columbia**, **Nova Scotia**, and **Saskatchewan**, employers are specifically required to post in the workplace a notice including information about the time at which work begins and ends.

In **Manitoba**, **New Brunswick**, **Newfoundland and Labrador**, **Prince Edward Island**, **Quebec**, **Northwest Territories**, **Nunavut**, and the **Yukon**, there is a requirement that employers post general conditions of employment or items required by employment standards officials. This general requirement can include changes to the standard workweek, hours of work, etc.

In **Ontario**, employers are required to display a government-provided poster in the workplace where it is likely to be seen by employees. This poster contains a summary of parts of the **Ontario** legislation, including hours of work.

In **Newfoundland and Labrador** employers are required to provide each employee with a written statement of the terms and conditions of employment, which would include hours of work.

Finally, **federally regulated** employers are required to post hours of work in a number of circumstances, including when a modified work schedule is introduced or revised.

TAKING A BREAK

Q. Are Employees Entitled To a Weekly Rest Period?

A. Yes. All employees are entitled to have some time off during each week of work.

- In the **federal** jurisdiction, **New Brunswick**, **Newfoundland and Labrador**, **Nova Scotia**, **Prince Edward Island**, and **Nunavut**, employees are entitled to at least one full day of rest in every seven days, which should be on Sunday whenever possible.

- In **British Columbia** and **Quebec**, employees are entitled to 32 hours free from work each week.

- In **Manitoba** and the **Northwest Territories**, employees have a right to a 24-hour rest period in each week, which may be on any day of the week.

- In **Alberta**, employees are entitled to one day of rest each week, two consecutive days of rest in each two consecutive workweeks, three consecutive days of rest in each period of three consecutive workweeks, or four consecutive days of rest in each period of four consecutive workweeks.

- In **Ontario**, 24 consecutive hours off work (free from active duties) each week, or at least 48 consecutive hours off in every two-week period of work are mandatory.

- **Saskatchewan** provides a rest period of one day in every seven for all employees who usually work 20 hours or more in a week. Where more than 10 employees work in the organization, the employer must grant a rest period of two consecutive days in every seven to each employee who works 20 hours or more in a week. One of these two days must be Sunday, if possible.

- In the **Yukon**, employees are entitled to two full days of rest in a week, one of them to be on a Sunday if possible.

In many cases there are exceptions to these rest provisions. For example, a number of provinces make exceptions for urgent work, seasonally operating industries, or operations in remote areas where employees would not benefit by the break.

Q. Are Employees Entitled To Meal and Rest Breaks During the Day?

A. The law makes provision for employees to take a break during the working day to eat and briefly rest.

- **Alberta**, **British Columbia**, **Manitoba**, **Ontario**, **New Brunswick**, **Nova Scotia**, **Prince Edward Island**, **Quebec**, the **Northwest Territories**, and **Nunavut** require employers to allow employees a rest period of at least half an hour each time they work at least five consecutive hours. In **Ontario**, where the employee agrees, the required half-hour meal break can be broken into two shorter periods that still total 30 minutes.

- In **Newfoundland and Labrador**, the required period of rest is one hour after every five consecutive hours of work.

- **Saskatchewan** requires a half-hour meal break within every five consecutive hours of work for all employees who work six or more hours in a day.

- In the **Yukon**, a half-hour break must be granted after five consecutive hours of work if the employee works fewer than 10 hours on that day, and after six hours if the employee works more than 10 hours.

- The **federal** jurisdiction makes no specific provisions for meal breaks.

Employers are not required to pay employees during this break.

Again, a number of provinces have exceptions to these requirements. The exceptions are for such things as emergencies and accidents, and agreements reached through collective bargaining.

Q. Can Employees Be Required To Work During Their Meal Breaks?

A. Of the provinces that mention daily breaks, some specify that employees may not be allowed to work during their meal breaks. In **British Columbia**, **Quebec**, and **Saskatchewan**, for example, the legislation provides that employees must be paid if they are required to be available for work during their meal breaks. **Prince Edward Island** legislation prohibits an employer from requiring an employee to remain at the workplace during the rest or eating break. In the **Northwest Territories** and **Nunavut**, the legislation prohibits employers from requiring employees to work during their meal breaks.

Q. Is There Any Protection for Shift Workers?

A. In **Alberta**, **British Columbia**, **Newfoundland and Labrador**, **Saskatchewan**, and the **Yukon**, the law specifically protects workers from being required to work shifts without a rest in between. In these jurisdictions, workers must be allowed at least eight hours of rest between each shift. In **Ontario**, employers must give employees at least eight hours of rest between shifts, unless the successive shifts do not exceed 13 hours or the employer and employee agree otherwise.

Q. Are Split Shifts Regulated?

A. In **British Columbia** and the **Yukon**, employers must limit their employees' standard hours of work to the 12-hour period immediately following commencement of each employee's shift.

DAYS OF REST

Historically, Sundays were considered a day of rest in Canada. On that day, shops were closed, business was not conducted, and employees rested. However, given the provisions of the *Canadian Charter of Rights and Freedoms*, the courts declared that, while governments could regulate civil rights on Sundays, they could not compel people to observe Sunday as a religious holy day. **Federal** legislation (the *Lord's Day Act*) prohibiting Sunday work was struck down. However, legislation governing hours of opening still places some restrictions on Sunday openings in some provinces. **Manitoba**, **New Brunswick**, **Ontario**, and **Prince Edward Island** have included provisions in their employment standards legislation protecting the right of workers (generally in retail trades) to refuse to work on Sunday under certain conditions.

It also needs to be borne in mind that, where an employee's religious convictions require that he or she not work on holy days, the employer has an obligation to try to reasonably accommodate those religious beliefs under human rights legislation.

OVERTIME PAY

Q. What Constitutes Overtime Work?

A. The point at which work becomes overtime work is different from jurisdiction to jurisdiction. As a general rule, after 40 or 44 hours in a week, employees start to log overtime. In some jurisdictions, however, there is also a daily standard. **Alberta**, **British Columbia**, **Manitoba**, **Saskatchewan**, the **Northwest Territories**, **Nunavut**, the **Yukon**, and the **federal** jurisdiction all provide for daily overtime over eight hours per day.

Proposed **Saskatchewan** legislation will require overtime pay after maximum daily hours of work are exceeded (eight hours, or 10 hours if a four-day workweek); and after 40 hours worked in a week. The chart on page 41 sets out overtime hours and rates for each jurisdiction in Canada.

Q. What if a Worker Is on a Shortened Workweek?

A. In some organizations, employees work longer hours on some days so that they may work a shorter week. This may cause workers to repeatedly exceed the daily standard hours beyond which overtime must be paid.

This is not of concern in those jurisdictions where only weekly standards are set out, and not daily standards. In jurisdictions where there is a daily standard in place, the law usually sets out special provisions to allow shortened workweeks to be worked without the necessity of paying overtime. Refer to the question concerning compressed workweeks at page 31.

Q. What if a Worker's Hours of Work Vary from Week-to-Week?

A. In some jurisdictions, the law specifically allows employers to average the number of hours worked over a number of weeks without the necessity of paying overtime. Refer to the question concerning averaging hours of work at page 30.

Q. What Rate of Pay Must Be Given for Overtime Work?

A. In most provinces and territories, the overtime rate is 1.5 times the employee's regular rate of pay. However, in **New Brunswick** and **Newfoundland and Labrador**, the overtime rate is 1.5 times the minimum wage. Similarly, in **Nova Scotia**, the overtime rate is 1.5 times the minimum wage for "excluded" employees such as those with professional designations and managers. For other employees it is

1.5 times the employee's regular rate. Finally, in **British Columbia**, the overtime rate is 1.5 times the employee's regular pay for hours in excess of eight in a day or 40 in a week and two times the employee's regular pay for hours in excess of 12 in a day. For more information on overtime, refer to the "Overtime Pay Chart" on page 41.

Q. Can Employers Force Employees To Work Overtime Hours?

A. Employees cannot generally be forced to work overtime unless they or their agent (i.e., a trade union), consent to the extra hours or it is defined as a clear condition of employment at the time of hire. In other words, an employer is generally prohibited from taking any sort of disciplinary action against an employee who chooses not to work overtime hours. Having said this, a number of jurisdictions declare that employees may be required to work overtime in the case of an emergency or accident.

Q. Are There Any Workers Who Are Excluded from Protection under Overtime Provisions?

A. There are employees who are exempted from overtime provisions. In most jurisdictions, professionals (for example, doctors, accountants, lawyers, architects, engineers, foresters) and persons in management positions are not allowed to claim overtime pay. In addition to managers, **Manitoba** law also excludes employees with substantial control over their hours of work and who earn twice the **Manitoba** industrial average wage for the previous year (i.e., who earn at least $84,043.44 *per annum* as of June 2013). As well, many jurisdictions exclude agricultural, emergency, and domestic workers from overtime provisions. Some jurisdictions exempt family members of the employer from overtime provisions. Again, the variation between jurisdictions in terms of exceptions is significant, and it is suggested that readers who are concerned regarding coverage contact the appropriate Employment Standards office for more information.

Q. Can Employers Give Time Off in Lieu of Overtime Pay?

A. With the changing nature of work and the increased pressure on employees with respect to work and family responsibilities, time off instead of overtime pay is becoming increasingly popular. Time off in lieu of overtime pay (i.e., setting up an overtime bank) is specifically permitted in nine jurisdictions: **Alberta**, **British Columbia**, **Manitoba**, **Newfoundland and Labrador**, **Ontario**, **Prince Edward Island**, **Quebec**, the **Northwest Territories**, and the **Yukon**. While this may seem to be an attractive alternative to the cost of overtime pay, employers need to be aware that the time off must be 90 minutes off for every 60 minutes worked (except in **Alberta**, where it is an hour off for an hour worked), and that if the time off is not taken by the time employment ends or within the time limit in the legislation is reached, it is converted to a cash payment. Good record keeping is essential when engaging in a lieu time program.

In **Alberta**, an employer and an employee or a group of employees may enter into a written agreement (including through a collective agreement) to provide, either wholly or in part, time off with pay instead of overtime pay. Under this agreement, overtime hours are taken as time off in lieu (hour-for-hour worked). The time off must be taken within three months of the end of the pay period in which it was earned, unless a collective agreement or permit authorizes otherwise. Banked time not taken within the three-month period must be paid out at time-and-a-half. An agreement regarding time off in lieu of overtime pay may terminate on one month's written notice by either party.

In **British Columbia**, at the written request of an employee, an employer may establish a time bank for an employee and credit overtime wages to the time bank instead of paying them to the employee. The wages must be credited at the overtime rate. The time bank may be used to take time off with pay at a time agreed to by the employer and the employee. The employee may ask the employer at any time to pay all or part of the banked overtime pay, close the bank, or allow for time off at a mutually agreed upon time.

In **Manitoba**, there must be a written agreement between the employer and the employee to permit overtime to be compensated for by the provision of time off rather than overtime pay. The time off must be not less than 150% of the number of hours or parts of hours of overtime, and the employee must be paid his or her regular wage rate for the time off. The time off must be provided during the employee's regular hours and the employee must take the time within three months after the end of the pay period in which the overtime occurred, unless the Director of Employment Standards has approved a longer period. If the employee does not take the time off within the required period, overtime wages must be paid out.

In **Newfoundland and Labrador**, where the employer and the employee agree, the employee may be credited with 1.5 hours of paid time off for each overtime hour worked instead of overtime pay. The time off instead of overtime pay is to be granted to the employee no later than three months after the week in which the overtime was worked or, if the employee agrees, the credited hours of time off can be accumulated or "banked" for up to 12 months from the week the overtime was worked. Where the employment of an employee ends before the paid time off is taken, the employer must pay the employee overtime pay for the overtime hours that were worked.

In **Ontario**, where the employer and employee agree, the employee may be credited with 1.5 hours of paid time off instead of overtime pay. The time off instead of overtime pay is to be granted to the employee no later than three months after the week in which the overtime was worked or, if the employee agrees, the credited hours of time off can be accumulated or banked for up to 12 months from the week the overtime was worked.

In **Prince Edward Island**, if requested in writing by the employee, 1.5 hours of paid time off may be given for each hour of overtime worked. The time off must be taken within three months of the work-week in which the overtime was worked.

In **Quebec**, either at the request of an employee or as provided in a collective agreement or decree, the payment of overtime may be replaced by paid leave equivalent to the overtime worked plus 50%. The paid leave must be taken during the 12 months following the working of the overtime, at a date agreed upon between the employer and the employee.

In the **Yukon** and the **Northwest Territories**, an employee or group of employees may enter a written agreement (or collective agreement) with the employer to take time off in lieu of overtime, either in whole or in part. The employees must be compensated for the overtime worked with time-and-a-half off. The time off must be taken within 12 months (**Yukon**) or three months (**Northwest Territories**) of the time it was earned.

Proposed **Saskatchewan** legislation will allow for the establishment of time banks for overtime hours on agreement of the employer and employee.

HOURS OF WORK CHART

Jurisdiction	Minimum Hours To Be Paid	Maximum Hours Permitted	Required Rest Periods
Federal	3	maximum 48 per week	1 full day of rest per week, on Sunday wherever practicable
Alberta	3		1 day per week; 2 consecutive days in each 14-day period; 3 consecutive days in each 21-day period; or 4 consecutive days in each 28-day period; at least 4 consecutive days of rest after 24 consecutive work days
British Columbia	2; 4 if more than 8 hours scheduled	excessive hours; hours detrimental to health or safety	32 consecutive hours per week
Manitoba	3		24 consecutive hours in each 7-day period
New Brunswick	3		24 consecutive hours per week, on Sunday if possible
Newfoundland and Labrador	3		24 consecutive hours per week, on Sunday wherever possible
Nova Scotia	3		24 consecutive hours in each 7-day period, on Sunday wherever possible
Ontario	3	48 per week	24 consecutive hours in every workweek; or 48 consecutive hours in every period of 2 consecutive workweeks; 11 consecutive hours per day
Prince Edward Island	3		24 consecutive hours in each 7 days, on Sunday wherever possible
Quebec	3	employee may refuse to work more than 50 hours per week; 60 hours per week in James Bay or isolated area; more than 4 extra hours in a day; more than 14 hours in a 24-hour period	32 consecutive hours per week

Jurisdiction	Minimum Hours To Be Paid	Maximum Hours Permitted	Required Rest Periods
Saskatchewan...........	3	44 per week, except with employee consent	1 day in every 7 days (persons usually employed for 20 hours or more in any one week); 2 consecutive days in every 7 days (more than 10 employees in any establishment), one of which is Sunday wherever possible
Northwest Territories ..	4	10 per day; 60 per week	1 day of rest per week; 2 consecutive days in every 2 weeks; 3 consecutive days in each period of 3 weeks
Nunavut	4	10 per day; 60 per week	1 full day of rest per week, on Sunday wherever practicable
Yukon	2		2 full days of rest per week, one being Sunday wherever practicable

OVERTIME PAY CHART

Jurisdiction	Overtime Rate
Federal	more than 8 hours in a day or 40 hours in a week: 1.5 times regular wage
Alberta	more than 8 hours in a day or 44 hours in a week: 1.5 times regular wage
British Columbia	more than 8 hours in a day or 40 hours in a week: 1.5 times regular wage; more than 12 hours in a day: double regular wage
Manitoba	more than 8 hours in a day or 40 hours in a week: 1.5 times regular wage
New Brunswick	more than 44 hours in a week: $15 per hour effective April 1, 2012
Newfoundland and Labrador	more than 40 hours in a week: $15 per hour, effective July 1, 2010
Nova Scotia	more than 48 hours in a week: 1.5 times regular hourly wage (1.5 times minimum wage for "exempt" employees)
Ontario	more than 44 hours in a week: 1.5 times regular wage
Prince Edward Island	more than 48 hours in a week: 1.5 times regular wage
Quebec	more than 40 hours in a week: premium of 50% of prevailing hourly wage
Saskatchewan	more than 8 hours in a day or 40 hours in a week: 1.5 times regular wage
Northwest Territories	more than 8 hours in a day or 40 hours in a week: 1.5 times regular wage
Nunavut	more than 8 hours in a day or 40 hours in a week: 1.5 times regular wage
Yukon	more than 8 hours in a day or 40 hours in a week: 1.5 times regular wage

Chapter 5

STATUTORY HOLIDAYS

Page

INTRODUCTION 44

TIME OFF FOR STATUTORY HOLIDAYS 44

What Is a Statutory Holiday? 44

Which Days Are Statutory Holidays? 44

Which Jurisdictions Have Legislated the First Monday in August as a Statutory
Holiday? 44

Which Jurisdictions Have Legislated the Second or Third Monday in February as
a Statutory Holiday? 45

Are Civic Holidays Statutory Holidays? 45

Are All Employees Entitled To Statutory Holidays? 45

Are Part-Time Workers Entitled To Statutory Holidays? 45

Can an Employer Require an Employee To Work on a Statutory Holiday? 45

Can Another Day Be Substituted for a Statutory Holiday? 46

What if a Statutory Holiday Falls on a Non-Working Day? 46

What if a Statutory Holiday Falls During an Employee's Vacation Time? 47

PAYMENT FOR STATUTORY HOLIDAYS 47

Is There a Qualifying Period Before Employees Are Entitled To Pay for Statutory
Holidays? 47

Are There Other Exceptions That Would Disentitle the Employee to a Statutory
Holiday with Pay if the Statutory Holiday Falls on a Working Day? 47

When an Employee Qualifies for a Statutory Holiday off Work with Pay but Does
Not Work That Day, How Is the Pay Calculated? 48

How Are Employees Paid Who Work on the Statutory Holiday? 48

How Are Employees Who Work in Continuous Operations or Special Industries
Paid for Work on Statutory Holidays? 49

What if an Employee's Employment Ends Before Payment for a Statutory Holiday
or a Substitute Holiday Is Received? 50

STATUTORY HOLIDAYS CHART 51

STATUTORY HOLIDAYS ENTITLEMENT CHART 52

INTRODUCTION

In every community, there are days of special significance that the public celebrates together. All federal, provincial, and territorial governments in Canada have recognized this by passing laws that allow employees time off from work to observe days of national or regional importance. These are called statutory holidays, public holidays, or general holidays, depending on the part of Canada in which you are located, but all of these terms mean the same thing.

TIME OFF FOR STATUTORY HOLIDAYS

Q. What Is a Statutory Holiday?

A. A statutory holiday is a day set aside by the federal, provincial, or territorial government in order to celebrate days of national or regional significance. Examples of national days of significance include Thanksgiving Day, Canada Day, and Labour Day. Provincial and territorial governments also proclaim public holidays for days of importance particular to their own regions. Examples of this include British Columbia Day in **British Columbia**, Saint-Jean-Baptiste Day in **Quebec**, St. George's Day in **Newfoundland and Labrador**, and National Aboriginal Day in the **Northwest Territories**. On these days, employees are not required to work, but nonetheless receive pay from their employers.

Q. Which Days Are Statutory Holidays?

A. There are some days that are recognized as holidays all across Canada, such as New Year's Day, Labour Day, and Christmas Day. Others, such as Remembrance Day, Victoria Day, and Thanksgiving Day are only recognized as statutory holidays in certain jurisdictions. The statutory holidays recognized in the various parts of Canada are set out in the "Statutory Holidays Chart" found on page 51.

Q. Which Jurisdictions Have Legislated the First Monday in August as a Statutory Holiday?

A. **British Columbia**, **New Brunswick**, **Saskatchewan**, the **Northwest Territories**, and **Nunavut** consider the first Monday in August to be a statutory holiday. This holiday is also customarily observed in **Manitoba** and **Ontario** as Civic Holiday, in **Alberta** as Heritage Day, and in **Nova Scotia** and **Prince Edward Island** as Natal Day, although it is not a legislated statutory holiday in those provinces.

Q. Which Jurisdictions Have Legislated the Second or Third Monday in February as a Statutory Holiday?

A. **Alberta**, **Manitoba**, **Ontario**, **Prince Edward Island**, and **Saskatchewan** all recognize the third Monday in February as a statutory holiday. **British Columbia** recognizes the second Monday as a statutory holiday. In **Alberta**, **British Columbia**, **Ontario**, and **Saskatchewan**, the holiday is called Family Day; in **Manitoba**, it is known as Louis Riel Day; and in **Prince Edward Island**, it is called Islander Day.

Q. Are Civic Holidays Statutory Holidays?

A. Civic holidays are not statutory holidays, and so employers are not obliged to observe these holidays unless they have agreed to do so in an employment contract or collective agreement. For example, while many employers in **Ontario**, **Manitoba**, **Prince Edward Island**, **Alberta**, and **Nova Scotia** provide their employees a day off with or without pay on the first Monday in August, they are not required by law to do so.

Q. Are All Employees Entitled To Statutory Holidays?

A. No, not all employees have the right to take a statutory holiday, because not all employees are covered by the statutory holiday provisions of employment standards laws. For example, in **British Columbia**, high technology professionals are exempted from the normal hours of work, overtime, and statutory holiday pay requirements.

Those employees who are not covered by the statutory holiday provisions of the employment standards laws may, however, still be entitled to statutory holidays. An employment contract or collective agreement may grant these employees certain statutory holiday rights and benefits.

Q. Are Part-Time Workers Entitled To Statutory Holidays?

A. Yes. Part-time employees are entitled to the same rights and benefits under employment standards law as are full-time employees, provided that they meet the qualifying requirements.

Q. Can an Employer Require an Employee To Work on a Statutory Holiday?

A. Except in continuous operations, the tourism industry, or special industries as described on page 49, employees generally cannot be required to work the statutory holiday. Employees can, however, agree in writing to do so. Where the employee agrees to work or the employer requires the employee to work, the employer must pay the employee the specified premium or provide the employee with an alternate day off for doing so.

Q. Can Another Day Be Substituted for a Statutory Holiday?

A. Most jurisdictions in Canada provide for substitution of statutory holidays. Generally, where employees are represented by a union, the employer and the union must both agree in writing to substitute another day for the statutory holiday. Where there is no bargaining agent and no collective agreement, the employer must obtain the agreement of a majority of employees (70% under **federal** law), generally under the supervision of an employment standards official. In **New Brunswick**, the employer must obtain the consent of each employee, if the employees are not represented by a union. In **Ontario**, the day substituted for the public holiday must be granted no later than three months after the public holiday or, if the employee and employer agree, no later than 12 months after the public holiday.

Q. What if a Statutory Holiday Falls on a Non-Working Day?

A. Generally speaking, if a statutory holiday falls on a day on which the employee does not usually work, the employee has a right to take a holiday with pay at some other time. The exception to this rule is **Alberta**. Employees in **Alberta** receive no compensation for statutory holidays that fall on their regular days off. **Quebec** has dealt with the issue by defining most of its statutory holidays as falling on weekdays rather than weekends (i.e., **Quebec** provides a statutory holiday on "the Monday preceding 25 May" rather than Victoria Day). **Saskatchewan** provides that, when Remembrance Day, New Year's Day, or Christmas Day fall on a Sunday, the following Monday will be observed as a statutory holiday. **British Columbia** permits the pay for the holiday to be credited to the employees' "time bank".

The **federal** government and **Manitoba** make special provisions for certain holidays, requiring that a substitute holiday be granted on a working day immediately before or after the holiday in the **federal** jurisdiction and on the first workday after the holiday in **Manitoba**. Statutory holidays to which this requirement applies are New Year's Day, Canada Day, and Christmas Day in **Manitoba**, with the addition of Remembrance Day and Boxing Day under the **federal** jurisdiction.

Q. What if a Statutory Holiday Falls During an Employee's Vacation Time?

A. In all jurisdictions, if a statutory holiday falls during an employee's vacation, another day of vacation will be given to the employee at a later time. Employees are usually entitled to extend their vacation by one day if a public holiday occurs during their time off. For example, if an employee's annual vacation is scheduled for the first two weeks of September, during which Labour Day occurs, the employee will return to work a day later than he or she would have if Labour Day was not a public holiday. The other option, where the employer and the employee agree, is that another substitute day off with pay can be granted prior to the employee's next annual vacation. In these situations, the employee will be paid for the statutory holiday, as well as all vacation days, including the compensatory vacation day.

PAYMENT FOR STATUTORY HOLIDAYS

Q. Is There a Qualifying Period Before Employees Are Entitled To Pay for Statutory Holidays?

A. There are no qualifying periods in **Manitoba**, **Nova Scotia**, **Ontario**, **Quebec**, or **Saskatchewan**. In the other jurisdictions, an employee must have been employed for a specified number of days before he or she qualifies for a paid statutory holiday. In **Alberta**, **British Columbia**, **Newfoundland and Labrador**, **Prince Edward Island**, the **Northwest Territories**, **Nunavut**, the **Yukon**, and the **federal** jurisdiction, there is a 30-day qualifying period. There is a 90-day qualifying period in **New Brunswick**.

Q. Are There Other Exceptions That Would Disentitle the Employee to a Statutory Holiday with Pay if the Statutory Holiday Falls on a Working Day?

A. Employees are entitled to a day off with pay when a statutory holiday falls on a working day, with the following exceptions:

- The employee does not work on the statutory holiday when required or scheduled to do so. This exception applies in **Alberta**, **Manitoba**, **New Brunswick**, **Nova Scotia**, **Ontario**, **Prince Edward Island**, the **Northwest Territories**, **Nunavut**, and the **Yukon**.

- The employee is absent without justification on the working day preceding or following the statutory holiday. This exception applies everywhere except in **British Columbia**, **Saskatchewan**, and the **federal** jurisdiction.

- The employee has not earned wages for 15 of the 30 calendar days preceding the statutory holiday. This exception applies in **British Columbia**, **Manitoba**, **Nova Scotia**, **Prince Edward Island**, the

Yukon, and the **federal** jurisdiction. In the **Yukon**, an employee is not eligible if the employee has been absent for 14 consecutive days immediately before the holiday on a "leave of absence without pay" requested by the employee.

- The employee works under an arrangement in which he or she chooses whether or not to work when requested to do so. This exception applies only in **New Brunswick** and **Prince Edward Island**.

Q. When an Employee Qualifies for a Statutory Holiday off Work with Pay but Does Not Work That Day, How Is the Pay Calculated?

A. The basic principle for calculating holiday pay is that employees receive as payment for the statutory holiday the wages that they would ordinarily receive for their normal hours of work, paid at the regular rate. This means, for example, that if an employee is paid on a weekly or monthly basis, the amount of pay he or she receives is not reduced because of the statutory holiday. Where employees are paid on a daily or hourly basis, they must be paid the equivalent of the wages they would have earned at their regular rate of wages for their normal hours of work. In cases where pay varies, the daily earnings of the employee are typically averaged over a period of time to come up with an average daily rate. This averaging does not include overtime, but would normally include vacation pay. The amount of time over which pay should be averaged varies from jurisdiction to jurisdiction. Some provinces calculate statutory holiday pay for certain industries, such as construction, differently.

Q. How Are Employees Paid Who Work on the Statutory Holiday?

A. Employees who work on a statutory holiday are compensated differently throughout the country.

- In the **federal** jurisdiction, **New Brunswick**, **Nova Scotia**, and **Saskatchewan**, employees are entitled to regular pay plus 1.5 times their regular pay for hours worked.

- In **Alberta**, **Prince Edward Island**, the **Yukon**, the **Northwest Territories**, and **Nunavut**, employees are entitled to regular pay plus 1.5 times the employee's regular rate for hours worked or the employee's rate for hours worked and a substitute paid holiday at a later date.

- In **British Columbia**, employees who work on a statutory holiday receive 1.5 times their regular wage for the first 12 hours of work and two times their regular wage for time worked over 12 hours in that day, plus an average day's pay.

- In **Manitoba**, employees are entitled to 1.5 times the employees' regular wage rate plus holiday pay. For an employee with regular hours of work, holiday pay will be the employee's regular wage for regular hours of work on a normal workday in the pay period. If the employee has varying wages, holiday pay will be 5% of the employee's total wages, excluding overtime, for the four-week period immediately preceding the holiday.

- In **Newfoundland and Labrador**, employees may receive twice the wages properly earned by the employee for the day as if the day were a normal working day, one full day holiday to be enjoyed as if that day were a public holiday within 30 days, or one additional full day of vacation as if that day were a public holiday.

- In **Ontario**, employees are entitled to regular wages plus a substitute paid holiday at a later date or, if the employee and employer agree, to public holiday pay plus 1.5 times regular pay. Public holiday pay is calculated as the total amount of regular wages and vacation pay payable to the employee during the four-week period right before the work week in which the public holiday falls, divided by 20.

- In **Quebec**, employees receive regular wages plus a compensatory holiday to be taken within three weeks of the statutory holiday or an amount equal to an average day's wages.

Q. How Are Employees Who Work in Continuous Operations or Special Industries Paid for Work on Statutory Holidays?

A. In some parts of Canada, employees who work in "continuous operations", the tourism industry, or other specialized industries are required to work on statutory holidays. A continuous operation is an industry or service that, in each seven-day period, continues operations without stopping once commenced until the completion of the regularly scheduled operation for that period. Typical examples of continuous operations are hotels or hospitals.

The entitlements to payment under the continuous operations or special industry provisions are as follows:

- **Federal:** Employees in a continuous operation receive regular pay plus 1.5 times that amount, a compensatory holiday with pay at some other time, or where there is a collective agreement, a compensatory holiday with pay on the first day on which they do not work after the holiday.

- **British Columbia:** There are special provisions for silviculture workers. A silviculture worker is a person working in the silviculture industry who is paid primarily on a piece rate basis and who is involved in reforestation field work. An employer can pay these workers an additional 3.6% of gross earnings on each paycheque. However, if the employer has been paying 3.6% of gross earnings on each paycheque, the employer only has to pay straight time (regular piece rate) for work done on a statutory holiday. An employer may substitute another day off for a statutory holiday if it is agreed to in writing by the majority of affected employees (silviculture workers) or negotiated under a collective agreement.

- **Manitoba:** Employees in a continuously operating business are paid regular pay plus time off with pay equal to the hours worked on the holiday, taken within 30 days of the holiday or, with the agreement of the employer and the employee, some other time not later than the next annual vacation day.

- **New Brunswick:** Employees in a hotel, motel, tourist resort, restaurant, tavern, or a continuous operation are entitled to regular pay plus 1.5 times regular pay or regular pay plus a substituted day off with pay on the first working day immediately following the next annual vacation or on a working day agreed upon.

- **Newfoundland and Labrador:** Employees in a continuous operation or working for a public utility are entitled to receive either twice their regular pay for that day, or regular pay for the day plus a substituted day off with pay.

- **Nova Scotia:** Continuous operations are defined broadly in this province and include industrial establishments with a scheduled seven-day operation, operations or services where trucks or other vehicles are run in scheduled or non-scheduled operations, telephone or other communications or services, and any other service normally conducted without regard to Sunday or other holidays. An employee in a continuous operation who works on a statutory holiday receives either regular pay plus 1.5 times that amount or a compensatory holiday with pay on the working day immediately after the employee's annual vacation or on another day agreed upon by the employer and employee.

- **Ontario:** Employees in a hotel, motel, tourist resort, restaurant, tavern, hospital, or continuous operation can be required to work on a public holiday, but receive either regular wages plus a substitute day off with pay or public holiday pay plus 1.5 times regular wages. The election does not, however, require employee agreement. There are also special provisions for farm workers and silviculture workers.

Q. What if an Employee's Employment Ends Before Payment for a Statutory Holiday or a Substitute Holiday Is Received?

A. When a worker's employment is terminated, whether voluntarily or involuntarily, any monies owing for statutory holiday pay must be paid to the worker at the same time as other wages owing to that employee. This also includes pay owed for a substituted holiday not yet taken and a holiday in compensation for time worked on a statutory holiday that has not been taken.

STATUTORY HOLIDAYS CHART

	Fed.	Alta.[4]	B.C.	Man.[4]	N.B.	Nfld. and Lab.	N.S.[4]	Ont.[4]	P.E.I.[4]	Que.[5]	Sask.	NWT[7]	Num.	Yukon[8]
New Year's Day	X	X	X	X	X	X	X	X	X	X	X	X	X	X
Family Day		X	X[1]	X[1]				X	X[1]		X			
Good Friday	X	X	X	X	X	X	X	X	X	X[6]	X	X	X	X
Victoria Day	X	X	X	X				X		X	X	X	X	X
Canada Day	X	X	X	X	X	X[3]	X	X	X	X	X	X	X	X
First Monday in August			X		X						X	X	X	X
Labour Day	X	X	X	X	X	X	X	X	X	X	X	X	X	X
Thanksgiving Day	X	X	X	X				X		X	X	X	X	X
Remembrance Day	X	X	X	X[2]	X	X	X[2]		X		X	X	X	X
Christmas Day	X	X	X	X	X	X	X	X	X	X	X	X	X	X
Boxing Day (Dec. 26)	X							X						

[1] In Manitoba, the third Monday in February is called Louis Riel Day instead of Family Day. In Prince Edward Island, the third Monday in February is called Islander Day instead of Family Day. In British Columbia, Family Day is celebrated on the second Monday in February.

[2] In Manitoba, employees need not be paid for Remembrance Day if they are not required to work. In Nova Scotia, if an employee is required to work, he or she shall be given a holiday with pay on another agreed-upon day.

[3] Newfoundland and Labrador also observe July 1 as a statutory holiday, but it is called Memorial Day, not Canada Day. The province also observes Easter Sunday, Victoria Day, Thanksgiving Day, and Boxing Day as unpaid holidays.

[4] Alberta, Manitoba, Nova Scotia, Prince Edward Island, and Ontario customarily observe an additional holiday not provided for by statute — on the first Monday in August.

[5] In Quebec, an additional National Holiday, Saint-Jean-Baptiste Day, is observed on June 24.

[6] In Quebec, the employer can choose whether Good Friday or Easter Monday is observed as a holiday.

[7] The Northwest Territories also observes National Aboriginal Day on June 21.

[8] The Yukon Territory also observes Discovery Day, the third Monday in August.

STATUTORY HOLIDAYS ENTITLEMENT CHART

Jurisdiction	Length of Service Entitlement	Wages for Work on Holiday
Federal	30 days	1½ times regular rate plus regular pay
Alberta	30 days	1½ times hourly wage plus average daily wage, or average wage rate for each hour worked plus one day's holiday
British Columbia	30 days	1½ times regular wage for first 11 hours; double regular wage for each hour thereafter, plus an average day's pay
Manitoba	not specified	1½ times regular rate plus regular pay
New Brunswick	90 days	1½ times regular rate plus regular pay
Newfoundland and Labrador	30 days	2 times regular wages, regular wages plus a day off with pay within 30 days, or regular wages plus one additional day of vacation with pay
Nova Scotia	not specified	1½ times regular rate plus regular pay
Ontario	not specified	regular wages plus a substitute holiday with pay, or 1½ times regular rate plus regular wages
Prince Edward Island	30 days	1½ times regular rate plus regular pay, or regular wages for the hours worked that day plus a holiday with pay
Quebec	not specified	regular day's pay plus wages for work done, or wages for the work done plus a compensatory holiday within 3 weeks
Saskatchewan	not specified	1½ times regular rate for hours worked plus regular pay
Northwest Territories	30 days	1½ times regular rate for time worked plus regular pay, or regular rate for time worked plus holiday with pay

Nunavut	30 days	1½ times regular rate for time worked plus regular pay, or regular rate for time worked plus holiday with pay
Yukon Territory	30 days	1½ times regular rate plus regular wages, or regular rate for hours worked plus day off with pay

Chapter 6

VACATIONS WITH PAY

	Page
INTRODUCTION	56
TIME OFF	56
Do All Employees Have a Right To Take a Vacation with Pay?	56
Do Part-Time Employees Have a Right to Vacations with Pay?	56
How Much Vacation Time Are Employees Entitled To?	56
Do Employees Have To Work for a Certain Length of Time Before Being Entitled To Take a Vacation with Pay?	57
How Is the Length of Employment Calculated for the Purpose of Vacation Entitlement?	57
Can Employees Take Vacation Whenever They Like?	57
When Must the Employer Grant the Vacation?	58
Must an Employer Provide Notice of When the Vacation Is To Begin?	58
Can Vacation Be Taken in More Than One Period?	58
Are Employees Required To Take an Annual Vacation?	59
What Happens if a Statutory Holiday Occurs During an Employee's Vacation?	60
If an Employee Takes Maternity or Parental Leave, Is Entitlement to Vacation Affected?	60
If an Employee Takes Maternity or Parental Leave, Is Entitlement to Vacation Pay Affected?	60
VACATION PAY	61
How Is Vacation Pay Calculated?	61
What Is Included in "Wages" or "Annual Wage"?	61
When Must Vacation Pay Be Paid?	61
Are Normal Salary Deductions Made from Vacation Pay?	62
TERMINATION OF EMPLOYMENT	62
What If an Employee Is Dismissed Before All Vacation Is Taken or All Vacation Pay Is Received?	62
How Is Vacation Pay Paid on Termination Calculated?	62
When Must an Employer Pay Any Vacation Pay Owed upon Termination?	63
Can an Employee's Vacation Be Used as Part of the Notice Period?	64
MINIMUM VACATION ENTITLEMENT CHART	65
VACATION WITH PAY REQUIREMENTS CHART	66
VACATIONABLE EARNINGS INCLUSION CHART	68

INTRODUCTION

Even the most dedicated employee occasionally needs a break. Governments across the country have recognized that employee well-being and productivity are improved when vacations are provided. While the details of the laws regarding vacations vary — for instance, in the length of the vacation that employees can take — the basic structures and philosophies are similar across the country. This chapter provides an overview of employees' entitlement to vacation time and vacation pay.

TIME OFF

Q. Do All Employees Have a Right To Take a Vacation with Pay?

A. While the federal government and every province and territory in Canada have laws requiring employers to provide periods of rest for their employees on a regular basis, not every employee is entitled to paid vacation as not all employees are covered by employment standards laws or provided with all the benefits set out under employment standards legislation. Having said that, even if an employee is not entitled to vacation pay under the employment standards legislation, he or she may still have a right to a paid vacation if this is provided for in his or her employment contract or collective agreement.

Q. Do Part-Time Employees Have a Right to Vacations with Pay?

A. All employees covered by employment standards laws are entitled to vacations with pay. The fact that some employees work shorter hours than some of their co-workers does not affect their right to take a vacation. However, because vacation pay is calculated as a percentage of annual earnings, part-time workers may receive less vacation pay than their full-time colleagues.

Q. How Much Vacation Time Are Employees Entitled To?

A. All Canadian governments have provided for at least two weeks of vacation for each employee per year. In **Saskatchewan**, employees are entitled to a minimum of three weeks' vacation each year. In addition, **Alberta**, **British Columbia**, **Manitoba**, **New Brunswick**, **Nova Scotia**, **Newfoundland and Labrador**, **Nova Scotia**, **Prince Edward Island**, **Quebec**, **Saskatchewan**, the **Northwest Territories**, **Nunavut**, and the **federal** government each provide for longer vacations for employees who have worked for one employer for a specified length of time. As well, in **Quebec**, employees who are not yet entitled to three weeks of vacation can apply to take the number of days required to increase their annual leave to three weeks as unpaid leave. For details regarding the amount of vacation time to which an employee is entitled, please refer to the "Minimum Vacation Entitlement Chart" found on page 65.

Q. Do Employees Have To Work for a Certain Length of Time Before Being Entitled To Take a Vacation with Pay?

A. In all parts of Canada, employees are required to complete a year of employment before they become entitled to a vacation with pay.

Q. How Is the Length of Employment Calculated for the Purpose of Vacation Entitlement?

A. A year of employment is defined as 12 consecutive months of continuous employment with the same employer. The employment year typically commences on the date on which employment began, or on any anniversary of that date.

In a number of jurisdictions, however, including **Alberta**, **Manitoba**, **Ontario**, and the **federal** jurisdiction, the employer can set up a common anniversary date for all employees for ease of administration. For example, an employer may decide to use January 1st of each year as its common anniversary date so that the vacation entitlements of all employees will be calculated based on their service as of that date. If the employer uses a common anniversary date, it must ensure that employees do not receive any less vacation time or vacation pay than they would by the regular method of calculation.

In two provinces, the employment year is defined in the legislation. In **New Brunswick**, the law states that the vacation year runs from the first of July until the last day of June each year. In **Quebec**, regardless of when the employee begins employment, the vacation year runs from the first of May until the last day of April.

Q. Can Employees Take Vacation Whenever They Like?

A. While employers will often consult with employees about the timing of vacations, employees are not entitled to take vacation whenever they choose. Vacations must be scheduled in an orderly manner to enable employers to operate their businesses effectively, and therefore, employers have the final say regarding when vacations are to be taken.

Q. When Must the Employer Grant the Vacation?

A. While employers have the final say on when vacations are granted, the vacation must be granted within specific time limits.

- In **Prince Edward Island** and **New Brunswick**, the annual vacation must be given within four months of the end of the year of employment during which the right to a vacation was earned.

- In **Alberta**, **British Columbia**, **Quebec**, and **Saskatchewan**, employees must be permitted to take their vacations within 12 months of the end of the vacation year.

- In the rest of Canada, vacations must begin not later than 10 months following the completion of the employment year during which the employee earned the vacation.

Q. Must an Employer Provide Notice of When the Vacation Is To Begin?

A. With the exception of **British Columbia**, **Ontario**, the **Northwest Territories**, and the **Yukon**, all of the other jurisdictions specifically require employers to notify employees about the start date of their vacations.

- In **Alberta**, **Newfoundland and Labrador**, and the **federal** jurisdiction, the employer must give notice at least two weeks before the planned beginning of the vacation.

- In **Quebec** and **Saskatchewan**, employers must provide four weeks' notice.

- In **Prince Edward Island**, **Nova Scotia**, and **New Brunswick**, one week's advance notice must be given to the employee.

- In **Manitoba**, at least three weeks' notice must be given to the employee.

The notice from the employer to the employee setting out the vacation dates should be in writing.

Q. Can Vacation Be Taken in More Than One Period?

A. Whether vacations can be taken in more than one period varies between jurisdictions. The **federal** jurisdiction, **New Brunswick**, the **Northwest Territories**, **Nunavut**, and the **Yukon**, have no provisions regarding how annual vacation is to be taken. In these jurisdictions, the way in which the vacation period is used is a matter to be worked out between the employee and the employer.

In other jurisdictions, governments have ensured that employees are not required by their employers to break their vacations up into short periods. **Alberta**, **Newfoundland and Labrador**, **Nova Scotia**, **Prince Edward Island**, **Quebec**, and **Saskatchewan** permit employees to take their vacation in one unbroken period if they choose. In **British Columbia**, **Manitoba**, and **Ontario**, employers are prohibited from requiring employees to take their annual vacations in periods of less than one week. **Alberta**, **Newfoundland and Labrador**, **Nova Scotia**, **Ontario**, **Prince Edward Island**, **Quebec**, and **Saskatchewan** permit the vacation period to be broken down into smaller sections if the employee so requests. In **Alberta**, **Saskatchewan**, and **Newfoundland and Labrador**, employees who wish to divide their vacation into periods of one week must give the employer written notice of their desire to do so by the date upon which their year of employment is completed.

Q. Are Employees Required To Take an Annual Vacation?

A. Generally, employers are required to ensure that employees take the vacation time required under employment standards law. Some jurisdictions, however, provide that employees may postpone their right to take a paid vacation or give up the time off altogether, if they choose.

- Under **federal** law, an employee may either postpone or give up his or her right to a vacation with pay for a particular year by entering into a written agreement with the employer. Even if the vacation with pay is waived, the employer is still obliged to provide the employee with vacation pay.

- In **Nova Scotia**, an employee who works for an employer for less than 90% of the regular working hours during a continuous 12-month period may waive his or her right to a paid vacation in writing. Where the employee chooses to exercise this option, the employer must still pay the employee vacation pay.

- In **Ontario**, if the Director of Employment Standards approves, and the employer agrees, an employee may be allowed to forgo taking the vacation to which he or she is entitled. However, the employer must still pay the employee vacation pay.

- In the **Northwest Territories** and **Nunavut**, an employee may waive his or her vacation leave by sending a joint employer–employee written application to the Labour Standards Officer setting out the exceptional circumstances that require the postponement of the vacation.

- In the **Yukon**, the employer and employee may enter into a written agreement that the employee will not take annual vacation and will receive vacation pay in lieu.

Q. What Happens if a Statutory Holiday Occurs During an Employee's Vacation?

A. In all jurisdictions, if a statutory holiday falls during an employee's annual vacation period, another day of vacation will be given to the employee at a later time. Employees are usually entitled to extend their vacation for one day if a statutory holiday occurs during it. For example, if an employee's annual vacation is scheduled for the first two weeks of September, during which Labour Day occurs, the employee will return to work a day later than he or she would have. The other option, where the employer and the employee agree, is that another substitute day off with pay can be granted prior to the employee's next annual vacation. In these situations, the employee will be paid for the statutory holiday, as well as all vacation days, including the compensatory vacation day.

Q. If an Employee Takes Maternity or Parental Leave, Is Entitlement to Vacation Affected?

A. When an employee is away on maternity or parental leave, her or his employment is deemed to be continuous. This means that the employee maintains and continues to accrue seniority for vacation purposes and continues to earn vacation time during his or her leave.

Q. If an Employee Takes Maternity or Parental Leave, Is Entitlement to Vacation Pay Affected?

A. Since vacation pay is usually calculated as a percentage of wages earned and employees usually earn less in wages during maternity or parental leave, an employee who takes such a leave will typically receive less vacation pay. **Newfoundland and Labrador** is an exception to this rule as employees are required to have worked 90% of the normal working hours in the year in order to be credited with a year's service. In **Quebec**, however, the right of employees who take either maternity or paternity leave to collect vacation pay is specifically protected. In the case of such a leave, vacation pay is calculated, for employees with more than one but less than five years of service, at twice the weekly average of the wage earned during the period of work; for employees with five years of service or more, it is calculated at three times the weekly average of wages earned during the period of work.

VACATION PAY

Q. How Is Vacation Pay Calculated?

A. Vacation pay is calculated as a percentage of the wages the employee was paid during the year of employment in which he or she earned the right to a paid vacation. If an employee is entitled to two weeks' paid vacation, he or she will receive 4% of his or her yearly wages. If the employee is entitled to three weeks' paid vacation, she or he will receive 6% of her or his yearly wages.

There are two exceptions to this method of calculating vacation pay:

- In **Alberta**, special provisions apply to workers who are paid monthly. In such cases, the normal monthly wage is divided by $4^{1}/_{3}$. For other employees, vacation pay is calculated as a percentage of the yearly earnings.

- In **Saskatchewan**, those who are entitled to three weeks' annual vacation receive $^{3}/_{52}$ of their annual wage as vacation pay, and those who are entitled to four weeks' vacation will receive $^{4}/_{52}$ of their annual wage. Because of this difference in calculation method, employees in **Saskatchewan** receive less vacation pay than their counterparts in other jurisdictions who are entitled to the same length of vacation.

Q. What Is Included in "Wages" or "Annual Wage"?

A. Employees receive payment for their services in many different ways, and which amounts are included when calculating an employee's "wages" or "annual wage" differs depending on the jurisdiction in which the employee works. For assistance in determining what is and what is not included in vacationable earnings, refer to the "Vacationable Earnings Inclusion Chart" on pages 68 to 69.

Q. When Must Vacation Pay Be Paid?

A. Generally, employers are required to pay employees the vacation pay due to them before the start of the vacation. There are, however, several exceptions:

- Under **federal** law, an employer must pay the vacation pay due within the 14-day period before the start of the employee's vacation. However, where it is not practical to do so, or where it is the established practice at the employer's place of business, vacation pay may be paid on the regular payday during or immediately following the vacation.

- In **Alberta**, the employee must request payment of vacation pay prior to the vacation, otherwise the employer may pay it on the next scheduled payday after the employee starts his or her annual vacation.

- In **British Columbia**, vacation pay may be paid on the employee's scheduled payday if it is so agreed by the employer and the employee, or by the collective agreement.

- In **Manitoba**, employees may agree to receive their vacation pay at another time.

- In **Ontario**, if the employee takes vacation in complete weeks, vacation pay must be paid in a lump sum prior to the start of the vacation. If the employee is paid his or her wages by direct deposit to a financial institution, or the employee does not take vacation in complete weeks, vacation pay may be paid on or before the payday for the pay period in which the vacation falls. If the employee agrees, vacation pay that an employee earns during the 12-month employment period may be paid on each pay period throughout the year. Finally, the employer may also pay vacation pay at a time agreed to by the employee.

Q. Are Normal Salary Deductions Made from Vacation Pay?

A. Yes, normal salary deductions are made from vacation pay because vacation pay is typically considered to fall under the definition of wages.

TERMINATION OF EMPLOYMENT

Q. What If an Employee Is Dismissed Before All Vacation Is Taken or All Vacation Pay Is Received?

A. If the employee is dismissed before all earned vacation is taken, the employee will receive the vacation pay, but not the time off. Upon termination, an employer must pay the employee vacation pay for:

- any vacation entitlement that the employee earned in a prior year of employment and has not yet used, and

- any vacation entitlement that the employee earned for the portion of the current year of employment that the employee has worked.

Q. How Is Vacation Pay Paid on Termination Calculated?

A. Any vacation pay owing with respect to a previous year of employment is calculated in the normal manner, as if employment had not been terminated before the employee used his or her vacation time.

For the current employment year, the employer must pay the employee a percentage of the wages earned so far in the year. The percentage will depend on how many weeks' vacation the employee would have been entitled to take in that year. For example, if the employee would have been entitled to two weeks' vacation, he or she will be entitled to 4% of the wages earned to date in that year.

Q. When Must an Employer Pay Any Vacation Pay Owed upon Termination?

A. In some jurisdictions, vacation pay owing must be paid at the same time as all other wages owing on termination; in other jurisdictions, vacation pay must be paid at a different time. The following list sets out the time for payment in each jurisdiction:

- The **federal** jurisdiction, **Newfoundland and Labrador**, the **Northwest Territories**, and **Nunavut** all require payment of vacation pay at the time of termination.

- In **Alberta**, where proper termination notice is given or notice is required to be given by the employer, vacation pay must be paid not later than three consecutive days after the last day of employment. Where an employer terminates an employee's employment and no termination notice or termination pay is required to be given, the employer must pay the employee within 10 consecutive days of the employee's last day of employment.

- In **British Columbia**, if the employer terminates the employment relationship, vacation pay must be paid 48 hours from the effective date of the termination; if the employee terminates the employment relationship, vacation pay must be paid by six days after the effective date of termination.

- In **Manitoba**, payment of vacation pay must be made within 10 working days of termination.

- In **New Brunswick**, payment must be made at the time of final pay.

- In **Nova Scotia**, the employee is entitled to his or her vacation entitlement within 10 days of the day of termination of employment.

- In **Ontario**, payment of vacation pay must be made by the later of seven days after the effective date of termination or by the date that would have been the employee's next payday.

- In **Prince Edward Island**, the vacation pay must be paid by the end of the next regular pay period following the termination of employment.

- In **Quebec**, the time limit for payment of vacation pay is not specified.

- In **Saskatchewan**, payment must be made within 14 days from the effective date of the termination.

- In the **Yukon**, the time limit for payment of vacation pay is seven days from the date of termination.

Q. Can an Employee's Vacation Be Used as Part of the Notice Period?

A. No. If an employee's employment is terminated, the employee must be fully compensated for any earned vacation time as well as receive any notice or pay in lieu of notice to which he or she is entitled.

MINIMUM VACATION ENTITLEMENT CHART

Jurisdiction	Length of Annual Vacation	Vacation Pay
Federal	2 weeks; 3 weeks after 6 years	4% of annual earnings; 6% after 6 years
Alberta	2 weeks; 3 weeks after completion of 5th and subsequent years	4% of annual earnings; 6% after 5th and subsequent years of service
British Columbia	2 weeks; 3 weeks upon completion of 5th and subsequent years	4% of annual earnings after 5 days; 6% after 5 years
Manitoba	2 weeks; 3 weeks upon completion of 5th and subsequent years	4% of annual earnings; 6% after 5th and subsequent years of service
New Brunswick	2 weeks; 3 weeks upon completion of 8th and subsequent years	4% of annual earnings; 6% after 8 years
Newfoundland and Labrador	2 weeks; 3 weeks after 15 years	4% of annual earnings; 6% after 15 years
Nova Scotia	2 weeks; 3 weeks after 8 years	4% of annual earnings; 6% after 8 years
Ontario	2 weeks	4% of annual earnings
Prince Edward Island	2 weeks; 3 weeks after 8 years	4% of annual earnings; 6% of annual earnings after 8 years
Quebec	2 weeks; 3 weeks after 5 years	4% of annual earnings; 6% of annual earnings after 5 years
Saskatchewan	3 weeks; 4 weeks on the 10th anniversary of employment and subsequent anniversaries	$3/52$ of annual earnings on completion of one year's service; $4/52$ of annual earnings on the 10th anniversary and subsequent anniversaries
Northwest Territories	2 weeks; 3 weeks upon completion of 6th and subsequent years	4% of annual earnings; 6% after 5th and subsequent years of service
Nunavut	2 weeks; 3 weeks upon completion of 6th and subsequent years	4% of annual earnings; 6% after 5th and subsequent years of service
Yukon Territory	2 weeks	4% of annual earnings

VACATION WITH PAY REQUIREMENTS CHART

Jurisdiction	Qualifying Period	Time of Vacation	Required Notice	How Vacation Taken	Waiver/ Postponement	Time for Payment
Federal	12 months	within 10 months of entitlement	2 weeks	not specified	yes	within 14 days preceding vacation
Alberta	12 months	within 12 months of entitlement	2 weeks	unbroken	no	next scheduled payday
British Columbia	12 months	within 12 months of entitlement	not specified	periods of at least 1 week	no	within 7 days preceding vacation
Manitoba	12 months	within 10 months of entitlement	15 days	periods of at least 1 week	no	by day preceding vacation
New Brunswick	12 months	within 4 months of entitlement	1 week	not specified	no	by day preceding vacation
Newfoundland and Labrador	12 months	within 10 months of entitlement	2 weeks	1 unbroken period or 2 unbroken periods of 1 week	no	by day preceding vacation
Nova Scotia	12 months	within 10 months of entitlement	1 week	unbroken	yes	by day preceding vacation
Ontario	12 months	within 10 months of entitlement	not specified	1 unbroken period or 2 unbroken periods of 1 week or shorter with agreement	yes	by day preceding vacation
Prince Edward Island	12 months	within 4 months of entitlement	1 week	unbroken	yes	by day preceding vacation

Jurisdiction	Qualifying Period	Time of Vacation	Required Notice	How Vacation Taken	Waiver/ Postponement	Time for Payment
Quebec	12 months	within 12 months of entitlement	4 weeks	1 or 2 unbroken periods	no	before beginning of vacation
Saskatchewan	12 months	within 12 months of entitlement	4 weeks	1 unbroken period or periods of at least 1 week	yes	on the employee's normal payday or before vacation upon the employee's request
Northwest Territories	12 months	within 6 months of entitlement	not specified	not specified	yes	by day preceding vacation
Nunavut	12 months	within 10 months of entitlement	not specified	not specified	yes	by day preceding vacation
Yukon	12 months	within 10 months of entitlement	not specified	not specified	yes	by day preceding vacation

VACATIONABLE EARNINGS INCLUSION CHART

Jurisdiction	Salary	Commission	Tips & Gratuities	Expenses	Vacation Pay	Overtime	Holiday Pay	Discretionary Bonuses
Federal	yes	yes	no	not specified	yes	yes	yes	yes
Alberta	yes	yes	no	no	yes	no	no	no
British Columbia	yes	yes	no	no	yes	yes	yes	no
Manitoba	yes	yes	not specified	not specified	no	no	yes	yes
New Brunswick	yes	yes	no	not specified	no	yes	no	yes
Newfoundland and Labrador	yes	yes	no	not specified	yes	yes	yes	yes
Nova Scotia	yes	yes	no	not specified	no	yes	yes	yes
Ontario	yes	yes	no	no	no	yes	yes	no

Jurisdiction	Salary	Commission	Tips & Gratuities	Expenses	Vacation Pay	Overtime	Holiday Pay	Discretionary Bonuses
Prince Edward Island	yes	yes	no	not specified	no	yes	yes	yes
Quebec	yes	not specified	not specified	not specified	not specified	yes	yes	yes
Saskatchewan	yes	yes	not specified	not specified	yes	yes	yes	yes
Northwest Territories	yes	yes	no	not specified	yes	yes	yes	yes
Nunavut	yes	yes	no	not specified	yes	yes	yes	yes
Yukon	yes	yes	no	no	yes	yes	yes	no

Chapter 7

LEAVES OF ABSENCE

	Page
INTRODUCTION	73
MATERNITY LEAVE	73
What Is Maternity Leave?	73
Are All Pregnant Employees Eligible for Maternity Leave?	74
Is There a Qualifying Period Before an Employee Is Entitled To Maternity Leave?	74
Can Part-Time Employees Take Maternity Leave?	74
What Must an Employee Do if She Wants To Take Maternity Leave?	74
Is an Employee Still Entitled To Maternity Leave if She Fails To Give Her Employer Sufficient Notice?	74
How Much Time Can an Employee Take Off?	75
Can the Leave of Absence Begin at Any Time During the Pregnancy?	75
Must at Least Part of Maternity Leave Be Taken after the Birth?	75
Can an Employee Take a Leave of Absence Following a Miscarriage?	76
Can Maternity Leave Be Extended?	76
Can an Employee Be Required To Take Maternity Leave?	76
Must Maternity Leave Be Taken All at Once?	77
What Must an Employee Do When She Wishes To Return To Work Following Maternity Leave?	77
PARENTAL LEAVE	77
What Is Parental Leave?	77
Are All Employees Eligible for Parental Leave?	78
Can an Employee Take Leave if Adopting a Child?	78
How Much Time Can an Employee Take Off for Parental Leave?	78
Can Either Parent Take Parental Leave?	78
Can an Employee Who Took Maternity Leave Take Parental Leave at Any Time?	79
What if a Child Is Hospitalized at the Time Maternity Leave Expires or after Parental Leave Has Begun?	79
When Must an Employee Who Did Not Take Maternity Leave Begin Parental Leave?	80
Can Parental Leave Ever Be Extended?	80
What Must an Employee Do if He or She Wishes To Take Parental Leave?	80

71

Page

EMPLOYEE PROTECTIONS WHILE ON MATERNITY AND PARENTAL LEAVE 81

Will an Employee's Job Be Jeopardized as a Result of a Decision To Take Leave? 81

What Happens to Seniority Status While on Leave? 81

Do Benefits Continue To Accrue During the Leave of Absence? 81

What Is the Effect of the Leave of Absence on Vacations with Pay? 81

What Happens if the Employer Discontinues the Business While an Employee Is
on Leave? 82

Can an Employer Retaliate Against an Employee for Exercising His or Her
Entitlement To Take Maternity or Parental Leave? 82

What Can an Employee Do if an Employer Refuses To Grant Maternity or
Parental Leave? 82

HEALTH AND SAFETY BENEFITS FOR PREGNANT EMPLOYEES 82

Can an Employee Take Time Off for Medical Examinations? 82

What if the Employee's Health or the Health of the Unborn or Newborn Child Is
Jeopardized by the Employee's Work? 83

MISCELLANEOUS LEAVES OF ABSENCE 83

Are Employees Entitled to Time Off in the Event of a Death in the Family? 83

Are Employees Entitled to Time Off When They Are Sick? 87

Can an Employee Take Time Off for a Family Emergency or Event? 89

Is an Employee Entitled to a Leave of Absence in Order To Donate an Organ
and/or To Recover from Organ Donation? 94

Is an Employee Entitled to Time Off To Attend at His or Her Citizenship
Ceremony? 95

How Much Time Off Must an Employer Give Employees To Vote in Federal
Elections? 96

Are Employees Also Entitled To Time Off To Vote in Provincial, Territorial, or
Municipal Elections? 96

If an Employee Is Called for Jury Duty, Must the Employer Grant Time Off? 96

Are Employees Entitled To a Leave of Absence To Care for a Dying Family
Member? 97

Are Employees Entitled To a Leave of Absence To Serve in the Canadian Forces? 98

RESERVIST LEAVE CHART 99

ENTITLEMENT TO EMPLOYMENT INSURANCE BENEFITS DURING LEAVES OF
ABSENCE 104

What Is the Relationship Between the Provincial Employment Standards Laws
and the Federal Employment Insurance Legislation? 104

What Life Changes or Situations May Result in an Employee Receiving EI
Benefits? 104

What Length of Employment or Employment Status Must an Employee Establish
To Be Eligible for EI Sickness, Maternity, Parental, and Compassionate Care
Benefits, or Special Benefits for Parents of Critically Ill Children? 104

What Is the EI Benefit Payment During Sickness, Maternity, Parental,
Compassionate Care, or Critically Ill Child Care Leaves? 104

What Are EI Sickness Benefits and for What Period Will an Employee Be Eligible
To Receive Them? 105

What Are Maternity Benefits and for What Period Will an Employee Be Eligible
To Receive Them? 105

What Is the Impact on EI Maternity Benefits if the Child Is Hospitalized? 105

What Are EI Parental Benefits and for What Period Will an Employee Be Eligible
To Receive Them? 105

Can Either Parent Receive EI Parental Benefits? 106

Can an Employee Claim Both Maternity and Parental Leave Benefits? 106

Page

What Happens if an Employee Gets Sick While Collecting Maternity or Parental
Benefits? 106

What Are Compassionate Care Benefits and What Is the Period During Which an
Individual May Receive Them? 106

Who Is a Family Member for the Purposes of Receiving EI Compassionate Care
Benefits? 107

What Happens if an Employee Needs To Care for a Dying Family Member after
Collecting Maternity, Parental, or Sick Benefits? 108

What Are Special Benefits for Parents of Critically Ill Children and What Is the
Period During Which an Individual May Receive Them? 108

Can Either Parent Receive the Special Benefits for Parents of Critically Ill
Children? 108

Is There Any Support for Parents of Murdered or Missing Children? 108

Can an Employee Work While Collecting EI Benefits? 109

How Does an Employee Apply for EI Benefits? 109

MATERNITY LEAVE CHECKLIST 110

MATERNITY/PARENTAL LEAVE CHART 111

INTRODUCTION

While paid vacations were well-developed by the 1960s, leaves of absence are a relatively new phenomenon and are a response to the changing and competing interests of our society. Recognizing the number of women now in the workforce, maternity and parental leaves are attempts to balance the competing interests of child-bearing, child rearing, and workforce involvement. Other leaves acknowledge the need to care for family members at later stages of life or to grieve the loss of loved ones when they pass on or for parents to cope with the crime-related death or disappearance of a child. Still others relate to our civic responsibilities, including donating an organ, becoming a Canadian citizen, voting at elections, attending jury duty, and serving in the Armed Forces.

This chapter will discuss leaves of absence for maternity, parental, bereavement, sickness, family responsibility, compassionate care, the crime-related death or disappearance of a child, special occasions, organ donation, voting, citizenship ceremony, jury duty, and serving in the armed forces. This chapter will conclude by providing an overview of the Employment Insurance sickness, maternity, parental, compassionate care benefits, and special benefits for parents of critically ill children.

MATERNITY LEAVE

Q. What Is Maternity Leave?

A. Maternity leave, also known as pregnancy leave, provides pregnant employees with some time off from work during and immediately after pregnancy to ensure a healthy pregnancy, childbirth, and recovery.

The right to take maternity leave exists in all Canadian jurisdictions, but employers are not required to pay employees who are on maternity leave. Requirements with respect to the continuation of benefits vary from jurisdiction to jurisdiction.

Q. Are All Pregnant Employees Eligible for Maternity Leave?

A. No, employment standards legislation does not apply to all employees. Nonetheless, if the employment standards legislation does apply to the pregnant employee, and she meets the legislative requirements, she will be eligible.

Q. Is There a Qualifying Period Before an Employee Is Entitled To Maternity Leave?

A. There is no qualifying period in **British Columbia**, **New Brunswick**, and **Quebec**. In the remaining jurisdictions, the provisions generally state that an employee who has worked for the same employer for a period ranging from 13 consecutive weeks to 12 consecutive months is entitled to an unpaid maternity/parental leave of up to 52 weeks. To determine the qualifying period for a particular jurisdiction, please refer to the chart on pages 111 to 117.

Q. Can Part-Time Employees Take Maternity Leave?

A. Yes. Employment and labour standards legislation makes no distinction between part-time and full-time employees, so long as any required period of continuous employment prior to the leave has been completed.

Q. What Must an Employee Do if She Wants To Take Maternity Leave?

A. An employee who wishes to take maternity leave must give her employer sufficient notice of her intent to take such leave before the leave begins. The required notice ranges from two weeks to four months. This notice must be in writing. The employer also has the right to request a medical certificate that sets out an estimated date for the birth. For the specific requirements for your jurisdiction, please refer to the chart on pages 111 to 117.

Q. Is an Employee Still Entitled To Maternity Leave if She Fails To Give Her Employer Sufficient Notice?

A. In most jurisdictions, an employee who fails to give her employer the required notice is still entitled to maternity leave if, within two weeks after leaving work, she gives her employer notice and provides a medical certificate that sets out the estimated date of delivery and states that she cannot work due to a medical condition resulting from the pregnancy.

Q. How Much Time Can an Employee Take Off?

A. Pregnant employees are entitled to 17 weeks of maternity leave in all jurisdictions except **Alberta**, **Quebec**, and **Saskatchewan**. Employees in **Alberta** are entitled to 15 weeks' maternity leave. Employees in **Quebec** and **Saskatchewan** are entitled to 18 weeks' maternity leave.

Q. Can the Leave of Absence Begin at Any Time During the Pregnancy?

A. No, each jurisdiction stipulates that a pregnant employee cannot begin her maternity leave before a certain stage in her pregnancy. In **British Columbia**, **New Brunswick**, **Prince Edward Island**, and the **federal** jurisdiction, employees cannot start maternity leave until 11 weeks before the expected delivery date. In **Alberta** and **Saskatchewan**, employees cannot start maternity leave until 12 weeks before the expected delivery date. In **Nova Scotia** and **Quebec**, employees cannot start maternity leave until 16 weeks before the expected delivery date. Finally, in **Manitoba**, **Newfoundland and Labrador**, **Ontario**, the **Northwest Territories**, **Nunavut**, and the **Yukon**, employees cannot start maternity leave until 17 weeks before the expected delivery date.

Q. Must at Least Part of Maternity Leave Be Taken after the Birth?

A. Some jurisdictions structure maternity leave so that a certain portion of the leave must be taken after the birth of the child. For example, **Alberta** specifically provides that the period of maternity leave is to include at least six weeks immediately following the actual date of delivery, unless the employer and employee agree to shorten the period and the employee provides a medical certificate indicating that she is able to return to work. In **British Columbia**, **New Brunswick**, **Prince Edward Island**, and the **federal** jurisdiction, employees cannot start maternity leave until 11 weeks before the expected delivery date and, therefore, at least six weeks of the leave would generally be taken after the birth. Other jurisdictions may require the presentation of medical documentation certifying the employee's ability to return to work if the planned return is very soon after the delivery.

Q. Can an Employee Take a Leave of Absence Following a Miscarriage?

A. Yes. Most jurisdictions protect an employee's right to have at least some period of time away from work if an employee has a miscarriage or stillbirth. However, that period may be shorter than the period of maternity leave that is otherwise available.

Q. Can Maternity Leave Be Extended?

A. Some jurisdictions permit the extension of the maternity leave for a few weeks due to medical reasons. However, with the extension of parental leave to between 35 and 52 weeks, this is becoming less common. In **British Columbia**, leave may be extended by six weeks, if the employee provides the employer with medical documentation demonstrating why she is unable to return to work. **Ontario**, **Saskatchewan**, the **Northwest Territories**, and **Nunavut** also provide that the maternity leave may be extended for up to six weeks where the birth is later than expected. In **Prince Edward Island**, where the employee's child (in respect of whom the leave is granted) has a physical, psychological, or emotional condition requiring an additional period of parental care, the employee is entitled to an additional five weeks of unpaid leave. In order to obtain such a leave, the employee must submit an application for extension to the employer along with supporting medical documentation if requested by the employer. In **Saskatchewan**, employees who are unable to return to work at the expiry of their maternity leave for *bona fide* medical reasons are entitled to further leave of up to six weeks. In **Quebec**, a pregnant woman who provides her employer with a medical certificate indicating that her health or the health of her unborn child is at risk will be entitled to special maternity leave without pay for the duration of the risk set out in the certificate. Nonetheless, this special maternity leave will be considered to be regular maternity leave from the first week preceding the expected delivery date onward.

Q. Can an Employee Be Required To Take Maternity Leave?

A. Generally speaking, it is up to the employee to decide how long she will take for maternity leave. She is not required to take the full entitlement of maternity leave, although, as noted above, in some provinces she will be required to take at least six weeks of leave following the delivery of her child unless she produces medical evidence that she is fit to work. However, in **New Brunswick**, **Nova Scotia**, **Prince Edward Island**, **Saskatchewan**, the **Northwest Territories**, **Nunavut**, the **Yukon**, and the **federal** jurisdiction, where pregnancy affects an employee's ability to perform her job, the employer may, in some cases, require the employee to take maternity leave. This enforced maternity leave lasts only as long as the employee is unable to effectively perform her job. In **Quebec**, an employer is entitled to require a pregnant employee to produce a medical certificate six weeks before the expected delivery date, indicating that she is fit for work. If the employee fails to provide the certificate within eight days, the employer may oblige her to take the maternity leave immediately.

Q. Must Maternity Leave Be Taken All at Once?

A. Yes. Once maternity leave has begun, all jurisdictions require maternity leave to be taken all at once — it cannot be split up. In **Quebec**, however, if the child is hospitalized during the maternity leave, the leave may be suspended during the period of hospitalization with agreement by the employer.

Q. What Must an Employee Do When She Wishes To Return To Work Following Maternity Leave?

A. Where an employee on maternity leave wishes to return to work, all jurisdictions require that the employee provide some form of notice to the employer. The simplest form of notice of return to work is provided with the notice of intention to take maternity leave. The notice of intention to take maternity leave must specify the start date and then, based on general entitlement, will have an end date and therefore a return-to-work date at the end of the period. If the employee does not specify a return date, the employer may assume that she will take the full maternity leave to which she is entitled. By contrast, **Alberta** and **Saskatchewan** both require that the employee provide a specific notice of return to work, and **Quebec** requires employees to provide three weeks' notice. Finally, **British Columbia**, **Manitoba**, **Newfoundland and Labrador**, **Nova Scotia**, **Ontario**, **Quebec**, the **Northwest Territories**, **Nunavut**, and the **Yukon** require employees to provide written notice, and, in some cases, a medical certificate, where the employee intends to return to work prior to the end of the full period of maternity leave.

PARENTAL LEAVE

Q. What Is Parental Leave?

A. Parental leave, or child care leave, as it is known in some jurisdictions, permits natural or adoptive parents to take time off without pay to adjust to their new familial responsibilities and to care for their new child. The right to parental leave exists in all jurisdictions in Canada.

Q. Are All Employees Eligible for Parental Leave?

A. No. As with maternity leave, in most jurisdictions, in order to be eligible for parental leave, an employee must be covered by employment standards legislation and have worked for the employer for a specified period of time. In each of the jurisdictions where a qualifying period is specified, it is the same period as is required to become eligible for maternity leave. For details, please refer to the chart on pages 111 to 117.

Q. Can an Employee Take Leave if Adopting a Child?

A. Yes. In all jurisdictions, adoption leave is included under parental leave, and adoptive parents have the same rights as natural parents. However, in addition to the entitlements related to maternity and parental leave, **Newfoundland and Labrador**, **Quebec**, and **Saskatchewan** provide for a specific leave of absence ranging from five days to 18 weeks for adoptive parents.

Q. How Much Time Can an Employee Take Off for Parental Leave?

A. The amount of leave to which parents are entitled varies between jurisdictions and ranges from 35 to 37 weeks throughout most of Canada, to a high of 52 weeks in **Nova Scotia** and **Quebec**. The amount of leave usually varies depending on whether or not maternity leave was taken and whether or not the parents are entitled to a combined or individual parental leave. To determine the length of the parental leave to which an employee is entitled, please refer to the chart on pages 111 to 117.

Q. Can Either Parent Take Parental Leave?

A. In all jurisdictions, parental leave is available to both fathers and mothers; however, most provinces and territories reduce the length of parental leave where maternity leave has also been taken. The majority of jurisdictions, namely **British Columbia**, **Manitoba**, **Newfoundland and Labrador**, **Nova Scotia**, **Ontario**, **Quebec**, **Saskatchewan**, the **Northwest Territories**, and **Nunavut**, permit both parents to take the full parental or adoption leave. In these provinces and territories, parental leave is generally limited to a maximum of 35 or 37 weeks for each parent. In other jurisdictions, **Alberta**, **New Brunswick**, the **Yukon**, and the **federal** jurisdiction, parental leave must normally be shared between parents. In these jurisdictions, the total combined parental or adoption leave cannot exceed 37 weeks.

Regardless of the total leave entitlement, some jurisdictions place restrictions on both parents taking parental leave at the same time. In

Alberta, where the parents are both employed by the same employer, the employer is not required to grant parental leave to more than one parent at a time. In the **Yukon**, where both parents take parental leave, they cannot take their leaves at the same time, unless the employee who is first on parental leave cannot reasonably be expected to care for the child by him or herself because of injury, illness, death, or other hardship in the family.

Q. Can an Employee Who Took Maternity Leave Take Parental Leave at Any Time?

A. No, except in exceptional circumstances. Unless her employer agrees otherwise, parental leave must begin when maternity leave ends. Thus, the employee cannot take her maternity leave, return to work for a limited period, and then take parental leave.

Q. What if a Child Is Hospitalized at the Time Maternity Leave Expires or after Parental Leave Has Begun?

A. **New Brunswick**, **Newfoundland and Labrador**, **Nova Scotia**, **Ontario**, and the **federal** jurisdiction make special provisions for such cases. In **New Brunswick** and **Newfoundland and Labrador** parental leave need not commence until the child actually comes into the care and custody of its parents. In **Nova Scotia**, where parental leave has begun and the child is hospitalized for a period exceeding or likely to exceed one week, the employee is entitled to resume work and defer the unused portion of the parental leave until the child is discharged from hospital. An employee is entitled to only one interruption and deferral of parental leave. An employee who intends to use the deferral option must give the employer as much notice as possible of the dates of resumption of work and resumption of leave and, where requested, provide the employer with whatever proof is reasonable to support the employee's entitlement to the option. In **Ontario**, the parental leave of a mother who has taken pregnancy leave must begin when the pregnancy leave ends, unless the child had not yet come into the custody and care of the parent for the first time. This exception recognizes situations where the child is hospitalized after birth. However, should the child first come home and then have to be hospitalized, the parental leave will continue to run. In all other cases, the parental leave must begin no later than 52 weeks after the child is born or first comes into the custody and care of the parent. In the **federal** jurisdiction, an employee who intends to interrupt his or her parental leave in order to return to work as a result of the hospitalization of his or her child shall provide the employer with notice in writing of the interruption as soon as possible after the child's hospitalization begins. The employer is required to advise the employee in writing of its decision to accept or refuse the employee's return to work within one week after receiving the notice. If the employer refuses the return to work, or does not advise the employee within one week of receiving the notice, the employee's parental leave will be extended by the number of weeks for which the child is hospitalized. Regardless of the duration of the hospitalization, parental leave must end no later than 104 weeks after the day on which the child is born or comes into the employee's actual care.

Q. When Must an Employee Who Did Not Take Maternity Leave Begin Parental Leave?

A. In most jurisdictions, unless a parent is also taking maternity leave, an employee can begin parental leave any time during the 52 weeks following the birth or adoption of the child, or its coming into the parents' care and custody. In **Manitoba** and **Ontario**, parents must commence their parental leave within 52 weeks of the birth, adoption, or arrival of the child into parental care and custody. In **Quebec**, parental leave must end within 70 weeks of the child's birth or 70 weeks after the adoption of a child by the employee.

Q. Can Parental Leave Ever Be Extended?

A. In **British Columbia** and **Prince Edward Island**, where the child has a physical, psychological, or emotional condition requiring an additional period of parental leave, the employee is entitled to up to five additional weeks of unpaid leave, beginning immediately after the end of the original parental leave. The employee must, however, submit an application for an extension and provide supporting medical documentation if requested by his or her employer.

Q. What Must an Employee Do if He or She Wishes To Take Parental Leave?

A. The employee must provide the employer with written notice of intent to take parental leave. Again, the length of the required notice varies from province to province, and the requirements are set out in the chart on pages 111 to 117. In the notice, the employee must specify not only the intention to take child care leave, but the dates on which the leave is proposed to commence and terminate. In some jurisdictions, the employee is required to provide a medical certificate confirming the pregnancy and the anticipated date of birth. If the employee is adopting a child, the employee must provide proof of the adoption to the employer. As with maternity leave, there are exceptions to the notice requirements if the child comes into parental care and custody earlier than was expected.

EMPLOYEE PROTECTIONS WHILE ON MATERNITY AND PARENTAL LEAVE

Q. Will an Employee's Job Be Jeopardized as a Result of a Decision To Take Leave?

A. No. The legislation in all jurisdictions protects parents' right to return to their jobs upon the expiry of their maternity or parental leaves. If their employer cannot return the employee to his or her former position, the employee must be placed in a comparable job with equivalent wages and benefits.

Q. What Happens to Seniority Status While on Leave?

A. **Alberta**, **New Brunswick**, **Nova Scotia**, **Prince Edward Island**, the **Northwest Territories**, and **Nunavut** provide that the leave will not result in any loss of seniority accrued to the time leave began. **Ontario**, **Saskatchewan**, and the **federal** legislation specify that seniority continues to accrue during maternity and parental leaves. **British Columbia**, **Manitoba**, **Newfoundland and Labrador**, and the **Yukon** legislation states that employment is deemed to be continuous during maternity and parental leaves. In **Quebec**, the employee is entitled to reinstatement to his or her former position with the same benefits, including the wage he or she would have been entitled to had he or she not taken leave.

Q. Do Benefits Continue To Accrue During the Leave of Absence?

A. In **Alberta**, **Manitoba**, **New Brunswick**, **Newfoundland and Labrador**, **Nova Scotia**, and **Saskatchewan**, benefits are protected at the level reached before leave was taken. In the **federal** jurisdiction, **British Columbia**, **Ontario**, **Prince Edward Island**, **Quebec**, the **Northwest Territories**, **Nunavut**, and the **Yukon**, benefits will continue to accrue during the period of leave as if there had been no loss of continuity in the employment. If benefits are to continue to accrue, the employee may be obliged to pay contributions to the benefit scheme during his or her absence from work, depending on the jurisdiction.

Q. What Is the Effect of the Leave of Absence on Vacations with Pay?

A. For those provinces in which employment is deemed to be continuous during an employee's leave, the employee will not be obliged to work an entire year after returning from leave before being entitled to a vacation with pay, as he or she would have if the employment was considered to have been interrupted.

Q. What Happens if the Employer Discontinues the Business While an Employee Is on Leave?

A. An employee's right to reinstatement does not necessarily disappear upon the suspension of the employer's operations. If the employer resumes operations, for example, the employee may be entitled to reinstatement.

Q. Can an Employer Retaliate Against an Employee for Exercising His or Her Entitlement To Take Maternity or Parental Leave?

A. No. Employment and labour standards legislation in all jurisdictions explicitly prohibits employers from dismissing, suspending, laying off, or otherwise discriminating against employees because they exercise their right to take maternity or parental leaves. As well, human rights legislation in all jurisdictions also prohibits discrimination in employment because of pregnancy or family status.

Q. What Can an Employee Do if an Employer Refuses To Grant Maternity or Parental Leave?

A. An employee who believes that his or her rights with respect to maternity or parental leave have been violated should contact the nearest Employment Standards or Labour Standards office. The contact information for those offices is located in the Appendix on page 249.

HEALTH AND SAFETY BENEFITS FOR PREGNANT EMPLOYEES

Quebec and the **federal** jurisdiction have unique health and safety benefits for pregnant employees, which are described below.

Q. Can an Employee Take Time Off for Medical Examinations?

A. In **Quebec**, women who, because of their pregnancy, require a medical examination or an examination by a midwife, are entitled to time off without pay to do so. The employee must inform her employer as soon as possible of her intended absence. In other provinces, although not expressly set out in the employment or labour standards legislation, employers typically accommodate employee time off for medical or midwife examinations if it is impossible for the appointments to be scheduled outside work hours.

Q. What if the Employee's Health or the Health of the Unborn or Newborn Child Is Jeopardized by the Employee's Work?

A. **Federally regulated** employees who are pregnant or breastfeeding are entitled, from the beginning of the pregnancy until 24 weeks after birth, to be reassigned or have their job duties modified, if the work is posing a risk to the health of the mother, the fetus, or the child. While the employer is examining the request, the mother is entitled to continue at her job, if she chooses, or, if the risk requires, to take a leave of absence with pay at her usual rate, until the employer has come to a decision. If it is not reasonably practicable to modify the job functions or reassign the employee, the employee is entitled to a leave of absence without pay for the duration of the risk.

In **Quebec**, an employer must, on its own initiative, transfer a pregnant employee if her conditions of employment are physically dangerous to her or the fetus. The employee may refuse the transfer by presenting a medical certificate attesting that her conditions of employment are not dangerous as alleged.

MISCELLANEOUS LEAVES OF ABSENCE

A number of jurisdictions have provisions for other forms of leave, such as bereavement, sick or emergency, family responsibility, compassionate care, organ donor, citizenship, voting, jury duty, reservist leave, critical illness, and the crime-related death or disappearance of a child. The eligibility requirements and entitlements for these leaves are summarized below.

Q. Are Employees Entitled to Time Off in the Event of a Death in the Family?

A. The following jurisdictions provide employees with time off in the event of a death in the family:

- **Federal:** In the event of the death of a member of an employee's immediate family, the employee is entitled to bereavement leave on any of his or her normal working days that occur during the three days immediately following the day of the death. The definition of immediate family includes the employee's spouse or common-law partner, father or mother and the spouse or common-law partner of the father or mother, children and the children of the employee's spouse or common-law partner, grandparents, grandchildren, brothers and sisters, father-in-law and mother-in-law and their spouses, and also includes any relative permanently residing in the employee's household or with whom the employee resides. For the purpose of bereavement leave, common-law partner means a person who has been cohabiting with an individual in a conjugal relationship for at least a year. If the employee has completed three consecutive months of continuous employment with the employer, he or she is entitled to bereavement leave with pay at his or her regular rate of wages for the normal hours of work, and such pay is, for all purposes, deemed to be wages.

- **British Columbia:** An employee is entitled to up to three days of unpaid leave on the death of a member of the employee's immediate family. An employee's immediate family includes his or her spouse, child, parent, guardian, sibling, grandchild or grandparent, as well as any person who lives with the employee as a member of the employee's family.

- **Manitoba:** An employee who has been employed for at least 30 days may take up to three days of unpaid leave on the death of a family member. Family member is defined as a spouse or common-law partner of the employee, a child of the employee or a child of the employee's spouse or common-law partner, a parent of the employee or parent of the employee's spouse or common-law partner, a brother, sister, stepbrother, stepsister, uncle, aunt, nephew, niece, grandchild, or grandparent of the employee or the employee's spouse or common-law partner, a current or former foster parent of the employee or employee's spouse or common-law partner, a current or former foster child, ward, or guardian of the employee or the employee's spouse or common-law partner, the spouse or common-law partner of any of the above individuals; or any other person whom the employee considers to be like a close relative, whether or not they are related by blood. A common-law partner means a person who is not married to the employee, but is cohabiting with him or her in a conjugal relationship of some permanence.

- **New Brunswick:** Employees are entitled to an unpaid leave of up to five consecutive days on the death of a person in a close family relationship with the employee. The leave is to be taken during the period of the bereavement and is to begin no later than the day of the funeral or memorial service. The employee is to inform the employer of the employee's intention to take the leave, the anticipated commencement date, and the anticipated duration of the leave. Close family relationship means the relationship between persons who are married to one another, between parents and their children, between siblings and between grandparents and their grandchildren, and includes a relationship between persons who, though not married to one another and whether or not a blood relationship exists, demonstrate an intention to extend to one another the mutual affection and support normally associated with those relationships first mentioned.

- **Newfoundland and Labrador:** All employees are entitled to a period of bereavement leave consisting of two days' unpaid leave in the event of the death of a spouse, child, grandchild, mother, father, brother or sister, grandparent, mother- or father-in-law, brother- or sister-in-law, or daughter- or son-in-law. Upon completion of 30 days' continuous service with the same employer, an employee is also entitled to one paid day in addition to the two unpaid days. An employee's wages during his or her one day of paid bereavement leave is calculated by multiplying the employee's normal hourly rate of pay by the average number of hours worked per day in the three weeks immediately preceding the bereavement leave. Where an entitlement to the one paid day of bereavement leave occurs during vacation leave, the vacation leave is extended by one day.

- **Nova Scotia:** An employee may be absent from work, without pay, for up to three consecutive working days on the death of the employee's spouse, parent, guardian, child or ward. The employee may also take unpaid bereavement leave of one working day on the death of the employee's grandparent, grandchild, sister, brother, mother-in-law, father-in-law, son-in-law, daughter-in-law, sister-in-law, or brother-in-law.

- **Ontario:** An employer who regularly employs 50 or more employees must grant employees up to 10 days of unpaid emergency leave per year. The leave applies to matters including the death of the following individuals:

  — the employee's spouse or same-sex partner;

  — the parent, step-parent, or foster parent of the employee or the employee's spouse or same-sex partner;

  — a child, stepchild, or foster child of the employee or the employee's spouse or same-sex partner;

  — a grandparent, step-grandparent, grandchild, or step-grandchild of the employee or the employee's spouse or same-sex partner;

  — the employee's brother or sister;

  — a spouse or same-sex partner of the child of the employee; and

  — a relative dependent on the employee for care or assistance.

- **Prince Edward Island:** An employee is entitled to one day of paid leave and up to two consecutive days of unpaid leave in the event of the death of an immediate family member. An immediate family member for the purpose of bereavement leave entitlement is defined as the spouse, child, parent, brother, or sister of an employee. For the paid day of leave, the employer must pay the employee for the day of leave at the employee's regular rate of pay for a day of work. Upon the death of a member of an extended family member of the employee, the employee is entitled to up to three consecutive days of unpaid leave. Extended family member means the grandparent, grandchild, aunt, uncle, brother-in-law, sister-in-law, mother-in-law, father-in-law, son-in-law, or daughter-in-law of the employee. The absence must begin no later than the day of the funeral of the immediate or extended family member. Where the paid leave falls during an employee's scheduled vacation, the employer is required to extend the employee's vacation by one day.

- **Northwest Territories:** An employee is entitled to three days of bereavement leave without pay in respect to the death of a family member. Family member, for the purpose of bereavement leave, is defined as the employee's spouse or the parent, child, brother, sister, grandparent, or grandchild of the employee or the employee's spouse, or any relative who lives with the employee. If the funeral or memorial service does not take place in the community in which the employee resides, the employee is entitled to seven days of bereavement leave.

- **Quebec:** An employee may be absent from work for one day with pay by reason of the death or funeral of the employee's spouse, child, child of the employee's spouse, father, mother, brother, or sister. The employee may also be absent from work for four more days, without pay, on such occasion. An employee may take bereavement leave of one day, without pay, on the death or funeral of a son-in-law, daughter-in-law, grandparents or grandchildren, or the father, mother, brother, or sister of his or her spouse. On such occasions, the employee must advise the employer of his or her absence as soon as possible.

- **Saskatchewan:** An employee who has completed three continuous months of employment with an employer is entitled to a leave of up to five working days without pay on the death of a member of the employee's immediate family. Immediate family is defined as spouse, parent, grandparent, child, or brother or sister of an employee or the employee's spouse. Spouse is defined as the wife or husband of an employee or a person with whom the employee cohabits as a spouse continuously for a period of at least two years, or in a relationship of some permanence if they are the parents of a child. The leave must be taken within one week before and ending one week after the funeral.

- **Yukon:** In the event of the death of an immediate family member, an employee is entitled to bereavement leave without pay for up to one week, provided that the funeral of the deceased falls within that week. Immediate family member means a spouse, parent, step-mother, stepfather, child, brother, sister, mother-in-law or father-in-law, grandparent, grandchild, son-in-law, daughter-in-law, any relative permanently residing in the employee's household or with whom the employee resides. If an employee is designated by the family of a deceased member of a First Nation as the person responsible for organizing the funeral potlatch for the deceased, the employee is entitled to one week of unpaid bereavement leave.

Q. Are Employees Entitled to Time Off When They Are Sick?

A. Employees are entitled to time off when they are sick in the following jurisdictions, subject to the following eligibility requirements:

- **Federal:** An employer shall not dismiss or lay off an employee solely because of absence due to illness or injury if the employee has completed three consecutive months of continuous employment with the employer; the period of absence does not exceed 17 weeks; and the employee, if requested in writing by the employer within 15 days after returning to work, furnishes a doctor's certificate confirming that the absence was legitimate.

  The pension, health, and disability benefits and the seniority of an employee who is absent from work due to illness or injury shall accumulate during the entire period of the absence. To that end, an employer is required to continue the payment of contributions to employee benefit plans while the employee is on sick leave. However, if the employee fails to pay any employee contributions required, the employer's obligation ceases.

- **Manitoba:** An employee who has been employed for at least 30 days may take up to three days of unpaid leave every year, but only to the extent that the leave is necessary for the health of the employee.

- **New Brunswick:** Upon completion of more than 90 days of employment, an employee is entitled to a period of five days of unpaid sick leave per year. Where the employee requests a leave of four or more days, the employer can require the employee to provide a certificate from a medical practitioner or nurse practitioner certifying that the employee is incapable of working due to illness or injury.

- **Newfoundland and Labrador:** Upon completion of 30 days of continuous service with the same employer, an employee is entitled to a period of seven days' unpaid sick leave or family responsibility leave per year. Where the employee requests sick leave of three or more consecutive days, the employee must provide the employer with a certificate from a qualified medical practitioner. Any unused leave expires at the end of the year in which it was granted.

- **Nova Scotia:** An employee is entitled to a maximum of three days of unpaid leave per year where the leave is required due to the sickness of a child, parent, or family member or for medical, dental, or other similar appointments during working hours.

- **Ontario:** An employer who regularly employs 50 or more employees must grant employees up to 10 days of unpaid leave per year, which can be used for an employee's personal illness, injury, or medical emergency.

- **Prince Edward Island:** Where an employee has been employed by an employer for a continuous period of six months or more, the employer shall, at the request of the employee, grant the employee a leave of absence without pay up to three days. After five years of continuous employment with the same employer, the employee is entitled to one paid day of sick leave per 12-month period in addition to the three days of unpaid leave. If the employee requests a leave of absence that is three consecutive days in length, the employer may require the employee to provide the employer with a certificate signed by a medical practitioner certifying that the employee is or was unable to work due to illness or injury.

- **Quebec:** After three uninterrupted months of service, an employee may be absent from work for a period of not more than 26 weeks over a period of 12 months without pay relating to sickness or accident other than an employment injury or occupational disease, and up to 104 weeks without pay if the employee suffers serious bodily injury during or resulting directly from a criminal offence.

- **Saskatchewan:** An employer may not dismiss, suspend, lay off, demote, or otherwise discipline an employee because he or she was absent due to his or her own illness or injury or the illness or injury of a dependent member of the employee's immediate family. In order to qualify for this protection, the employee must have been employed for at least 13 consecutive weeks prior to the absence. The absence cannot exceed 12 weeks in a period of 52 weeks for a serious illness or injury or 12 days in a calendar year for a non-serious illness or injury. Where requested in writing by the employer, the employee must provide medical documentation certifying that the employee was incapable of working due to his or her own illness or injury.

- **Northwest Territories:** An employee who has been employed by an employer for at least 30 days is entitled to sick leave without pay for a period of five days during each 12-month period. To be eligible for sick leave, the employee must be incapable of working because of illness or injury and must submit to the employer a request for the sick leave. If the duration of the sick leave exceeds three consecutive days, the employee must, on the employer's request, provide a medical certificate stating that he or she is incapable of working due to illness or injury.

- **Yukon:** An employee is entitled to one day of sick leave without pay for every month employed by that employer minus the number of days on which the employee has previously been absent due to illness or injury. However, an employee's maximum net entitlement at any time shall not exceed 12 days. An employer may require the certificate of a qualified medical practitioner to confirm entitlement.

Q. Can an Employee Take Time Off for a Family Emergency or Event?

A. The following jurisdictions provide time off as described below for family emergencies or events:

- **Federal:** Employees in the **federal** jurisdiction are entitled to the following leaves of absences related to family emergencies or events:

  — *Leave Related to Critical Illness:* An employee who has been employed for at least six consecutive months and who is the parent of a critically ill child may take up to 37 weeks in order to care for or support that child. Employees must provide their employers with a medical certificate that states that the child is a critically ill child and requires the care or support of one or more of his or her parents and sets out the period during which the child requires that care or support. A "critically ill child" is defined as a person whose baseline state of health has significantly changed and whose life is at risk as a result of an illness or injury. While both parents are entitled to take this leave of absence, the total combined leave for critical illness cannot exceed 37 weeks for the same child.

  — *Leave Related to Death or Disappearance:* An employee who has been employed for at least six consecutive months may be absent for up to 104 weeks if the employee is the parent of a child who has died and it is probable, considering the circumstances, that the child had died as a result of a crime. Where an employee is the parent of a child who has disappeared and it is probable, considering the circumstances, that the child disappeared as a result of a crime, the employee may be absent for up to 52 weeks. An employee will not be entitled to any time off if the employee is charged with the crime or it is probable, considering the circumstances, that the child was a party to the crime. While both parents are entitled to take this leave of absence, the total combined leave related to the death or disappearance of a child cannot exceed 104 or 52 weeks respectively for the same child.

- **British Columbia:** An employee is entitled to up to five days of unpaid leave during each employment year to meet responsibilities related to the care, health or education of a child in the employee's care, or the care or health of any other member of the employee's immediate family.

- **Manitoba:** Employees are entitled to the following leaves of absence related to family emergencies or events:

  — *Family Leave:* An employee who has been employed for at least 30 days may take up to five unpaid days of leave every year, but only to the extent that the leave is necessary for the health of the employee or for the employee to meet his or her family responsibilities to his or her family members. Family member is defined in the same way as for the purpose of bereavement leave in Manitoba, which is set out on page 84.

  — *Leave Related to Critical Illness of a Child:* An employee who has been employed for at least 30 days may take up to 37 weeks of unpaid leave to provide care and support to a critically ill child. To be eligible for this leave, an employee must provide a medical certificate stating that the child is critically ill and requires the care or support of the employee and setting out the period during which the child requires that care and support. A "critically ill child" is defined as a person whose baseline state of health has significantly changed and whose life is at risk as a result of an illness or injury. If the employee wishes to take this leave he or she must give the employer notice of at least one pay period unless the circumstances necessitate a shorter period of time.

  — *Leave Related to Death or Disappearance of a Child:* An employee with 30 days of service may be absent for up to 104 weeks if the employee's child has died and it is probable, considering the circumstances, that the child died as a result of a crime. Similarly, where an employee's child has disappeared and it is probable, considering the circumstances, that the child disappeared as a result of a crime, the employee will be entitled to a leave of absence for up to 52 weeks. An employee will not be entitled to this particular leave of absence if he or she is charged with the crime.

- **New Brunswick:** An employee is entitled to up to three days of unpaid leave during each employment year to meet responsibilities related to the care, health or education of a person in a close family relationship with the employee.

- **Newfoundland and Labrador:** Upon completion of 30 days of continuous service with the same employer, an employee is entitled to a period of seven days of unpaid sick leave or family responsibility leave per year. Where the employee requests family responsibility leave of three or more consecutive days, the employee must provide the employer with a written statement of the nature of the family responsibility. Any unused leave expires at the end of the year in which it was granted.

- **Nova Scotia**: Employees are entitled to the following leaves of absences related to family emergencies or events:

  — *Emergency Leave:* Employees are entitled to take an unpaid leave of absence during a natural disaster or public health risk to attend to their own needs or the needs of a family member. The employee is entitled to unpaid emergency leave when the emergency declaration applies to the employee and prevents him or her from performing his or her work duties. The employee is also entitled to the unpaid leave where the declaration applies to a family member of the employee, the family member requires care or assistance as a result, the employee is the only reasonable person to provide the assistance, and this has the effect of preventing the employee from performing his or her duties. The leave continues as long as the emergency continues and the employee remains unable to perform his or her duties.

  — *Critically Ill Child Care Leave:* An employee who has been employed for at least three months is entitled to an unpaid leave of absence of up to 37 weeks to provide care or support to the critically ill child. The employee may be required to provide his or her employer with a medical certificate which states that the child is a critically ill child and requires the care or support of the employee and sets out the period during which the child requires the care or support. A critically ill child is defined as a person whose baseline state of health has significantly changed and whose life is at risk as a result of an illness or injury. The leave of absence must be taken in periods of not less than one week's duration.

  — *Crime-Related Child Death or Disappearance Leave:* An employee who has been employed for at least three months is entitled to an unpaid leave of absence of up to 104 weeks if the employee is the parent of a child who dies and it is probable, considering the circumstances, that the child died as a result of a crime. Where an employee is the parent of a child who has disappeared and it is probable, considering the circumstances, that the child disappeared as a result of a crime, the employee may be absent for up to 52 weeks. An employee will not be entitled to any time off if the employee is charged with the crime or it is probable, considering the circumstances, that the child was a party to the crime.

- **Ontario:** An employer who regularly employs 50 or more employees must grant its employees up to 10 days of unpaid personal emergency leave per year for reasons including the illness, injury, or medical emergency of the family members set out on page 85 with respect to bereavement leave. An employee who wishes to take emergency leave must notify the employer as soon as possible that he or she wishes to do so. Employees are also eligible for unpaid declared emergency leave where the employee is unable to perform his or her work duties because of an emergency declared by the government under particular emergency management and civil and health protection legislation.

  Under proposed legislation, the Ontario government has proposed three additional categories of unpaid leaves of absence:

  — *Family Caregiver Leave:* This proposed leave of absence would entitle an employee to take up to eight weeks of unpaid leave to provide care and support to a family member who has a serious medical condition. The proposed legislation does not define serious medical condition and therefore could apply to any number of medical conditions.

  — *Critically Ill Child Care Leave:* This proposed leave of absence would entitle an employee with six months of service to take a leave of absence of up to 37 weeks to support an employee's critically ill child.

  — *Crime-Related Death or Disappearance Leave:* This proposed leave of absence would entitle an employee with six months of service to take an unpaid leave of absence of 104 weeks for the crime-related death of the employee's child and 52 weeks for the crime-related disappearance of the employee's child.

- **Prince Edward Island:** Where an employee has been employed by an employer for a continuous period of six months or more, the employer shall, at the request of the employee, grant the employee a leave of absence without pay of up to three days in total per year to meet responsibilities related to the health care of a person who is a member of the immediate family or extended family of the employee.

- **Quebec:** Employees are entitled to the following leaves of absences related to family emergencies and events:

  — *Family Responsibilities:* An employee may be absent from work without pay for 10 days per year to fulfill obligations relating to the care, health, or education of the employee's child or the child of the employee's spouse, or because of the state of health of the employee's spouse, father, mother, brother, sister, or one of the employee's grandparents.

  — *Disappearance of Minor:* An employee may be absent from work for a period of not more than 52 weeks if the employee's minor child has disappeared. If the child is found before the expiry of the period of absence, the leave shall end on the eleventh day that follows the day on which the child is found.

  — *Suicide:* An employee may be absent from work for a period of not more than 52 weeks if the employee's spouse or child commits suicide.

  — *Criminal Offence:* An employee may be absent from work for a period of not more than 104 weeks if the death of the employee's spouse or child occurs during or results directly from a criminal offence.

  — *Paternity/Adoption Leave:* In addition to the entitlements related to maternity and parental leave, an employee may be absent from work for five days upon the birth of his child, the adoption of a child, or where there is a termination of pregnancy after the twentieth week. The first two days will be with pay if the employee has 60 days of continuous service with the employer. The leave may be broken into separate days at the request of the employee. In the case of birth or adoption, the leave must be taken within 15 days of the child's arrival at the employee's residence.

  — *Special Occasion Leave:* An employee may be absent from work for one day with pay on his or her wedding day or civil union. An employee may also be absent from work, without pay, on the wedding day or civil union of his or her child, father, mother, brother or sister, or of a child of his or her spouse. The employee must advise the employer of his or her request for this leave at least one week in advance.

- **Saskatchewan:** Under proposed legislation, an employee will be entitled to an unpaid leave of absence of up to 37 weeks to care and support his or her critically ill child. In addition, the proposed amendments also provide for leaves of absence of up to 104 weeks and 52 weeks due to the crime-related death or disappearance of a child.

- **Yukon:** Employees are entitled to the following leaves of absences related to family emergencies and events:

  — *Leave Related to Critical Illness of a Child:* An employee who has completed 12 months of continuous employment and who is the parent of a critically ill child may take up to 37 weeks in order to care or support that child. The employee must provide his or her employer with a medical certificate stating that the child is a critically ill child and requires the care or support of one or more of their parents and sets out the period during which the child requires that care or support. A "critically ill child" is defined as a person whose baseline state of health has significantly changed and whose life is at risk as a result of an illness or injury. While both parents are entitled to take this leave of absence, the total combined leave cannot exceed 37 weeks. In addition, the leave of absence must be taken in periods of not less than one week's duration.

  — *Leave Related to Disappearance or Death of a Child:* An employee who has been employed for at least 12 months of employment may be absent for up to 35 weeks if the employee is the parent of a child who has died or disappeared and it is probable, considering the circumstances, that the child died or disappeared as a result of a crime. An employee will not be entitled to any time off if the employee is charged with the crime or it is probable, considering the circumstances, that the child was a party to the crime. While both parents are entitled to take this leave of absence, the total combined leave related to the death or disappearance of a child cannot exceed 35 weeks for the same child.

Q. Is an Employee Entitled to a Leave of Absence in Order To Donate an Organ and/or To Recover from Organ Donation?

A. Currently, only **Manitoba, Ontario**, and **Quebec** grant employees entitlement to an unpaid leave of absence to donate an organ. However, under proposed legislation, **Saskatchewan** is set to offer employees with the same entitlement.

In **Manitoba**, an employee who has been employed by an employer for 30 days is entitled to an unpaid leave of up to 13 weeks for the purpose of donating an organ. An employee donates an organ when he or she undergoes a surgical procedure that involves the removal of an organ or tissue from the employee for the purpose of it being transplanted into another individual. An employee who wishes to take organ donor leave must provide his or her employer with notice in writing with as much notice as is reasonable and practicable, as well as a medical certificate stating the start and end date of the period necessary for the organ donation and to recover from the procedure. The organ donor leave may be extended for up to 13 weeks if the employee provides a medical certificate indicating that the employee requires additional time to recover from donating the organ.

In **Ontario**, employees who have been employed by the employer for at least 13 weeks and who undergo surgery in order to donate organs to other persons are entitled to 13 weeks of unpaid leave from work. Currently, the leave entitlement applies only to kidney, liver, lung, pancreas, and small bowel donations, although the scope of organ and tissue donation may be expanded in future by regulation. The employee is required to give the employer at least two weeks' notice in writing. The employer may require the employee to provide a medical certificate confirming that the employee had undergone or will undergo surgery for the purpose of organ donation. The employee is entitled to extend his or her leave more than once if necessary, up to an additional 13 weeks, if a medical certificate is issued stating that the employee is not yet able to return to work and will not be able to do so for a specified time.

In **Quebec**, an employee with three months of uninterrupted service with the same employer may be absent from work without pay for up to 26 weeks to donate an organ. If the employee continues to make contributions to the various group insurance and pension plans during his or her leave, the employer must also do so. The employee must notify his or her employer as soon as possible of his or her absence. When the employee returns to work, the employer must reinstate the employee to his or her former position and grant him or her the wages and benefits to which he or she would have been entitled had the employee remained at work.

Under **Saskatchewan's** proposed legislation, employees who have been employed for more than 13 weeks and who undergo surgery in order to donate organs to other persons will be entitled to an unpaid leave of up to 26 weeks. The employer may require the employee to provide a medical certificate confirming the reasons for the employee's leave of absence.

Q. Is an Employee Entitled to Time Off To Attend at His or Her Citizenship Ceremony?

A. Currently, only **Manitoba** and **Nova Scotia** grant employees entitlement to an unpaid leave of absence to attend at his or her citizenship ceremony. However, under proposed legislation, **Saskatchewan** is also set to offer employees with the same entitlement.

In **Manitoba**, an employee who has been employed with an employer for at least 30 days may take up to four hours of unpaid leave to attend a citizenship ceremony to receive a certificate of citizenship. The employee must provide the employer with 14 days' notice or, if it is not possible to provide 14 days' notice, as much notice as is reasonable and practicable in the circumstances.

In **Nova Scotia** and under **Saskatchewan's** proposed legislation, employees may be absent for one day to attend a citizenship ceremony to receive a certificate of citizenship.

Q. How Much Time Off Must an Employer Give Employees To Vote in Federal Elections?

A. All employees who are qualified electors, that is, who are 18 years of age or older and Canadian citizens on polling day, are entitled to three consecutive hours free from work while the polls are open for the purpose of casting vote ballots. If an employee's hours of work do not allow the employee three consecutive hours to vote, an employee must be granted sufficient time off for this purpose.

It is the employer's obligation to ensure that an employee has three consecutive hours in which to vote. The additional time necessary for voting may be granted at the employer's convenience and need be extended only to eligible voters.

Q. Are Employees Also Entitled To Time Off To Vote in Provincial, Territorial, or Municipal Elections?

A. All provinces and territories require that employees be given time off to vote in provincial and territorial elections. **Prince Edward Island** requires that employees be granted one hour off to vote. **British Columbia**, **Newfoundland and Labrador**, **Quebec**, and the **Yukon** require that employees be granted four hours to vote. All other provinces and territories require that employees have three hours to vote.

Only **Alberta**, **New Brunswick**, **Newfoundland and Labrador**, **Ontario**, **Quebec**, and the **Yukon** have enacted legislation with regard to time off for voting at municipal elections. In **Alberta**, **New Brunswick**, and **Ontario**, employees are entitled to three consecutive hours for the purpose of voting. In **Newfoundland and Labrador**, **Quebec**, and the **Yukon**, employees are entitled to four consecutive hours for the purpose of voting in municipal elections.

Q. If an Employee Is Called for Jury Duty, Must the Employer Grant Time Off?

A. All jurisdictions except **Nunavut** have enacted legislation requiring employers to grant employees time off if they are summoned for jury duty.

Only **Newfoundland and Labrador** requires that the time off be paid at the employee's regular wage. All the other jurisdictions either make no statement regarding pay or state that the leave may be either paid or unpaid.

Q. Are Employees Entitled To a Leave of Absence To Care for a Dying Family Member?

A. All jurisdictions in Canada now permit employees to take eight weeks off work (12 in **Quebec** and **Saskatchewan** (under proposed legislation, **Saskatchewan's** compassionate care leave would be reduced to eight weeks) to care for a dying family member. (At the time of writing, **Alberta** has passed legislation, but it is not yet in force.) This leave is called either compassionate care, family medical, family care, or sick leave. Although the leave is unpaid under employment or labour standards legislation, Employment Insurance (EI) benefits are available for up to six weeks, subject to meeting the compassionate care eligibility requirements (see the discussion in the last section of this chapter, on page 104). In most jurisdictions, the leave period may be shared between different family members, but the aggregate time cannot exceed the leave entitlement.

In order to be eligible for the compassionate care leave, an employee must provide a medical certificate stating that the eligible family member has a serious medical condition with a significant risk of death within 26 weeks.

Each jurisdiction provides a detailed list of the eligible family members. The family members for whom an employee may receive paid EI compassionate care benefits are also set out in the chart on page 107.

Depending on the jurisdiction, an employee may also be required to provide the employer with notice subject to certain requirements. Employees in **Newfoundland and Labrador** are required to provide their employers with at least two weeks' written notice of the employee's intention to take the leave, as well as the length of the leave. Any change to the leave must also be provided in writing two weeks in advance. In **Manitoba**, if possible, employees should provide notice of at least one pay period that he or she requires the leave. The family medical leave provisions in **Ontario** state that the employer must be advised in writing as soon as possible before the leave commences.

In **Manitoba**, **New Brunswick**, **Newfoundland and Labrador**, **Nova Scotia**, **Prince Edward Island**, the **Northwest Territories**, **Nunavut**, the **Yukon**, and the **federal** jurisdiction, the leave days need not be taken consecutively, but must be taken in periods of not less than one week. In **Alberta**, employees may take up to two periods of compassionate care leave; however, any second period of leave must end no later than 26 weeks after the first period of leave began. Regardless, no period of leave may be less than one week's duration.

In most jurisdictions, compassionate care leave ends upon the death of the family member or within a week thereafter. Unless otherwise agreed to, in **Manitoba**, employees must provide 48 hours' notice if they wish to return to work. In **Alberta**, employees must provide two weeks' written notice of the date they intend to return to work.

In the event that the family member does not die within the leave period, in **British Columbia** and **Ontario**, the employee may take a further leave after obtaining a new medical certificate.

Q. Are Employees Entitled To a Leave of Absence To Serve in the Canadian Forces?

A. All jurisdictions now permit employees to take reservist leave. Eligibility requirements for reservist leave (including the minimum notice the employee must provide and its form and the employment service eligibility), as well as the entitlement (including benefit continuation and protection of seniority), vary by jurisdiction. The chart below summarizes the differences in eligibility requirements and entitlement by jurisdiction.

RESERVIST LEAVE CHART

Jurisdiction	Reservist Leave	Minimum Notice	Service Eligibility	Certificate	Benefit Continuation	Protection of Seniority
Federal	Yes	4 weeks' written notice (or as soon as possible)	6 consecutive months	If requested, within 3 weeks after the leave starts (unless valid reason provided)	No	Yes
Alberta	Yes	4 weeks' written notice or as soon as reasonable and practical	26 consecutive weeks	An employer may request proof that the employee is entitled to reservist leave	No	Yes
British Columbia	Yes	4 weeks' written notice of the date the leave will begin and end (or as much notice as practicable)	N/A	Employers may require the employee to provide further information respecting the leave	No	Not specified

Jurisdiction	Reservist Leave	Minimum Notice	Service Eligibility	Certificate	Benefit Continuation	Protection of Seniority
Manitoba	Yes	As much notice as reasonable and practicable in the circumstances	7 consecutive months	Employer may request a certificate	Not specified (although employment deemed continuous)	Yes
New Brunswick	Yes	4 weeks' written notice of the date the leave will begin and end (or as much notice as practicable)	6 months (for a second or subsequent leave, 12 months must elapse)	Employer may require a certificate	Not specified	Yes
Newfoundland and Labrador	Yes	At least 60 days' notice in writing (reasonable notice where compliance is not possible)	6 consecutive months (for a second or subsequent leave, 12 months must elapse)	Employer may require a certificate	No (unless otherwise agreed)	Not specified
Northwest Territories	Yes	4 weeks' written notice or at earliest reasonable opportunity	6 consecutive months	Employer may request certificate	No	Yes

Jurisdiction	Reservist Leave	Minimum Notice	Service Eligibility	Certificate	Benefit Continuation	Protection of Seniority
Nova Scotia	Yes, but reservist leave for training must not be longer than 20 days, including travel time, per calendar year	4 weeks' notice of training except in an emergency in which case as much notice as reasonably practical; 90 days' notice for active duty or what is reasonably practical	1 year	Employer may require a certificate	Yes/No (the reservist has the option to prepay and continue benefit plans)	Yes
Nunavut	Yes	4 weeks' written or at earliest reasonable opportunity	6 consecutive months	Employer may request certificate	No	Yes
Ontario	Yes	Reasonable notice in writing	6 consecutive months	Employer may require a certificate	No	Yes
Prince Edward Island	Yes	As much as reasonable and practical	6 consecutive months	Employer may require a certificate	No	Yes

Jurisdiction	Reservist Leave	Minimum Notice	Service Eligibility	Certificate	Benefit Continuation	Protection of Seniority
Quebec	Yes, but employee who is absent on reservist leave for a period of greater than 12 weeks cannot be absent again on reservist leave until 12 months from the date of his or her return to work	4 weeks' written notice of the reason for the leave, the date it is to begin, and its duration	12 months of uninterrupted service	Employer may require a certificate	No	Yes
Saskatchewan	Yes	At least 6 weeks' notice for training; 6 weeks' notice for deployment; and reasonable notice for emergencies	N/A	Employer can ask the employee for a certificate	Not specified	Yes

Jurisdiction	Reservist Leave	Minimum Notice	Service Eligibility	Certificate	Benefit Continuation	Protection of Seniority
Yukon	Yes	4 weeks' written notice	6 months	Employer can ask the employee for a certificate, which the employee must provide within 3 weeks of beginning the leave	No	Yes

ENTITLEMENT TO EMPLOYMENT INSURANCE BENEFITS DURING LEAVES OF ABSENCE

Q. What Is the Relationship Between the Provincial Employment Standards Laws and the Federal Employment Insurance Legislation?

A. There are two separate types of legislation that need to be considered when dealing with sickness, maternity, parental, compassionate care, critical illness, and crime-related death or disappearance leaves. Provincial employment or labour standards legislation dictates how much unpaid time an employee can take off work for maternity and parental leave with protection, while the **federal** legislation administered by Human Resources and Social Development Canada (HRSDC), and in **Quebec**, by the Parental Insurance Plan, govern the amount of Employment Insurance (EI) benefits that are available and how and when they will be paid.

Q. What Life Changes or Situations May Result in an Employee Receiving EI Benefits?

A. In addition to providing benefits for persons who lose their jobs, HRSDC provides eligible employees with special benefits in relation to sickness, pregnancy, parental, or family care responsibilities. Because eligibility requirements and benefit levels for employment insurance change frequently, it is advisable to check entitlement with HRSDC. Please see the HRSDC contact information in the Appendix on page 249.

Q. What Length of Employment or Employment Status Must an Employee Establish To Be Eligible for EI Sickness, Maternity, Parental, and Compassionate Care Benefits, or Special Benefits for Parents of Critically Ill Children?

A. In order to be entitled to sickness, maternity, parental, compassionate care benefits, or special benefits for parents of critically ill children, an employee must show that the employee's regular weekly earnings have been decreased by more than 40% and the employee has accumulated 600 insured hours in the last 52 weeks or since his or her last claim.

Q. What Is the EI Benefit Payment During Sickness, Maternity, Parental, Compassionate Care, or Critically Ill Child Care Leaves?

A. While an employee is on a leave of absence from work due to sickness, maternity, parental, compassionate care, or critically ill child leave, in 2013, the employee is entitled to receive 55% of his or her average weekly insurable earnings, up to a maximum of $501 per week.

Q. What Are EI Sickness Benefits and for What Period Will an Employee Be Eligible To Receive Them?

A. Sickness benefits may be paid to an employee for up to 15 weeks when the employee is unable to work because of sickness, injury, or quarantine. A medical certificate must be obtained to confirm the duration of the employee's incapacity. The fees payable to the employee's doctor or dentist for such a medical certificate are entirely at the employee's own expense.

Q. What Are Maternity Benefits and for What Period Will an Employee Be Eligible To Receive Them?

A. Maternity benefits are payable to the birth mother or surrogate mother for a maximum of 15 weeks. The employee will need to prove pregnancy by signing a statement declaring the expected due date or actual date of birth.

The mother can start collecting maternity benefits either up to eight weeks before she is expected to give birth or during the week in which she gives birth.

Q. What Is the Impact on EI Maternity Benefits if the Child Is Hospitalized?

A. If the child is hospitalized after birth, the benefit period in which maternity benefits may be paid may be extended by the period of time the child is hospitalized up to a maximum of 52 weeks.

Q. What Are EI Parental Benefits and for What Period Will an Employee Be Eligible To Receive Them?

A. Parental benefits are payable to either the biological or adoptive parents while they are caring for a newborn or an adopted child, up to a maximum of 35 weeks. An employee must sign a statement declaring the newborn's date of birth or, when there is an adoption, the child's date of placement for the purpose of the adoption, and the name and address of the adoption authority.

Q. Can Either Parent Receive EI Parental Benefits?

A. EI parental benefits are available to either parent, or parents can share the benefits between them if they wish. Employees applying for parental benefits must provide the name and Social Insurance Number (SIN) of the other parent for cross-reference purposes, as the total parental benefits payable cannot exceed 35 weeks.

Q. Can an Employee Claim Both Maternity and Parental Leave Benefits?

A. An employee can receive both maternity and parental benefits within one benefit period. The maximum allowable combined claim is 50 weeks. An employee can also receive maternity and parental benefits in combination with regular benefits so long as the total benefits do not exceed 50 weeks or the maximum regular benefit entitlement, whichever is greater.

Q. What Happens if an Employee Gets Sick While Collecting Maternity or Parental Benefits?

A. Employment insurance also provides sick benefits for a period of up to 15 weeks. Sick benefits can be combined with maternity or parental benefits, up to a maximum of 65 weeks in total.

Q. What Are Compassionate Care Benefits and What Is the Period During Which an Individual May Receive Them?

A. Compassionate care benefits are paid to employees who have to be away from work temporarily to provide care or support to a family member who is gravely ill with a significant risk of death. An employee may receive a maximum of six weeks of compassionate care benefits within the 26-week period that starts with the earlier of:

- the week the doctor signs the medical certificate;
- the week the doctor examines the gravely ill family member; or
- the week the family member became gravely ill, if the doctor can determine that date (e.g., the date of the test results).

  The benefits end when:

- six weeks of compassionate care benefits have been paid;
- the gravely ill family member dies or no longer requires care or support (benefits are paid to the end of the week);
- the 26-week period has expired; or
- the individual has exhausted the maximum benefits payable combining compassionate care benefits with other types of EI benefits.

Q. Who Is a Family Member for the Purposes of Receiving EI Compassionate Care Benefits?

A. Individuals are eligible to receive compassionate care benefits to care for the following family members:

FAMILY MEMBERS

Employee can receive compassionate care benefits to care for his or her:	**Or to care for the following family members of the employee's spouse or common-law partner:**
Child	Child
Wife/husband or common-law partner	
Father or mother	Father or mother, either married or common-law
Father's wife or mother's husband	Father's wife or mother's husband
Common-law partner of father or mother	Common-law partner of father or mother
Brothers or sisters and stepbrothers or stepsisters	Brothers or sisters and stepbrothers or stepsisters
Grandparents and step-grandparents	Grandparents
Grandchildren and their spouses or common-law partners	Grandchildren
Son-in-law and daughter-in-law, either married or common-law	Son-in-law and daughter-in-law, either married or common-law
Father-in-law and mother-in-law, either married or common-law	
Brother-in-law and sister-in-law, either married or common-law	
Uncle and aunt and their spouses or common-law partners	Uncle and aunt
Nephew and niece and their spouses or common-law partners	Nephew and niece
Current or former foster parents	Current or former foster parents
Current or former foster children and their spouses or common-law partners	
Current or former wards	Current or former wards
Current or former guardians and their spouses or common-law partners	

Note: Common-law partner means a person who has been living in a conjugal relationship with that person for at least a year.

An employee can also receive compassionate care benefits to care for a gravely ill person who considers the employee to be like a family member. In such cases, a signed Compassionate Care Benefits Attestation from the gravely ill person or his or her representative is required from the gravely ill person or his or her legal representative.

Q. What Happens if an Employee Needs To Care for a Dying Family Member after Collecting Maternity, Parental, or Sick Benefits?

A. Having collected other EI benefits will not necessarily preclude an individual from receiving compassionate care benefits. When compassionate care benefits are combined with maternity, parental, and sickness benefits, an employee can receive up to a combined maximum of 71 weeks, subject to certain conditions.

Q. What Are Special Benefits for Parents of Critically Ill Children and What Is the Period During Which an Individual May Receive Them?

A. Special benefits for parents of critically ill children are paid to employees who have to be away from work to provide care or support to their critically ill or injured child. A critically ill child is one who has a life-threatening illness or injury, that can include various acute phases of illness and for which continued parental care or support is required. The definition does not include a child with a chronic illness or condition that is his or her normal state of health. There must be a significant change from the child's normal or baseline state of health at the time he or she is assessed by a specialist medical doctor.

These special benefits are payable to the parent for a maximum of 35 weeks within the 52-week period that starts on the day the doctor issues the medical certificate; or, if the claim is made before the certificate is issued, from the date the specialist medical doctor certifies that the employee's child is critically ill or injured.

The benefits end when:

- 35 weeks of parents of critically ill children benefit have been paid;
- the critically ill child no longer requires the care or support of a parent or dies;
- the 52-week period has expired; or
- the individual has exhausted the maximum benefits payable combining parents of critically ill children benefits with other types of EI benefits.

Q. Can Either Parent Receive the Special Benefits for Parents of Critically Ill Children?

A. The EI Special Benefits for Parents of Critically Ill Children are available to either parent, or parents can share the benefits between them if they wish.

Q. Is There Any Support for Parents of Murdered or Missing Children?

A. Yes. Parents of murdered or missing children who have suffered a loss of income due to taking time away from work to deal with the death or disappearance of a child may apply for a special income support grant. Eligible employees may receive up to 35 weeks of income support during the 52-week period immediately following the incident. The maximum grant payable is $350 per week, paid biweekly.

Q. Can an Employee Work While Collecting EI Benefits?

A. As is the case with regular EI benefits, persons claiming sickness, maternity, parental, or compassionate care benefits can work and earn income while collecting parental benefits. Generally speaking, employees can earn up to $50 or 25% of their weekly benefit, whichever is higher. However, beginning on August 7, 2008, the "Working While on Claim" measure was implemented. Under this measure, claimants were permitted to earn $75 per week or 40% of the employee's weekly earnings, whichever is higher. Any earnings above this allowable amount would be deducted from that week's benefit.

More recently, on August 5, 2012, a new "Working While on Claim" Pilot Project was implemented. Under this pilot project, employees are able to keep 50 cents of their EI benefits for every dollar they earn, up to 90% of the weekly insurable earnings used to calculate the employees' EI benefit amount. After the 90% threshold is met, earnings are deducted dollar-for-dollar from the benefits.

Employees are permitted to choose between the above two methods for deducting earnings from their EI benefits for any claims during the period of August 5, 2012 to August 1, 2015.

Q. How Does an Employee Apply for EI Benefits?

A. Once the employee has obtained a Record of Employment from the employer, the employee can file a claim at the local HRSDC office. If the employer opts to submit the Record of Employment electronically, an employee will be able to apply as soon as the Record of Employment is submitted. Once the claimant has applied for benefits, there is a two-week waiting period while the claim is processed. It is therefore important for an employee to make claim as soon as the leave begins.

MATERNITY LEAVE CHECKLIST

❏ Is the employee covered by employment standards laws?

❏ Has the employee worked continuously for the same employer for the required period of time?

❏ Has the employee obtained and submitted

- a medical certificate certifying the pregnancy and the expected date of delivery, or

- proof of adoption in those jurisdictions where it is required?

❏ Has the employee given the employer the required notice of her intent to take leave?

❏ The required notice should:

- be in writing,

- include the date on which the employee intends to begin leave, and

- include the date on which the employee intends to return to work.

❏ If benefits are to continue to accrue during the absence from work, have arrangements been made to continue any employee contributions to benefit plans during the leave?

❏ Has the employer issued the Record of Employment necessary for the employee to apply for Employment Insurance maternity/parental benefits?

MATERNITY/PARENTAL LEAVE CHART

Jurisdiction	Qualifying Period	Length of Leave	Extension	Required Notice	Reinstatement	Seniority/Benefits
Federal (pregnancy)	6 months	17 weeks	not specified	4 weeks	same/similar position with same wages/benefits	employment deemed continuous; employer to continue making payments to benefit plans
(parental)	6 months	37 weeks	not specified	4 weeks		
Alberta (pregnancy)	52 weeks	15 weeks	not specified	6 weeks	same/comparable position with same wages	same wages/benefits that accrued to date leave commenced
(parental)	52 weeks	37 weeks	not specified	6 weeks		

Jurisdiction	Qualifying Period	Length of Leave	Extension	Required Notice	Reinstatement	Seniority/ Benefits
British Columbia (pregnancy)	not specified	17 weeks	6 weeks	4 weeks	same/comparable position with all increments/ benefits as if leave not taken	services deemed continuous; employer to continue making payments to benefit plans
(parental)	not specified	37 weeks; 35 weeks if pregnancy leave is taken	5 weeks	4 weeks		
Manitoba (pregnancy)	7 months	17 weeks	not specified	4 weeks	same/ comparable position wages/benefits as before leave began	services deemed continuous
(parental)	7 months	37 weeks	not specified	4 weeks		
New Brunswick (pregnancy)	not specified	17 weeks	not specified	4 months notice of intent to take leave; 2 weeks notice of commencement of leave	same/ equivalent position	no loss of seniority/ benefits/ wages accrued to date leave commenced
(child care)	not specified	37 weeks	not specified	4 weeks		

Jurisdiction	Qualifying Period	Length of Leave	Extension	Required Notice	Reinstatement	Seniority/ Benefits
Newfoundland and Labrador (pregnancy)	20 weeks	17 weeks	not specified	2 weeks	wages, duties, benefits, and position not less beneficial than before leave	employment deemed continuous; benefits do not accrue unless agreed to
(parental)	20 weeks	35 weeks	not specified	2 weeks		
Nova Scotia (pregnancy)	1 year	17 weeks	not specified	4 weeks	same/comparable position; same wages, benefits	no loss of seniority/ benefits accrued to date leave commenced; employee has option to maintain benefits at own expense
(parental)	1 year	52 weeks; 35 weeks if pregnancy leave is taken	not specified	4 weeks		

Jurisdiction	Qualifying Period	Length of Leave	Extension	Required Notice	Reinstatement	Seniority/ Benefits
Ontario (pregnancy)	13 weeks prior to estimated delivery date	17 weeks	not specified	2 weeks	same/comparable work; same wages as at date leave commenced	period of leave included in calculation of length of employment/ seniority; employer to continue making payments to benefit plans
(parental)	13 weeks	37 weeks; 35 weeks if pregnancy leave is taken	not specified	2 weeks		
Prince Edward Island (maternity)	20 weeks	17 weeks	5 weeks	4 weeks	same/comparable work; same wages/ benefits as if leave not taken	no loss of seniority/ benefits accrued to date leave taken/employer not obliged to pay pension benefits during leave; employee has option to maintain benefits at own expense
(parental)	20 weeks	35 weeks	5 weeks	4 weeks		

Jurisdiction	Qualifying Period	Length of Leave	Extension	Required Notice	Reinstatement	Seniority/ Benefits
Quebec (pregnancy)	none	18 weeks	not specified	3 weeks	same position	same rights and benefits as if no leave taken; employer to continue making payments to group insurance and pension plans
(parental)	none	52 weeks	not specified	3 weeks		
Saskatchewan (pregnancy)	20 weeks in the immediately preceding 52-week period (under proposed legislation, the qualifying period would be reduced to 13 weeks)	18 weeks	6 weeks	4 weeks	same/compara- ble position; not less than same wages/ benefits	seniority and recall rights continue to accrue no loss of accrued benefits; employee has option to maintain benefits at own expense

Jurisdiction	Qualifying Period	Length of Leave	Extension	Required Notice	Reinstatement	Seniority/ Benefits
Saskatchewan — *cont'd* (parental)	20 weeks in the immediately preceding 52-week period (under proposed legislation, the qualifying period would be reduced to 13 weeks)	37 weeks; 34 weeks if pregnancy leave is taken	not specified	4 weeks		
Northwest Territories (pregnancy)	12 months	17 weeks	6 weeks	4 weeks	same/compara- ble position; with same/ wages/benefits	no loss of seniority accrued to date leave commenced; wage/benefit increments as if leave not taken
(parental)	12 months	37 weeks	not specified	4 weeks		
Nunavut (pregnancy)	12 months	17 weeks	6 weeks	4 weeks	same/compara- ble position; with same/ wages/benefits	no loss of seniority accrued to date leave commenced; wage/benefit increments as if leave not taken
(parental)	12 months	37 weeks	not specified	4 weeks		

Jurisdiction	Qualifying Period	Length of Leave	Extension	Required Notice	Reinstatement	Seniority/ Benefits
Yukon (pregnancy)	12 months	17 weeks	not specified	4 weeks	same/comparable position; same wages/ benefits as if leave not taken	employment deemed continuous; increase to wages and benefits as if leave not taken
(parental)	12 months	37 weeks	not specified	4 weeks		

Chapter 8

PAYMENT OF WAGES

Page

INTRODUCTION 119
PAYMENT OF WAGES 120
    How Often Must Employees Be Paid Their Wages? 120
    How May Wages Be Paid? 120
    What if an Employee Is Absent at the Time of Payment? 120
    What Happens if an Employer Cannot Locate an Employee To Pay Him or Her? .. 120
    When Must Wages Be Paid on Termination of Employment? 121
    What Deductions Can Be Made from an Employee's Wages? 121
STATEMENT OF WAGES 121
    Must Employees Receive a Statement of Wages? 121
    How Can the Statement of Wages Be Given To Employees? 122
ENFORCEMENT OF PAYMENT 122
    What Can an Employee Do if an Employer Does Not Pay Wages Owing? 122
    How Do Employment Standards Branches Enforce Payment of Wages? 122
    Can an Organization's Directors Be Held Liable for Unpaid Wages? 123
    Are There Limits on the Amount of Unpaid Wages That Can Be Recovered? 124
    What Recourse Does an Employee Have To Recover Unpaid Wages if His or Her
        Employer Is Bankrupt or Goes into Receivership? 124
PAYMENT OF WAGES CHART 125
STATEMENT OF WAGES CHART 127

INTRODUCTION

Payment of wages is one of the most important areas for an employer and involves much more than just cutting a cheque or making a deposit to an employee's bank account. Complaints of unpaid wages are amongst the most common that employees make to employment or labour standards branches. Failure to properly pay employees the wages to which they are entitled can leave an organization and its directors open to liability and penalties, as well as to intrusive and costly investigations. In this section, we will examine when wages are to be paid, how they may be paid, permitted and prohibited deductions, proceedings for the recovery of unpaid wages, and employer and director liability for unpaid wages.

PAYMENT OF WAGES

Q. How Often Must Employees Be Paid Their Wages?

A. All jurisdictions have established a "pay period", which requires employers to pay employees at least that frequently. As well, all jurisdictions, except **Ontario** and **Quebec**, also specify that the payment of wages must include all wages earned up to a cut-off date. For example, in **Prince Edward Island**, wages must be paid at least every 16 days and pay must include all wages earned up to five working days before the payment date. For information specific to each jurisdiction consult the chart on pages 125 to 126.

Q. How May Wages Be Paid?

A. All jurisdictions except the **federal** jurisdiction state that wages must be paid in Canadian currency, in cash or by cheque or bill of exchange, or by direct deposit to a specified financial institution such as a bank or trust company. While the **federal** jurisdiction is silent with respect to how wages are to be paid, the methods set out for the rest of the country would apply.

Q. What if an Employee Is Absent at the Time of Payment?

A. Generally speaking, if an employee is absent at the time fixed for the payment of wages, he or she is entitled to be paid at any time thereafter during normal working hours.

Q. What Happens if an Employer Cannot Locate an Employee To Pay Him or Her?

A. In **British Columbia**, **Manitoba**, **Nova Scotia**, **Nunavut**, **Ontario**, and the **Yukon**, if an employee cannot be located for the payment of wages owing, the employer is required to remit the wages to the Director of Employment or Labour Standards in that province or territory. The Director will then hold the money in trust for the employee, and the employer is considered to have fulfilled its obligation to pay the wages. The deadline for remitting the wages to the Director varies by jurisdiction and ranges from 60 days to six months. In **Saskatchewan**, the employer must send the employee's wages by registered mail to his or her last known address. There is no specific procedure set out for this situation in the remaining jurisdictions.

Q. When Must Wages Be Paid on Termination of Employment?

A. Each jurisdiction sets out different time frames within which an employer must pay the wages owing to a terminated employee. For example, in **Ontario**, all wages owing at the time of termination are to be made by the later of seven days after termination and the next payday. The time frames for each jurisdiction are set out in the chart on pages 125 to 126.

Q. What Deductions Can Be Made from an Employee's Wages?

A. Typically, the only deductions that can be made from an employee's wages are those required by law or those that the employee authorizes.

- **The following deductions are required by law:**
    - statutory deductions, including Canada Pension Plan, Quebec Pension Plan, Employment Insurance, income tax (federal and provincial), and Quebec income tax;
    - court-ordered deductions, including garnishments and family support orders;
    - overpayments of wages by the employer; and
    - payroll tax (**Northwest Territories**).
- **The following deductions are permitted with employee consent:**
    - pension and group benefit plan deductions;
    - trade union dues; and
    - room and board.

STATEMENT OF WAGES

Q. Must Employees Receive a Statement of Wages?

A. All jurisdictions require that employers provide a "statement of wages" (also known as "statement of earnings") to their employees. Statements of wages must, in most parts of Canada, be provided to employees at the end of each pay period, or on each payday. However, some provinces, such as **British Columbia** and **Manitoba**, provide that, if statements of wages are the same from pay period to pay period, a new statement need not be given until a change occurs. Generally speaking, a statement of wages must include the hours worked, the rate of pay, the amount and purpose of deductions, and the net pay. Details on the required contents of statements of wages in each jurisdiction can be found in the chart on pages 127 to 128.

Q. How Can the Statement of Wages Be Given To Employees?

A. Most jurisdictions specify that the statement of wages must be in writing. Increasingly, Canadian jurisdictions are expressly permitting delivery of statements of wages in electronic format. **Alberta, British Columbia, Manitoba, Ontario, Prince Edward Island, Quebec, Saskatchewan** (proposed legislation), the **Northwest Territories**, and the **federal** jurisdiction all now explicitly state that the statement of wages may be given to an employee electronically or by email, rather than in paper form. Due to concerns with respect to employee privacy, however, in some of these jurisdictions, an employer will only be able to provide statements of wages electronically if the employee is able to access the electronic pay statement confidentially and the employee has a means of printing a paper copy of the pay statement if he or she so chooses.

ENFORCEMENT OF PAYMENT

Q. What Can an Employee Do if an Employer Does Not Pay Wages Owing?

A. Where an employee believes that a past or current employer has improperly failed to pay wages which are owing, he or she may file a complaint with the local employment standards branch. Generally speaking, there is a time limit on when such a complaint can be filed, although this time limit varies across the country. In most parts of the country, such a complaint must be filed within six months of when employment with the employer ceased, or when the wages became due. Employees may also have avenues of redress through their collective agreement if they are unionized, or by pursuing a civil action in the courts.

Q. How Do Employment Standards Branches Enforce Payment of Wages?

A. Generally speaking, once a complaint has been filed, an Employment Standards Officer will investigate to determine whether and how much wages are owing. The officer may attempt to settle the matter informally between the parties. If it is determined that there are wages owing, the Director of Employment Standards will issue an order to pay against the employer. If it is determined that the complaint is unfounded, it will be dismissed. If either party is dissatisfied with the determination, it can be appealed.

Employment and labour standards branches generally have a variety of powers at their disposal to enforce the payment of wages owing. Although there is some variance across the country, some of the most common methods of enforcement are listed below:

- **Filing an order with the court:** In all parts of the country, an order for unpaid wages may be filed with the court, in which case it is enforceable in the same manner as a judgment of the court. These powers of enforcement include the power to garnish and to seize and sell property belonging to the employer.

- **Attachment of debts:** Where an order for payment of wages has been issued against an employer, and the Director learns or suspects that a person is or is about to become indebted to the employer, the Director may demand that the money be paid to the Director in trust.

- **Registration in Land Titles Office:** In some parts of the country, the Director has the power to register an order for unpaid wages in the Land Titles Office against property of the employer. Once an order is registered in this manner, it becomes a secured charge against the employer's interests in the land.

- **Liability of associated firms:** Where it is found that a business, undertaking, or other activity is being carried on by two or more employers, the employers may both be deemed to be the employer for the purposes of employment standards, and the associated entities will be jointly and severally liable for the unpaid earnings.

- **Seizure of assets:** As noted above, Directors have the power to file an order with the court, in which case the order may be enforced by the seizure and sale of assets. As well, some jurisdictions give directors the power to seize assets belonging to the employer in order to secure payment of the unpaid wages.

Q. Can an Organization's Directors Be Held Liable for Unpaid Wages?

A. In a number of jurisdictions, directors of a corporation can be held personally liable for unpaid wages that accrued while they were directors. However, limitations are placed on this liability. In some parts of the country, employees who are owed wages must first pursue the corporation before seeking compensation from directors. As well, limitations are placed on the amount of unpaid wages for which directors can be held liable. The jurisdictions with specific provisions are as follows:

- In **Alberta**, **Manitoba**, **Ontario**, **Saskatchewan**, and the **federal** jurisdiction, directors are liable for up to six months' wages that became due while they were directors. Similarly, under **Prince Edward Island's** legislation, directors of corporations may now also be held liable for up to six months of unpaid wages in certain limited circumstances.

- In **British Columbia**, **Newfoundland and Labrador**, the **Northwest Territories**, **Nunavut**, and the **Yukon**, directors are liable for up to two months' wages that became due while they were directors.

- Directors are also liable for all outstanding vacation pay in **Manitoba**. In the **Yukon**, directors may be liable for the greater of the vacation pay set out in the employment standards legislation and the amount contractually agreed to between the employer and the employee for 12 months.

- Some jurisdictions, such as **New Brunswick** and **Quebec**, do not indicate specific liability or amounts, but rather state that an offence, such as non-payment of wages, committed by a corporation, is also held to be an offence by each officer and director of the corporation.

Q. Are There Limits on the Amount of Unpaid Wages That Can Be Recovered?

A. Some provinces place a limit on the amount of wages that can be recovered through employment standards legislation. For example, in **Alberta** and **Saskatchewan**, recovery is limited to wages payable in the year preceding the complaint, or the last year of employment if employment has been terminated. In **British Columbia** and **Manitoba**, recovery of wages is capped at six months from the date of the complaint. In **Ontario**, an Employment Standards Officer may not make an order to pay for wages greater than $10,000 for any employee.

Q. What Recourse Does an Employee Have To Recover Unpaid Wages if His or Her Employer Is Bankrupt or Goes into Receivership?

A. In most jurisdictions, statutes set out both the priority that unpaid wages receive as compared to other creditors, as well as the amount an employee is entitled to recover. Where the employer is bankrupt or goes into receivership, employees who have been terminated and had been working for the employer for more than three months, can now pursue up to six months' unpaid wages (including salaries, commissions, compensation for services rendered, vacation pay, severance pay, and termination pay) through the Wage Earner Protection Program under the *Wage Earner Protection Program Act*. An individual who has occupied a managerial position, was an officer or director of the employer, or had a controlling interest in the employer's business, is not eligible for the program. Wages recoverable are those earned in the last six months before the bankruptcy, less any applicable provincial or federal deductions, to a maximum of the greater of $3,000 and four times the maximum weekly insurable earnings under the *Employment Insurance Act*.

PAYMENT OF WAGES CHART

Jurisdiction	Regular Payments	Payment upon Termination
Federal	to be paid on regular payday within 30 days of entitlement arising	within 30 days of entitlement
Alberta	to be paid within 10 days of each pay period; pay periods not to exceed 1 month	within 3 consecutive days after last day of employment where employment terminated with notice or pay in lieu of notice; within 10 consecutive days after last day of employment where employment terminated without notice or pay in lieu of notice
British Columbia	to be paid at least semi-monthly within 8 days after the expiration of each pay period	within 48 hours of termination; where employee terminates, within 6 days after the termination
Manitoba	to be paid at least semi-monthly within 10 days after the expiration of each pay period (pay period defined as not more than 16 consecutive days)	within 10 working days of termination
New Brunswick	to be paid at least every 16 days which is to include all wages earned up to a day no more than 7 calendar days prior to the date of payment	no later than the next regular payday; never more than 21 days from date of termination
Newfoundland and Labrador	to be paid at least half-monthly, within 7 days after the end of the pay period, and must include all wages earned by the employee in a pay period	within 1 week of the date of termination
Nova Scotia	to be paid at least semi-monthly within 5 days after the expiration of each pay period	payment on expiry of termination notice

Jurisdiction	Regular Payments	Payment upon Termination
Ontario	to be paid on regular payday established by employer	payment to be made by the later of 7 days after termination and the next payday
Prince Edward Island	intervals between paydays cannot be more than 16 days; pay must include all wages earned up to and including a day that is not more than 5 working days prior to the date of payment	payment to be made no later than the last day of the next pay period after termination
Quebec	regular intervals of not more than 16 days or 1 month if employee is an executive or party to a contract payment in lieu of notice of termination due at the time of termination	not specified
Saskatchewan	wages to be paid at least semi-monthly or at the end of every 14-day period, to include all wages earned up to 6 days before payday	within 14 days of the termination
Northwest Territories	pay periods not to exceed 1 month; all wages earned during a pay period are due within 10 days after the end of the period	within 10 days after termination
Nunavut	pay periods not to exceed 1 month; all wages earned during a pay period are due within 10 days after the end of the period	within 10 days after termination
Yukon	pay periods not to exceed 16 days; all payments are due no later than 10 days after end of pay period	within 7 days of the date of termination

STATEMENT OF WAGES CHART

Jurisdiction	Information Recorded on Statement of Wages
Federal	period for which payment is made, number of hours worked, rate of wages, details of all deductions, actual sum being received by the employee
Alberta	regular and overtime hours of work, wage rate and overtime rate, earnings paid showing separately each component of the earnings for each pay period, deductions from earnings and the reason therefore, time off instead of overtime pay provided and taken, and the period of employment covered by the statement
British Columbia	name, address, hours worked, wage rate and basis, overtime wage rate and hours worked at this rate, any money, allowance or other payment the employee is entitled to, amount and purpose of each deduction, how wages are calculated if other than hourly or salaried, gross and net wages, how much money the employee has taken from the employee's time bank and how much remains
Manitoba	regular hours of work and overtime for which wages are being paid, wage rates, deductions and the reason for deductions, net wages
New Brunswick	dates of pay period, gross pay, deductions, net pay
Newfoundland and Labrador	gross wages, pay period, wage rate and hours worked, deductions, net wages, vacation pay
Nova Scotia	pay period, hours of work, wage rate, details of deductions, actual sum received by employee
Ontario	pay period, rate of wages, amount of entitlement, amount and purpose of deductions, net wage, any amount with respect to room or board (living allowance) that is deemed to be paid to the employee, the method of arriving at gross wages unless that information is provided to the employee in some other manner and with respect to vacation pay, if one or more vacation days are taken during the pay period, the following information is required: • the amount of vacation pay accrued in previous calendar years that has not yet been paid; • the amount of vacation pay accrued in the current calendar year; • the amount of vacation pay paid for that pay period; and

Jurisdiction	Information Recorded on Statement of Wages
	• the total amount of vacation pay that has been accrued but not yet paid where the employer pays vacation pay on a pay period by pay period basis throughout the year, the information regarding vacation pay does not have to appear on the statement of wages if:
	— the amount of vacation pay paid appears on the pay statement separately from the amount of other wages being paid, or
	— a separate vacation pay statement setting out the amount of vacation pay for the pay period is given to the employee
Prince Edward Island	name and address of employer, name of employee, pay period, rate of wages, hours worked, gross wages, gross vacation pay, gross amount of any pay in lieu of notice of termination, amount and purpose of each deduction, bonus, gratuity, or living allowance, net wages
Quebec	name of employer, name of employee, identification of occupation, date of payment and work period covered by payment, hours paid at the regular rate, hours being paid at overtime rate or hours off in lieu of overtime, nature and amount of bonuses, indemnities, allowances or commissions, wage rate, amount of wages before deductions, nature and amount of deductions, net wages paid to employee, information on gratuities where applicable
Saskatchewan	name of employee, period for which payment of wages is made, hours for which payment is made, rate of wages, category or class of employment, amount of total wages, any deductions from wages, actual amount of payment made
Northwest Territories	period for which payment is made, hours for which payment is made, number of hours for which the payment is made in respect of any statutory holiday, rate of wages, details of deductions, actual sum received
Nunavut	period for which payment is made, hours for which payment is made, rate of wages, details of deductions, actual sum received
Yukon	period for which payment is made, hours for which payment is made, rate of wages, details of deductions, actual sum received by employee

Chapter 9

PERSONNEL RECORDS

Page

INTRODUCTION 129
RECORDING REQUIREMENTS 129
    What Kinds of Records Are Employers Required To Keep about Their
        Employees? 129
    Where Must These Records Be Kept? 130
    How Long Must These Records Be Kept? 130
ACCESS TO RECORDS 130
    Can the Government Access These Records? 130
    Can the Information in Personnel Records Be Disclosed To Anyone Else? 131
    What Information Must Be Provided To Employees? 132
    Can Pay Statements Be Provided Electronically? 132
PERSONNEL RECORDS CHART 133

INTRODUCTION

Employers across the country are subject to detailed record-keeping requirements. Due to the varying lengths of record retention by jurisdiction, it is recommended that employers keep all records for the longest retention period required. This is especially true when employers have operations and employees in numerous provinces or territories.

RECORDING REQUIREMENTS

Q. What Kinds of Records Are Employers Required To Keep about Their Employees?

A. All employers are required to keep records for each employee detailing compliance with employment standards requirements. For example, records must indicate the hours worked by each employee, both regular and overtime, the wage rate, the dates on which wages are paid, and information on annual vacations and statutory holidays taken by each employee. The requirements as to the personnel records that must be kept are detailed, and vary slightly from province to province. For details on the required contents of personnel records, please refer to the chart on page 133.

Q. Where Must These Records Be Kept?

A. A number of jurisdictions, such as **British Columbia**, **Manitoba**, **Nova Scotia**, **Prince Edward Island**, the **Northwest Territories**, and the **Yukon**, require employers to keep their personnel records at their principal place of business within the province or territory. In **Saskatchewan** and **Nunavut**, employers are required to keep records within each place of business within the jurisdiction. In **New Brunswick**, the employer is simply required to keep the records within the province. **Ontario** does not specify where the records are to be kept, but does require that the records be readily available for inspection by an Employment Standards Officer. The other jurisdictions do not specify a required location for the maintenance of personnel records.

Q. How Long Must These Records Be Kept?

A. The length of time for which personnel records must be retained varies across the country, from one year to five years. For details on the requirement to retain records, please refer to the chart on page 133.

Aside from employment standards retention rules, it is advisable to retain records for unsuccessful job candidates for the period allowed for filing a human rights complaint of discrimination in the selection process; these run from six to 24 months, depending on the province (see chart at page 133). Records for former employees should be retained for at least the limitation period for filing a wrongful dismissal claim (i.e., two to six years, depending on the province). Finally, under the *Income Tax Act*, payroll records should be kept for at least seven years to meet Canada Revenue Agency audit purposes.

ACCESS TO RECORDS

Q. Can the Government Access These Records?

A. Part of the rationale for record keeping is to assist the government in monitoring and enforcing compliance with employment standards legislation. Therefore, inspectors from employment standards departments are entitled to request that these records be produced for inspection. A person who is requested by an inspector to produce personnel records must do so when and as required.

Q. Can the Information in Personnel Records Be Disclosed To Anyone Else?

A. In today's world of email, Internet, digital data storage, and expanding e-commerce, many Canadians have increased concerns regarding the amount of personal data that is being collected, how it is stored, and who has access to it. However, in the case of the workplace, that concern can be heightened, given the amount of sensitive personal data collected and its concentration in one place, and the potential for identity theft.

Privacy protection is an evolving concept and there is still relatively little legislation or case law in the area. Most jurisdictions in Canada have public sector privacy legislation protecting the confidentiality and limiting the use of personal information in the control of the government.

The extent to which an employee's personal information is protected from disclosure to a third party by an employer depends on the particular jurisdiction, whether the employee is in the public or private sector, and occasionally the contents of a collective agreement where the employee is in a union.

The *Personal Information Protection and Electronic Documents Act* ("PIPEDA") governs personal employee and job candidate information collected and/or stored by **federally regulated** employers such as banks, telecommunication companies, broadcasters, airlines, and interprovincial railways and trucking companies. Employees have a right of access to their own records, and disclosure to third parties is regulated.

In **Alberta**, **British Columbia**, and **Quebec**, personal information protection legislation limits the collection, use, and disclosure of personal information relating to private sector employees in those provinces. The legislation also allows for employee access to personal information about the employee.

For places of employment not covered by any protective legislation, safeguards on the personal information of employees will depend largely upon the policies which the company voluntarily chooses to adopt. However, the common law has recently accepted a concept of invasion of privacy described by the Ontario Court of Appeal as "intrusion upon seclusion" (see *Jones v. Tsige*, 2012 CLLC ¶210-012). The proliferation of personal information protection statutes across the country makes it advisable for an employer to provide reasonable protection for employee data, and establish a protocol for access and disclosure. Social Insurance Numbers ("SINs"), in particular, must be securely guarded against disclosure and hacking. The *Jones* case involved a bank employee who, contrary to the bank's policies, repeatedly accessed the banking records of a customer for personal reasons. Although the bank customer suffered no actual financial loss, she was awarded $10,000 in damages.

Q. What Information Must Be Provided To Employees?

A. Employers are required to provide "statements of earnings" to their employees. Statements of earnings must, in most parts of Canada, be provided to employees at the end of each pay period, or on each payday. However, some provinces, such as **British Columbia** and **Manitoba**, provide that, if statements of earnings are the same from pay period to pay period, a new statement need not be given until a change occurs. Generally speaking, a statement of wages must include the hours paid for, the rate of pay, the amount and purpose of deductions, and the net pay. Details on the required contents of statements of earnings in each jurisdiction can be found in Chapter 8, "Payment of Wages" generally, and specifically in the chart on page 125.

Q. Can Pay Statements Be Provided Electronically?

A. Legislation has not kept pace with technology and we are a long way from the paperless workplace. An employer wishing to provide electronic pay statements needs to consult first with the local employment standards office, as policy and legislation on electronic records are evolving slowly and without consistency across Canada. For example, the **British Columbia** *Employment Standards Act* allows an employer to provide an electronic pay statement if the employer provides the employee, through the workplace, confidential access and a way of printing a paper copy. **Ontario** legislation now allows an employer to provide a pay statement using a confidential email system, but only if the employee has access in the workplace to a way of printing a paper copy. **Prince Edward Island** legislation also allows electronic pay statements if the employer provides the employee, through the workplace, confidential access and a way of printing a paper copy. To date, employers in the **Northwest Territories** and **federally regulated** employers also have the option of using paperless pay statements. Most statutes remain silent on this point and refer simply to a requirement to provide a "statement in writing" and, as indicated above, it is advisable to check first with the regulator in the jurisdiction before making a change.

PERSONNEL RECORDS CHART

Jurisdiction	Information Recorded with Respect to Each Employee	Length Retained
Federal	dates of commencement and termination of employment, name, address, SIN, occupational classification, gender, and where under the age of 17, the age of the employee, rate of wages and basis for rate, daily hours of work, actual earnings, payments made after deductions and details of deductions, information on annual vacations, information on maternity or parental leave, information on general holidays, information on averaging where hours of work are averaged, employer's pay periods, information on sick leave, notice of termination or intention to terminate, information on bereavement leave, notice of work schedules which exceed either the standard or maximum hours of work, information on absence due to work-related injury or illness (*Canada Labour Code*)	3 years after work performed
Alberta	regular and overtime hours of work, wage rate and overtime rate, earnings paid showing separately each component, deductions from earnings and the reasons therefore, time off instead of overtime pay provided and taken, hours of work, name, address, and date of birth, date of commencement of present employment, dates on which general holidays are taken, dates of vacations and periods of employment in which the vacation was earned, wage rate and overtime rate and dates and particulars of any changes to these rates, documentation relating to maternity, parental, and reservist leaves, and copies of termination notices and written requests to employees to return to work after a temporary layoff (*Employment Standards Code*)	3 years from date record made
British Columbia	name, date of birth, occupation, telephone number, residential address, date of commencement of employment, wage rate, hours worked each day, any hours of work averaging agreements, benefits paid to the employee by the employer, gross and net wages for each pay period, each deduction made from the employee's wages and the reason for it, dates of statutory holidays taken by the employee and the amounts paid by the employer, dates of the annual vacation taken by the employee together with the amounts paid by the employer and the days and amounts owing, the amount of money taken by the employee from the employee's time bank, how much time remains, and the amounts paid and the dates taken (*Employment Standards Act*)	2 years after termination of employment

Jurisdiction	Information Recorded with Respect to Each Employee	Length Retained
Manitoba	name, address, date of birth, and occupation, date on which employment commenced, regular wage rate and overtime wage rate when employment starts, and particulars of any change to the regular or overtime wage rates, including date of change, regular hours of work if they vary from day-to-day and overtime hours, recorded separately and daily, copies of any work schedules that were required to be posted, dates on which wages are paid, and amount of wages paid on each date, deductions from wages and reason for each deduction, time off provided and taken in lieu of overtime wages, date on which each general holiday is taken, wage rate for work performed or hours on duty on a general holiday, for each annual vacation, the date on which it begins and ends, the period of employment in which it is earned, and the date and amount of vacation allowance paid, amount of vacation allowance paid in lieu of vacation upon termination of employment, and the date of payment, copies of documents relating to maternity, parental or other leave, including the dates and number of days taken as leave, date of termination of employment (*The Employment Standards Code*)	3 years from date record made
New Brunswick	name, address, date of birth, social insurance number, date of commencement of employment, hours worked by day and by week, wage rate and gross earnings for each pay period, particulars of deductions, living allowance, vacation periods, vacation pay, public holiday pay due or paid, net payments, any leaves of absence and the reasons and documents relating thereto, dates of all dismissals, suspensions or lay offs, and corresponding notices (*Employment Standards Act*)	3 years after work performed
Newfoundland and Labrador	name, address, date of birth, wage rate, daily hours worked, wages paid and deductions, dates of commencement, termination, notice of termination and notice of intention to terminate, particulars of annual vacation and wages paid, date of rest periods, date of expiry of contract or specific task for which the employee was hired if applicable (*Labour Standards Act*)	4 years from date of last entry
Nova Scotia	name, age, sex, address, wage rate, hours of work, vacation periods, leaves of absence, pay and vacation pay, dates of commencement and termination of employment, dates of all layoffs or discharges and corresponding notices, cumulative wages, date and amount of any payment made for recruitment of the employee, and name and address of recruiter (*Labour Standards Code*)	3 years after work performed

Jurisdiction	Information Recorded with Respect to Each Employee	Length Retained
Ontario	name, address, employment commencement date — kept for 3 years after employment ceases (separate recording rules for homeworkers), date of birth (if student under 18) — kept for 3 years after employee's 18th birthday or employment ceases, daily and weekly hours worked — kept for 3 years after day or week to which information relates, pay period, wage rate, gross wages (and manner calculated, if not provided elsewhere), particulars of payments made when employment terminated, particulars of deductions, amounts for room or board, net wages — kept for 3 years after information was given to employee, documentation relating to pregnancy, parental, emergency, and reservist leave — kept for 3 years after leave expired, particulars on vacation time and pay — kept for 3 years after records made, copies of extended or averaging hours of work agreements — kept for 3 years after agreement terminates (*Employment Standards Act, 2000*)	3 years
Prince Edward Island	name, address, Social Insurance Number, date of birth, wage rate and actual earnings, number of hours worked in each day and week, gross earnings per pay period, deductions from gross earnings and nature of each deduction, starting date of employment and date of termination, type of work performed by the employee, period in which employee received vacation with pay, amount of vacation pay paid to the employee in lieu of vacation, number of overtime hours accumulated and used (*Employment Standards Act*)	3 years after work performed
Quebec	name, address, Social Insurance Number, occupation, date employment commenced, number of hours of work per day and per week, number of overtime hours paid or taken as time off in lieu, wage rate, nature and amount of premiums, indemnities, allowances or commissions, gross wages, nature and amount of all deductions, net wages, work period corresponding to payment, date of payment, reference year, duration and departure dates of annual vacation, details on general holidays, tips reported by employee, tips attributed to employee pursuant to *Taxation Act*, and date of birth of employees under 18 (*Labour Standards Act Regulation respecting a registration system or the keeping of a register*)	3 years

Jurisdiction	Information Recorded with Respect to Each Employee	Length Retained
Saskatchewan	particulars of any unwritten contract and copies of written contracts relating to wages or monetary benefits, name, sex, date of birth, address, rate of wages, total wages for each pay period, time when work and meal breaks begin and end each day, total number of hours each day and week, total number of hours each day and week that employee is required to be at employer's disposal, amount and purpose of deductions, date of each payment of wages, commencement and termination of employment, information on annual holidays, termination pay, register of work performed at home where applicable and address of home worker (*The Labour Standards Act*)	5 years after termination
	copy of written contract or collective bargaining agreement dealing with wages or monetary benefits, name, sex, date of birth, address, description of job, rate of wages and particulars of any change, wages paid for each pay period, total hours worked each day and week, amount and purpose of deductions (*The Wages Recovery Act*)	2 years after entry made
Northwest Territories	hours worked each day, gross and actual payments, name, age, address, date of commencement of employment and anniversary date, rate of wages and particulars of any changes, information on annual vacations, amount paid in lieu of vacation on termination, amount paid for statutory holidays, amount and purpose of deductions, copy of any notice of termination, amount paid in lieu of notice of termination (*Employment Standards Act*)	2 years from date record made
Nunavut	hours worked each day, gross and actual payments, name, age, address, date of commencement of employment and anniversary date, rate of wages and particulars of any changes, information on annual vacations, amount paid in lieu of vacation on termination, amount paid for general holidays, amount and purpose of deductions, copy of any notice of termination, amount paid in lieu of notice of termination (*Labour Standards Act*)	2 years from date record made
Yukon	name, address, daily and weekly hours worked, gross wages and particulars of deductions, weekly overtime hours, paid time off in lieu of overtime accumulated and taken weekly, annual vacations taken, leaves of absence taken, and conditions of employment (*Employment Standards Act*)	1 year

Chapter 10

TERMINATION OF EMPLOYMENT

Page

INTRODUCTION 138

UNJUST DISMISSAL 139

    Are There Circumstances in Which an Employer Cannot Dismiss an Employee?... 139

INDIVIDUAL TERMINATION... 140

    How Much Notice Is an Employer Required To Give an Employee upon
    Termination of Employment?... 140

    What if an Employer Does Not Provide an Employee with the Required Notice?... 140

    Is Everyone Entitled To Notice of Termination?...................................... 140

    Are There Any Reasons for a Termination Which Do Not Require Notice of
    Termination? 141

    How Must the Notice Be Given?... 143

    Can an Employer Offer an Employee a Combination of Notice and Pay in Lieu?... 143

    Does Overtime Count Towards Calculating Pay in Lieu of Notice?................... 143

    When Calculating an Employee's "Normal" Hours, What if the Hours Are Not the
    Same from Week-to-Week? 143

    Do Employee Benefits Continue Once an Employee Has Received Notice of
    Termination or Pay in Lieu?... 144

    What if the Conditions of Employment Are Changed Once Notice of Termination
    Is Given?... 144

    Can an Employee's Vacation Be Used as Part of the Notice Period?................. 144

    When Must Employers Pay Employees Their Wages Owing?......................... 145

    When Must an Employer Pay Any Vacation Pay Owed at the Time of
    Termination? 145

    What Happens if an Employee Is Still Employed after the Date of Official
    Termination? 146

    Must Employment Have Been Continuous for the Notice Requirements to Apply? 146

    What if an Employee Has Been Hired for a Fixed Term of Employment, but
    Continues To Work Beyond This Term? 147

    If an Employer Sells the Business, Can the New Owners Terminate the
    Employees' Employment and Treat Them Like New Employees? 148

	Page
SEVERANCE PAY	149
What Is Severance Pay?	149
When Are Employees Entitled To Severance Pay?	149
How Is Severance Pay Calculated?	149
TERMINATION BY EMPLOYEE	150
Do Employees Owe Their Employers Any Notice if They Choose To Terminate Their Employment?	150
Are There Any Situations in Which Employees Would Be Justified in Not Giving the Minimum Notice?	151
What if an Employer Decides To Terminate the Employment of an Employee after the Employee Has Given Notice?	152
What if an Employer Tries To Force an Employee To Resign?	153
GROUP TERMINATION	153
Are There Any Jurisdictions That Do Not Have Group Termination Provisions?	154
What Constitutes a Group Termination?	154
What Are the Notice Requirements for Group Terminations?	155
Which Jurisdictions Require Employers To Participate in Planning Committees or the Equivalent?	156
Is Anyone Excluded from Group Termination Provisions?	156
What if Employees Wish To Give Notice after Receiving a Notice of Group Termination?	156
LAYOFFS	156
COLLECTIVE AGREEMENTS	160
INDIVIDUAL TERMINATION NOTICE REQUIREMENTS CHART	162
GROUP TERMINATION NOTICE REQUIREMENTS CHART	165
PAYMENT OF WAGES ON TERMINATION CHART	167

INTRODUCTION

The termination of the employment contract is one of the most important and difficult areas of employment law. The action of terminating the employment of a worker carries with it specific legal rights and obligations for both the employee and the employer. A misunderstanding as to its rights and duties upon the termination of the relationship can be costly for an employer.

All jurisdictions have enacted laws that require an employer to provide minimum notice of termination or payment in lieu of notice of termination. Some jurisdictions also require minimum notice from the employee terminating his or her own employment, and two jurisdictions require that an employee receive severance pay.

This series of questions and answers will discuss issues arising when an employer decides to terminate the employment of an employee, either individually or as part of a group, or when an employee decides to resign. As well, issues related to layoffs and the effect of collective agreements will be discussed.

This discussion will cover issues only as they arise under employment standards legislation across the country. While the parties also have rights and obligations under the common law upon termination of employment, these are discussed separately in the series of questions and answers on "wrongful dismissal".

UNJUST DISMISSAL

Q. Are There Circumstances in Which an Employer Cannot Dismiss an Employee?

A. Generally speaking, so long as an employer complies with its obligations under employment standards, human rights, and the common law, an employer may terminate the employment of non-union employees for any reason and without cause. However, the **federal** government, **Nova Scotia**, and **Quebec** have special protections for employees, restricting the right of employers to dismiss them. Essentially, these three jurisdictions grant rights equivalent to the rights of unionized employees to be let go only for cause, to contest the dismissal, and to seek reinstatement.

Under **federal** legislation, employees who have been employed at least 12 months and who are not covered by a collective agreement may file a complaint if they believe the dismissal was unjust. Complaints are not accepted for a hearing by an adjudicator if an employee was laid off for lack of work or because of the discontinuance of a function. Where a complaint of unjust dismissal is upheld, employees may be entitled not only to compensation, but to reinstatement to their former position.

In **Nova Scotia**, the law provides that employees with 10 years or more of service with an employer may file a complaint to the Labour Standards Tribunal if they allege that there was a discharge or suspension without just cause. There are certain exceptions such as: the reason for the dismissal was beyond the control of the employer, the employee has been offered reasonable alternative employment, the employee is retiring, or the employee is employed in the construction industry or an industry or profession exempted by regulation. The Tribunal has broad powers to "rectify injury" or order compensation.

A **Quebec** employee with at least two years of service may file a complaint if he or she believes the dismissal was not for a "good and sufficient" reason. If the matter proceeds to arbitration, the arbitrator may order reinstatement or damages.

INDIVIDUAL TERMINATION

Q. How Much Notice Is an Employer Required To Give an Employee upon Termination of Employment?

A. When the employment of an employee is terminated, the employer is required to provide notice of the termination. Each jurisdiction sets out minimum notice requirements based upon the employee's length of service. The chart on page 162 specifies the minimum requirements for each jurisdiction. Remember, again, that these are minimum requirements.

Other than in the **federal** jurisdiction, the notice periods generally increase from one to eight weeks with increasing length of service.

Q. What if an Employer Does Not Provide an Employee with the Required Notice?

A. If an employer does not provide the employee with the required notice, it must provide the employee with "pay in lieu of notice" or "termination pay". Essentially, the employer must give the employee the money he or she would have earned if he or she had worked during the required notice period.

Q. Is Everyone Entitled To Notice of Termination?

A. While most employees are entitled to notice of termination, some workers are generally excluded from protection under employment standards laws.

In many jurisdictions, certain employees are not entitled to notice of termination. Workers who have been hired for a definite term of employment, who are let go for cause, who have been offered and have refused reasonable alternate work, whose contracts have become impossible to fulfill, who are hired on a seasonal basis, or who work in the construction industry may very well not be entitled to notice of termination. In the **Northwest Territories** and **Nunavut** an unusual provision excludes part-time employees (working less than 25 hours per week) from the notice of termination requirements. Generally speaking, as noted earlier in this book, employment standards legislation applies to both full-time and part-time employees.

In every jurisdiction, a worker who has not completed the minimum length of service (see chart on page 162) is not entitled to notice of termination.

Finally, certain layoffs are not considered to be terminations. Since the whole issue of layoffs is a rather complicated one, we have included a section to deal specifically with the topic, beginning on page 156.

Even if an employee is not entitled to notice of termination under employment standards law, he or she may still have a right to notice under the common law, an employment contract, or collective agreement, if one applies.

Q. Are There Any Reasons for a Termination Which Do Not Require Notice of Termination?

A. Yes. A number of industries, occupations, and seasonal work arrangements are exempt from the requirement to provide notice of termination or pay in lieu of notice. The following are the most significant and common additional exemptions from any requirement to provide notice:

- **Termination for just cause — Federal, Alberta, British Columbia, Manitoba**, the **Northwest Territories, Nunavut, Prince Edward Island, Quebec** (where an employee commits a serious fault), **Saskatchewan**, and the **Yukon**. While the **New Brunswick** legislation does not require notice of termination in the case of dismissal for just cause, the employer dismissing for cause must do so in writing, setting out the reasons for the action, and, unless this provision is complied with, the legislation states that no dismissal without notice is valid, despite the fact that there is cause for the dismissal. In *Lindsay v. Peace Hills Trust* (2008 NBQB 303), the employer had dismissed the employee with an offer of pay in lieu of notice. Subsequent to dismissal, management learned of misconduct by the employee and asserted just cause for dismissal in its statement of defence in response to the former employee's wrongful dismissal claim. The Court looked at the legislation, but held that the employer had complied with the requirement for written reasons for a dismissal, even though it had not asserted cause in writing at the time of dismissal. Cause was asserted in writing less than two months later in the statement of defence. While this approach was recently confirmed by the New Brunswick Court of Appeal in *Doucet and Dauphinée v. Spielo Manufacturing Incorporated and Manship* (2011 NBCA 44), the Court nonetheless noted that employers will not be able to escape the legislation's application where the employer knew, or ought to have known, about the earlier misconduct but failed to specify this as a ground of dismissal.

- **Employee guilty of wilful misconduct, disobedience, or neglect of duty — Newfoundland and Labrador, Nova Scotia**, and **Ontario**. In *Oosterbosch v. FAG Aerospace Inc.* (2011 ONSC 1538), the employer dismissed the employee for just cause due to the employee's continued failure to meet certain performance standards. While the Court ruled that the employer had demonstrated just cause for the employee's dismissal, it did not accept that the employee's misconduct was intentional. Accordingly, as the employee's behaviour did not constitute *wilful misconduct, disobedience, or neglect of duty,* he therefore remained entitled to receive his statutory termination and severance payments.

- **Casual on-call arrangements — Alberta, British Columbia,** and **Manitoba.**

- **Employment for a definite term — British Columbia, Manitoba, New Brunswick,** and **Quebec.**

- **Employed for a definite term of 12 months or less — Alberta, Newfoundland and Labrador,** the **Northwest Territories, Nova Scotia, Nunavut,** and **Ontario.**

- **Employed for a definite task not exceeding 12 months — Alberta, British Columbia, Manitoba, New Brunswick, Newfoundland and Labrador,** the **Northwest Territories, Nova Scotia, Nunavut, Prince Edward Island, Ontario, Quebec** (no time limit), and the **Yukon.**

- **Employment agreement has become frustrated (i.e., impossible to perform due to an unforeseeable event or circumstance) — Alberta, British Columbia, Manitoba, Newfoundland and Labrador, Nova Scotia, Prince Edward Island, Ontario** (unless the frustration is the result of the employee's illness or injury), **Quebec,** and the **Yukon.**

- **The employee has refused an offer of reasonable alternative employment made by the employer — Alberta, British Columbia, New Brunswick, Newfoundland and Labrador,** the **Northwest Territories, Nova Scotia, Nunavut, Ontario, Prince Edward Island,** and the **Yukon.**

- **Failure to return to work after notice of recall — Alberta,** the **Northwest Territories, Nunavut,** and **Ontario.**

- **Employment terminates in connection with a strike or lockout — Alberta** (no work due to strike or lockout at the workplace), **Manitoba** (employee is on strike or locked out), **Ontario** (termination during or as a result of a strike or lockout), and **Prince Edward Island** (labour dispute directly affects employer's operations).

Q. How Must the Notice Be Given?

A. In all jurisdictions, except **Manitoba**, notice is explicitly required in writing.

Q. Can an Employer Offer an Employee a Combination of Notice and Pay in Lieu?

A. The **Alberta**, **British Columbia**, **Manitoba**, **Ontario**, and **Quebec** statutes deal specifically with this issue, and their answer is yes. Although the issue is not dealt with specifically in other jurisdictions, there would appear to be no reason why an employer could not offer an employee a combination of notice and pay in lieu of the remainder of the notice.

Q. Does Overtime Count Towards Calculating Pay in Lieu of Notice?

A. No. Pay in lieu of notice is defined in most jurisdictions as the amount of pay an employee would have earned had he or she worked his or her normal hours during the notice period. Generally, overtime is not considered part of an employee's normal hours. A number of jurisdictions state that overtime pay is not to be taken into account when calculating normal hours of work.

The exception is **Newfoundland and Labrador**, where the law states that "normal wages" include the amount of overtime pay that might have been earned by the employee, calculated on the basis of the overtime hours in the month preceding the termination.

Q. When Calculating an Employee's "Normal" Hours, What if the Hours Are Not the Same from Week-to-Week?

A. If an employee's weekly hours of work are not standard, some type of averaging will need to take place in order to figure out what the employee's normal hours of work are and to compensate the employee properly. This issue is addressed in the **federal** jurisdiction, **Alberta**, **British Columbia**, **Ontario**, **Quebec**, and **Saskatchewan**.

In the **federal** jurisdiction, the actual number of hours, excluding overtime, worked over the four complete weeks prior to the termination are calculated and divided by four. In **Alberta**, the sum to be paid is determined by calculating the average of the wages made by the employee over the three months prior to the termination. In **British Columbia**, the amount owed to an employee is based upon the average weekly wage earned in the last eight weeks in which the employee worked normal or average hours of work. In **Ontario**, where the employee does not have a regular workweek or is paid on a basis other than time, the employer must pay the employee a weekly wage equal to the average regular weekly wage earned by the employee in the 12 weeks immediately prior to the date the notice of termination was given. In **Quebec**, where an employee is remunerated partly or entirely by commission, the payment in lieu of notice is based on the average weekly wage during the three months preceding the termination. Finally, in **Saskatchewan**, an employee's regular weekly rate is determined by averaging the wage he or she made in the four weeks prior to the termination.

Q. Do Employee Benefits Continue Once an Employee Has Received Notice of Termination or Pay in Lieu?

A. If an employee has received notice of termination and remains actively employed until the notice period runs out, then yes, any benefit programs that are in place in the workplace still apply to the employee.

If, on the other hand, the employee has received pay in lieu of notice, he or she is generally not entitled to benefits since he or she is technically no longer employed.

However, the **Ontario** legislation is very clear that, where pay in lieu of notice is provided, the employer is required to continue benefit plan contributions, and employees are deemed to be actively employed for the purposes of benefit plans (and vacation accrual) during the period that they would have continued working for their employer had they received working notice.

Q. What if the Conditions of Employment Are Changed Once Notice of Termination Is Given?

A. All jurisdictions, with the exception of **New Brunswick**, **Newfoundland and Labrador**, **Prince Edward Island**, **Quebec**, and **Saskatchewan**, provide that an employer cannot alter a worker's conditions of employment once notice of termination has been given. This prevents an employer from intentionally reducing termination costs by reducing hours of work or benefits.

Q. Can an Employee's Vacation Be Used as Part of the Notice Period?

A. In **British Columbia**, **Manitoba**, **Newfoundland and Labrador**, **Nova Scotia**, **Ontario**, **Saskatchewan**, the **Northwest Territories, Nunavut**, and the **Yukon**, the laws specify that vacation to which an employee is entitled cannot be used as part of the notice period, unless the employee agrees otherwise. If an employee's employment is terminated, the employee must be fully compensated for any earned vacation time.

Q. When Must Employers Pay Employees Their Wages Owing?

A. Each jurisdiction sets out different time frames within which an employer must give monies owed to a terminated employee. These monies include pay in lieu of notice, and overtime pay. The time frames are set out in the chart found on page 167.

Q. When Must an Employer Pay Any Vacation Pay Owed at the Time of Termination?

A. In some jurisdictions, vacation pay owing must be paid at the same time as all other wages owing on termination; in other jurisdictions, vacation pay must be paid at a different time. Note that accrued vacation pay must be paid out even if the employment is terminated for cause and there is no notice or pay in lieu of notice owing. The following list sets out the time for payment in each jurisdiction:

- The **federal** jurisdiction, **Newfoundland and Labrador**, the **Northwest Territories**, and **Nunavut** require payment at the time of termination.

- In **Alberta**, where termination notice is given, or notice is required to be given by the employer, vacation pay must be paid within three days of termination. Where neither the employer nor employee is required to give termination notice, vacation pay must be paid within 10 days. If an employee quits without giving proper termination notice, the employer must pay vacation pay to the employee within 10 days after the date on which the notice would have expired if it had been given.

- In **British Columbia** a time limit of 48 hours is set from the effective date of termination if the employer terminates the relationship, and six days from the effective date of termination if the employee terminates the relationship.

- In **New Brunswick**, payment must be made at the time of final pay, not later than 21 days after the last day of employment.

- In **Manitoba** and **Nova Scotia**, the time limit is 10 days (10 working days in Manitoba) from the day of termination.

- In **Ontario**, payment must be made within seven days after termination or on the next regular payday, whichever is later.

- In **Prince Edward Island** the time limit is the end of the next regular pay period after employment ceases.

- In **Quebec** the time limit is not specified.

- In **Saskatchewan**, payment must be made within 14 days from the effective date of the termination.

- In the **Yukon**, the time limit is seven days from the date of termination.

Q. What Happens if an Employee Is Still Employed after the Date of Official Termination?

A. This issue is addressed in most jurisdictions — the **federal** jurisdiction, **Alberta**, **British Columbia**, **New Brunswick**, **Newfoundland and Labrador**, **Nova Scotia**, the **Northwest Territories**, **Nunavut**, **Ontario**, **Prince Edward Island**, and the **Yukon**. Each of these jurisdictions requires that, if an employee is still working a specified length of time after the notice of termination should have expired, then the notice of termination is no longer valid. As such, if an employer wishes to terminate an employee's employment at that point, it must again provide the employee with the full notice requirement or pay in lieu of notice as required by law.

The specified lengths of time that an employee may work before the original notice of termination ceases to be valid are set out in the chart below.

Jurisdiction	Specified Period
Federal	two weeks after the date specified for termination
Alberta	after the date specified for termination
British Columbia	after the expiry of the period of notice
New Brunswick	one month or more beyond the end of the notice period
Newfoundland and Labrador	after the expiry of the period of notice
Nova Scotia	after the expiry of notice for a period exceeding the length of notice
Northwest Territories	after the expiry of the period of notice
Nunavut	after the expiry of the period of notice
Ontario	up to 13 weeks of temporary work may be provided
Prince Edward Island	one month or more beyond the end of the notice period
Yukon	after the expiry of the period of notice

Q. Must Employment Have Been Continuous for the Notice Requirements to Apply?

A. Not necessarily. In eight jurisdictions, namely the **federal** jurisdiction, **Alberta**, **Manitoba**, **Newfoundland and Labrador**, **Nova Scotia**, **Ontario**, the **Northwest Territories**, and **Nunavut**, interruptions in employment history are ignored for the purposes of calculating length of service at the time of termination if these interruptions fit certain criteria. Since the criteria are significantly different from jurisdiction to jurisdiction, they are discussed separately below.

- **Federal:** Employment is considered to be continuous if an employee's absence from employment is due to a layoff that is not a termination, such as a layoff of less than three months (see the section on "Layoffs" on page 156 for clarification).

- **Alberta:** If an employee has been employed by the same employer more than once, if not more than three months has elapsed between periods of employment, the employee's employment is considered to be continuous.

- **Manitoba:** Consecutive periods of employment are treated as continuous and temporary interruptions are disregarded.

- **Newfoundland and Labrador:** Seasonal workers engaged under a contract of service for two or more consecutive seasons of at least five months in each season are considered to have been "continuously employed".

- **Nova Scotia:** Successive periods of employment constitute one period of employment, unless the periods are more than 13 weeks apart, in which case the last period of employment constitutes the period of employment for purposes of termination.

- **Ontario:** Successive periods of employment with the same employer are considered to constitute one period of employment, unless the successive periods are more than 13 weeks apart.

- **Northwest Territories** and **Nunavut:** An employee who has been employed by the same employer more than once is understood to have had continuous employment, as long as not more than 90 days has elapsed between each period of employment.

Q. What if an Employee Has Been Hired for a Fixed Term of Employment, but Continues To Work Beyond This Term?

A. In **British Columbia**, **New Brunswick**, **Nova Scotia**, **Ontario**, **Prince Edward Island**, and the **Yukon**, persons who work beyond the period for which the term of their employment is fixed become eligible for the same rights as other workers upon termination. The specific provisions are as follows:

- **British Columbia:** If a worker continues to work for a period of three months or more beyond the completion of the definite term of employment, that worker is no longer considered to be employed for a fixed term, and is entitled to notice of termination rights. The worker's length of employment is calculated from the beginning of his or her employment.

- **New Brunswick:** If an employee continues to work for a period of three months beyond the period fixed in the employment contract, the usual notice provisions apply if the employee's employment is terminated.

- **Nova Scotia:** When an employee who was originally hired for a definite term or task continues to work for a period of three months or more after the expiry of the term of employment or the completion of the task, that employee is no longer considered to have been hired for a definite term or task, and if the employee is terminated, the normal notice requirements apply. The employee's length of service is considered to have begun at the beginning of the term or task.

- **Ontario:** If an employee is employed for three months or more after the completion of the term or task or if the fixed term or task lasts more than 12 months, the general notice provisions apply.

- **Prince Edward Island:** The notice provisions do not apply to an employee employed to perform a definite task not exceeding 12 months.

- **Northwest Territories:** The notice provisions do not apply to someone employed for less than 180 days in a year, or a definite term or task not exceeding 365 days.

- **Yukon:** If an employee is employed for more than one month after the completion of the term or task, the general notice provisions apply.

Q. If an Employer Sells the Business, Can the New Owners Terminate the Employees' Employment and Treat Them Like New Employees?

A. Generally, when an employer sells its business and the purchaser hires the employees, they are protected in that their length of employment is considered to be continuous from the original date of hire with the seller. Accordingly, the new employer cannot simply dismiss employees without giving them the length of notice or pay in lieu of notice that they would have received had the business not been sold.

SEVERANCE PAY

Q. What Is Severance Pay?

A. Severance pay is payment that is required in addition to notice or pay in lieu of notice. The amount of severance pay is based on length of service. Severance pay is a cash payment and it cannot be replaced by working notice. In terms of individual termination, the only jurisdictions in which an employee is entitled to severance pay are the **federal** jurisdiction and **Ontario**. The severance pay requirements for these two jurisdictions are summarized below.

Q. When Are Employees Entitled To Severance Pay?

A. In the **federal** jurisdiction, an employee with at least 12 consecutive months of employment with the same employer is entitled to severance pay upon termination.

In **Ontario**, where 50 or more employees are terminated in a period of six months or less as a result of the discontinuance of all or part of the employer's business, OR one or more employees are terminated by an employer with an annual **Ontario** payroll of at least $2.5 million, the employer is required to pay severance pay to each employee who has been employed for *five years or more.*

Q. How Is Severance Pay Calculated?

A. In the **federal** jurisdiction, the amount of severance pay is the greater of: (a) two days' wages at the employee's regular rate of pay for each year of employment; or (b) five days' wages. It is payable in addition to the statutory notice.

In **Ontario** an employee eligible for severance pay is entitled to receive one week's pay multiplied by the sum of: (a) the number of completed years of employment; and (b) the number of completed months of employment not included in the number of completed years, divided by 12, to a maximum of 26 regular weeks' pay. For example, an employee with 10 years and 6 months of service receives 10.5 weeks of severance pay. The severance pay provided by the Act is payable in addition to any other payments, including payment in lieu of notice of termination. Therefore, this employee is entitled to a total of eight weeks of notice (or pay in lieu) *plus* 10.5 weeks of severance pay.

All time spent in the employment of the employer, whether or not continuous, and whether or not active, is included in determining entitlement to severance pay and in calculating the amount of severance pay. The one exception applies to an employee in receipt of an actuarially unreduced pension benefit who has his or her employment severed after November 5, 2009. Periods of employment for which the employee received pension service credits are not included in determining eligibility for severance pay or the amount of severance pay.

If the employer terminates the employment of an employee without providing notice of termination, the required notice period (eight weeks, for example), is included in the employee's length of service when calculating the amount of severance pay.

Where the employer and the employee agree, or with the approval of the Director of Employment Standards, severance pay can be paid in instalments. However, the instalments must be paid out during a period of not more than three years. There are a number of cases where severance pay is not required, including dismissal for cause and where there are certain pension entitlements. In **Ontario**, exceptions include: where employment is severed as a result of the permanent discontinuance of all or part of the business that the employer establishes was caused by the economic consequences of a strike; where the employee refuses an offer of reasonable alternative employment or refuses to exercise a seniority right; an employee is in the construction industry; or the employee is guilty of wilful misconduct, disobedience or wilful neglect of duty. Severance pay is not payable under the **federal** legislation in the case of dismissal for cause.

TERMINATION BY EMPLOYEE

Q. Do Employees Owe Their Employers Any Notice if They Choose To Terminate Their Employment?

A. Some jurisdictions specify minimum periods of notice that must be provided to the employer based upon how long the employee has worked for the employer. The chart on page 162 outlines what employees are legally required to offer their employers in terms of the minimum notice of termination. The **Yukon** legislation stipulates that, where an employee resigns without giving the required notice, the employer, with the consent of the employee, may deduct one week's wages from any wages owing. Similarly, in **Newfoundland and Labrador**, the employer may, with employee consent, deduct from unpaid wages the amount the employee is permitted to pay in lieu of giving notice.

The proposed **Saskatchewan** legislation will require employees with at least 13 weeks of service to provide at least two weeks of written notice of resignation.

Q. Are There Any Situations in Which Employees Would Be Justified in Not Giving the Minimum Notice?

A. Yes, there are a number of situations in which notice is unnecessary. If an employee's term of employment is less than the length of service required for notice to be necessary (see chart on page 162), then the employee is not required to give notice. Employees are also not required to give notice if they are hired for a fixed term or task and the term or task comes to an end.

As well, **Alberta**, **Manitoba**, **Newfoundland and Labrador**, **Nova Scotia**, and the proposed **Saskatchewan** legislation set out a number of specific situations in which an employee may terminate his or her employment without providing the minimum notice. These situations are listed below.

- **Alberta:** Employees are not required to give notice of termination when:
  - there is an established custom or practice in the industry that is different from the termination requirements;
  - the termination is the result of a danger to the health or safety of the employee;
  - the contract of employment has become impossible to perform as the result of unforeseeable or unpreventable causes beyond the control of the employee;
  - the employee has been employed for three months or less;
  - the employee is a casual employee;
  - in the case of a strike or lockout;
  - the employee terminates his or her employment because of a reduction in wage rate, overtime rate, vacation pay, or holiday pay.
- **Saskatchewan:** Pursuant to the draft legislation, employees are excused from giving notice when:
  - there is an established custom or practice in an industry;
  - the employee's health or safety would be in danger if the employee remained in employment;
  - the contract of employment has become impossible to perform;
  - it is a temporary layoff;
  - the employee is laid off after refusing reasonable alternative work;

— the employee is leaving because of a reduction in wage rate, overtime rate, vacation pay, public holiday pay or termination pay; or

— the employee is a casual on-call employee.

- **Manitoba:** Employees are not required to give notice of termination when:

  — the employee has less than 30 days of service or is a probationary employee covered by a collective agreement;

  — the contract of employment has become impossible to perform as the result of a fortuitous or unforeseeable circumstance;

  — the employer acts in a manner that is violent or improper towards the employee;

  — in the case of a strike or lockout;

  — the employee is a casual employee or employed in construction.

- **Newfoundland and Labrador:** Employees are not required to give notice of termination when:

  — the employer has mistreated the employee, acted in a manner that has or might endanger the health or welfare of the employee, or otherwise has been in breach of a material condition of employment;

  — the employee pays to the employer an amount equal to the amount the employee would normally earn during the period of notice that the employee would otherwise be required to give;

  — the employee is employed for a non-renewable term or for a specific task;

  — the employee has been employed for less than one month.

- **Nova Scotia:** Employees are not required to give notice of termination:

  — if they have less than three months of service; or

  — the employer has violated the terms and conditions of employment.

Q. What if an Employer Decides To Terminate the Employment of an Employee after the Employee Has Given Notice?

A. **Alberta** and **Ontario** are the only jurisdictions that explicitly deal with this issue.

In **Alberta**, if the employee has given the minimum notice, in order to terminate employment the employer must give the employee pay in lieu of notice for the remainder of the notice period. If the employee has given notice greater than the minimum, the employer must give the employee pay in lieu of notice for the remainder of the period of termination notice that the employer would have been obliged to give the employee if it had been the employer who originally gave notice of termination of the employment relationship.

In **Ontario**, where an employee with five or more years of service who is eligible for severance pay has received notice of termination and provides the employer with at least two weeks' written notice of resignation during the statutory notice period, the employee remains entitled to severance pay.

Q. What if an Employer Tries To Force an Employee To Resign?

A. Constructive dismissal occurs where an employer unilaterally changes fundamental terms and conditions of employment, such as salary or scope of responsibility. Depending upon how detrimental these changes are, they could amount to termination. **British Columbia**, **Ontario**, the **Northwest Territories**, **Nunavut**, and the **Yukon** all deal with constructive dismissal in their termination provisions. In **British Columbia**, the **Northwest Territories**, **Nunavut**, and the **Yukon**, the major criterion for determining constructive dismissal is a labour officer's decision that substantial change has occurred and, other than in **British Columbia**, a belief that the primary reason for changing the employment conditions is to discourage the employee from continuing work.

In **Ontario**, constructive dismissal is included in the definition of "termination". A constructive dismissal may occur where the employer makes a significant change to a fundamental term or condition of an employee's employment without the employee's actual or implied consent, following which the employee resigns within a reasonable time of learning of the change.

GROUP TERMINATION

Group terminations or "collective dismissals" generally take place when a business closes or significantly downsizes. The **federal** government and most of the provinces have instituted special laws in an attempt to "cushion the blow" caused by the termination of significant numbers of workers within one labour market. Generally, the issues surrounding group termination are similar to those encountered by employees who are terminated individually, except that employers have the added responsibility of notifying the Minister of Labour (or equivalent), and may have to provide employees with longer notice periods. As well, employers may have to take responsibility for organizing a joint planning committee to consider ways in which the terminations can be avoided, or to help employees find alternative employment.

As with individual termination, certain types of layoffs do not count as group termination. This issue, as noted earlier, is dealt with under the section entitled "Layoffs", beginning on page 156.

Q. Are There Any Jurisdictions That Do Not Have Group Termination Provisions?

A. Yes. **Prince Edward Island** is without group termination provisions. As such, the rules that apply to individual terminations apply when larger groups of employees have their employment terminated in this jurisdiction.

Q. What Constitutes a Group Termination?

A. In those jurisdictions that have group termination provisions, the criteria for group termination differ, but are always based on a certain number of dismissals within a defined time frame. These different criteria are listed below:

- The **federal** jurisdiction, **Alberta**, **Manitoba**, **Newfoundland and Labrador**, and **Ontario:** 50 or more employees within a period of not more than four weeks. (In **Ontario**, where 50 or more persons have their employment terminated in a four-week period and this number does not comprise more than 10% of the employees at the establishment, individual notice of termination provisions apply, unless the terminations are caused by the permanent discontinuance of all or part of the business at the establishment where the employees are employed.)

- **British Columbia:** 50 or more employees at a single location within a two-month period.

- **New Brunswick:** more than 10 employees in a four-week period, where the 10 or more employees represent at least 25% of the employer's workforce.

- **Nova Scotia** and **Saskatchewan:** 10 or more employees in a period of four weeks or less.

- **Quebec:** 10 or more employees within a period of two consecutive months where the terminations are for technological or economic reasons, except for businesses whose activities are seasonal or intermittent.

- **Northwest Territories, Nunavut**, and the **Yukon:** 25 or more employees within a four-week period.

Q. What Are the Notice Requirements for Group Terminations?

A. Generally, employers must provide notice to the workers who are having their employment terminated, the Minister of Labour or equivalent, and the union, if there is one in the workplace. Some jurisdictions specify the information that must be contained in notices. **Federal** employees are entitled to receive, in their notice, information outlining the employee's vacation benefits, wages, severance pay and any other benefits and pay arising from the employment. The notice to the Minister must also be given to the union, and must either be given to the non-union employees or posted in the workplace. The notice must include specified information, including the estimated number of employees by occupational classification and the reason for the group termination. The specific details for the other jurisdictions are as follows:

- **Alberta:** Notice is given to the Ministry, and there are no special notice requirements for the employees. The notice must be given four weeks in advance and must include the number of employees to be terminated and the effective date of the terminations.

- **British Columbia:** Notice to the Minister must include the number of employees being terminated, the effective dates of the terminations, and the reasons for the terminations.

- **Manitoba:** The notice to the Minister, trade union (if any), and affected employees must include the reasons for the terminations, the names of at least two persons who are to be appointed to a joint planning committee as employer representatives, and the estimated number of employees in each occupational classification whose employment will be terminated.

- **New Brunswick:** Notice must be given to the Minister, the affected employees, and any union and be posted in the workplace at least six weeks in advance.

- **Newfoundland and Labrador:** Notice must be given to the affected employees, and notice must be given to the Minister that sets out the numbers and the reasons. It is noteworthy that, where an employer fails to give the required notices, the employer may not proceed with the terminations.

- **Ontario:** The information required includes the economic circumstances surrounding the intended terminations, the company's total number of hourly and salaried employees, and the number of affected hourly and salaried employees. There is a government form which must be filed with the Ministry and posted in the workplace.

- **Quebec:** Notice to the Minister must contain the reason for the collective dismissal, the date, the sector of business activity, and the number of affected employees.

- **Saskatchewan:** Notice must include the number of employees to be terminated, the effective date of the terminations, and the reasons for the terminations.

The amount of notice that must be given is specified in the "Group Termination Notice Requirements Chart" on page 165.

Q. Which Jurisdictions Require Employers To Participate in Planning Committees or the Equivalent?

A. The **federal** jurisdiction, **British Columbia**, **Manitoba**, and **Quebec** all either require or may require the employer to set up a committee to deal with the issue of re-employment for those workers who are having their employment terminated.

Q. Is Anyone Excluded from Group Termination Provisions?

A. Yes, generally the same types of exclusions apply to group terminations as apply to individual terminations.

Q. What if Employees Wish To Give Notice after Receiving a Notice of Group Termination?

A. In **Manitoba** and **Ontario**, individual employees who wish to terminate their employment after notice of group termination has been given must still give notice to the employer — in **Manitoba**, employees must give notice in accordance with individual termination requirements.

In **Ontario**, those employed less than two years must give one week's notice, while those employed for two years or more must give two weeks' notice. In **Newfoundland and Labrador**, the legislation specifically permits employees to give notice of termination after they have received notice of group termination.

LAYOFFS

In most jurisdictions, being laid off does not automatically qualify employees for rights under termination provisions. Generally, however, there is a length of time after which a layoff is considered a termination. In several jurisdictions, there are also other more specific issues that need to be discussed in terms of layoffs and their relationship to the termination process. The highlights are set out below.

- **Federal:** A layoff is not considered to be termination for the purposes of severance pay, group or individual termination if the layoff:

  — is the result of a strike or lockout;

  — is 12 months or less, and is mandatory pursuant to a minimum work guarantee in a collective agreement;

  — is three months or less;

  — is between three and 12 months, during which time the employee maintains recall rights under a collective agreement;

  — is more than three months and the worker has been notified in writing at or before the layoff that he or she will be recalled on a fixed date or within a fixed period, neither of which is more than six months from the date of layoff and the worker is in fact recalled in accordance with this provision;

  — is more than three months and the worker continues to be paid an agreed-upon amount, the employer continues to make pension payments for the employee, or the worker receives supplementary Unemployment Insurance benefits or would be entitled to supplementary unemployment benefits, but is disqualified from receiving them under the *Employment Insurance Act.*

  It is important to note that in calculating the length of a layoff, any period of re-employment of less than two weeks is not included in the calculation. Any layoffs that do not fall into one of the preceding categories count as either an individual or group termination, at which point the termination provisions take effect.

- **Alberta:** A temporary layoff is defined as a layoff of less than 60 days, or a layoff of 60 days or more during which the employee receives an agreed-upon wage or the employer makes payments into a pension or insurance plan for the employee or the employee retains recall rights under a collective agreement. Any layoff which fits this definition is not considered a termination. Once the layoff becomes a termination, however, individual termination requirements come into play.

  It is also important to note that a non-union employee on temporary layoff who does not return to work within seven days after being requested to do so in writing loses his or her right to notice of termination.

- **British Columbia:** A temporary layoff is defined as a layoff of not more than 13 weeks in a period of 20 consecutive weeks or a layoff where an employee with recall rights is recalled within a fixed time. Where a period of temporary layoff exceeds the defined time limits, the employee is considered to have been terminated at the beginning of the temporary layoff and is entitled to termination pay.

  The Employment Standards Branch has revised its application of the *Employment Standards Act*'s temporary layoff provisions following the decision of the B.C. Supreme Court in *Besse v. Dr. A.S. Machner Inc.* (2009 BCSC 1316). In that case, the Court awarded damages for constructive dismissal where the employer temporarily laid off an employee for under 13 weeks. The Branch now interprets the Act to mean that even a layoff of less than 13 weeks constitutes termination of employment, unless temporary layoff is expressly provided for in the employment contract, is agreed to by the employee, or is implied by well-known industry-wide practice (such as in the logging industry).

- **Manitoba:** A layoff is not considered to be a termination where:

  — the layoff totals eight weeks or less in a period of 16 weeks;

  — seasonal layoffs are customary in the industry; or

  — the layoff is more than eight weeks and the employee either continues to receive an agreed-upon wage or the employer continues to make payments, for the employee, to a pension and insurance plan.

  Once a worker is no longer considered to be laid off, he or she is considered to have been terminated as of the first day of layoff and is entitled to payment in lieu of notice.

- **New Brunswick:** An employer can lay off an employee for any reason, for a period of up to six days, and where there is a lack of work due to any reason unforeseen by the employer, for as long as the lack of work continues.

- **Newfoundland and Labrador:** A temporary layoff is defined as not lasting more than 13 weeks in a period of 20 consecutive weeks. Any day during which an employee receives pay from the employer, including statutory holiday pay, is not included as a day of layoff. Once the layoff goes beyond 13 weeks, the employee is considered to have been terminated at the beginning of the temporary layoff. At this point, pay in lieu of notice requirements come into effect. No notice is necessary when the layoff does not exceed one week, but notice is required for other layoffs.

- **Nova Scotia:** A temporary layoff is one that does not exceed six days.

- **Ontario:** A temporary layoff gives rise to a termination of employment if the layoff is longer than a temporary layoff, which is described as:

  — not more than 13 weeks in any period of 20 consecutive weeks;

  — a layoff that exceeds 13 weeks in any period of 20 consecutive weeks but is less than 35 weeks in any period of 52 weeks, and the employee continues to receive substantial payments, the employer continues to make payments on behalf of the employee under a pension or insurance plan, the employee receives supplementary unemployment benefits, the worker is entitled to receive supplementary unemployment benefits, but does not because he or she is employed elsewhere during the layoff, the employer recalls the worker within the time approved by the Director of Employment Standards or where the employee is not represented by a union, when the employer recalls the employee within the time set out in an agreement between the employee and the employer; or

  — where the employee is represented by a union and the layoff is longer than described above but the employee is recalled within the time stipulated in the collective agreement.

  Where an employee entitled to termination or severance pay has a right to recall, the employee may elect to be paid the termination/severance pay immediately or may elect to maintain the right to recall. If the employee elects to be paid, the employee is deemed to have abandoned the right to be recalled.

  Where the employee elects to maintain the right to recall or fails to make an election, the employer is required to pay the termination pay to the Director of Employment Standards in trust or as otherwise negotiated between the employer and the union.

  The money in trust is returned to the employer if the employee is recalled, or paid to the employee if recall rights are renounced or expire.

- **Prince Edward Island:** An employer is required to give notice of a discharge or a layoff.

- **Quebec:** A temporary layoff is six months or less. If a layoff that was expected to last less than six months exceeds that period, termination pay must be paid at the six-month date.

- **Saskatchewan:** A layoff refers to the temporary termination of an employee's employment for a period longer than six consecutive days. However, an employer is not required to pay anything in lieu of notice to an employee who is laid off for a period of six days or less.

- **Northwest Territories** and **Nunavut:** A temporary layoff is defined as an interruption of employment for a period of not more than 45 days in a period of 60 consecutive days, or more than 45 days where the worker is recalled within a time fixed by the Labour Standards Officer.

  In order to lay off an employee temporarily, the employer must give the worker written notice of the layoff and indicate the expected date upon which the employee will be asked to return to work.

  A temporary layoff is understood to be a termination if the employer fails to provide the worker with written notice. As well, if a temporary layoff exceeds the limit, the employee is considered to have been terminated on the last day of temporary layoff and the employer must pay the worker termination pay.

- **Yukon:** A temporary layoff is defined as a layoff of not more than 13 weeks in a period of 20 consecutive weeks or a period of more than 13 weeks where the employer recalls the employee to employment within a time fixed by the Director of Employment Standards.

  Once a temporary layoff exceeds the time limit, the worker is understood to have had his or her employment terminated at the commencement of the temporary layoff.

COLLECTIVE AGREEMENTS

Collective agreements cannot generally put employees in a position where they are entitled to less than the minimum required by law. Discussed below are the provisions concerning collective agreements, by jurisdiction, only as they are addressed in the laws dealing specifically with termination of employment.

- **Federal:** Where a unionized employee with bumping rights is to have his or her employment terminated, the employer must give the union two weeks' advance written notice and post a copy of the notice in a conspicuous place in the workplace.

- **Alberta:** If an employee has recall rights under a collective agreement, an employee who is laid off is entitled to termination pay under employment standards law only when those rights expire.

- **British Columbia:** If a collective agreement includes provisions concerning seniority retention, recall, terminations, or layoffs, the notice or termination requirements of the employment standards legislation do not apply.

- **Manitoba:** Where a collective agreement deals with when a layoff may be treated as a termination, the statutory definition of temporary layoff does not apply.

- **New Brunswick:** The provisions for individual termination notice only apply to workers who are not covered by a collective agreement.

- **Newfoundland and Labrador:** The period of notice required by the employer and the employee can be altered by a collective agreement, as long as the employer and the employee are both required to provide the same length of notice.

- **Nova Scotia:** Employees covered by a collective agreement are excluded from the termination provisions of the employment standards legislation.

- **Ontario:** An employee who is entitled to termination pay (and severance pay, if applicable) once a layoff has exceeded 35 weeks in a 52-week period, but who has the right of recall under a collective agreement, may choose to either take the termination pay or retain the right to be recalled. Once the employee chooses to take the termination pay and any severance pay, he or she loses the right to recall.

  If an employee represented by a union chooses to maintain the right to recall, or fails to make a choice, the employer and the trade union must try to come to an arrangement to hold the termination pay and severance pay in trust for the employee. If they cannot come to an arrangement, the employer must send the termination pay (and severance pay, if any) to the Director of Employment Standards, to be held in trust.

- **Prince Edward Island:** Notice of termination provisions do not apply to employees covered by a collective agreement.

- **Quebec:** Where an employee is entitled, under a collective agreement, to recall rights for more than six months, termination pay must be paid upon the expiry of the recall rights, or after one year of layoff, whichever occurs first.

- **Yukon:** The individual termination provisions do not apply to workers who are represented by a trade union.

INDIVIDUAL TERMINATION NOTICE REQUIREMENTS CHART

Jurisdiction	Length of Service	Required Notice	Notice by Employee
Federal	3 mos.	2 wks.	none
Alberta	more than 3 mos. less than 2 yrs.	1 wk.	1 wk.
	2 yrs. or more, less than 4 yrs.	2 wks.	2 wks. if employed 2 yrs. or more
	4 yrs. or more, less than 6 yrs.	4 wks.	
	6 yrs. or more, less than 8 yrs.	5 wks.	
	8 yrs. or more, less than 10 yrs.	6 wks.	
	10 yrs. or more	8 wks.	
British Columbia	3 to 12 mos.	1 wk.	none
	12 mos. to 3 yrs.	2 wks.	
	3 yrs.	3 wks.	
	4 yrs. or more	1 additional week for each subsequent yr. up to a max. of 8 wks.	
Manitoba	more than 30 days, less than 1 yr.	1 wk.	1 wk.
	1 yr. or more, less than 3 yrs.	2 wks.	1 yr. or more, 2 wks.
	3 yrs. or more, less than 5 yrs.	4 wks.	
	5 yrs. or more, less than 10 yrs.	6 wks.	
	10 yrs. or more	8 wks.	
New Brunswick	6 mos. to 5 yrs.	2 wks.	none
	5 yrs. or more	4 wks.	
Newfoundland and Labrador	3 mos. or more, less than 2 yrs.	1 wk.	same as notice by employer
	2 yrs. or more, less than 5 yrs.	2 wks.	
	5 yrs. or more, less than 10 yrs.	3 wks.	
	10 yrs. or more, less than 15 yrs.	4 wks.	
	15 yrs. or more	6 wks.	

Jurisdiction	Length of Service	Required Notice	Notice by Employee
Nova Scotia	3 mos. or more, less than 2 yrs.	1 wk.	1 wk. notice if 3 mos.or more and less than 2 yrs. service; 2 wks. notice if 2 yrs. or more service
	2 yrs. or more, less than 5 yrs.	2 wks.	
	5 yrs. or more, less than 10 yrs.	4 wks.	
	10 yrs. or more	8 wks.	
Ontario	3 mos. or more, less than 1 yr.	1 wk.	none
	1 yr. or more, less than 3 yrs.	2 wks.	
	3 yrs. or more, less than 4 yrs.	3 wks.	
	4 yrs. or more, less than 5 yrs.	4 wks.	
	5 yrs. or more, less than 6 yrs.	5 wks.	
	6 yrs. or more, less than 7 yrs.	6 wks.	
	7 yrs. or more, less than 8 yrs.	7 wks.	
	8 yrs. or more	8 wks.	
Prince Edward Island	6 mos. or more, less than 5 yrs.	2 wks.	1 wk. if employed 6 mos. or more but less than 5 yrs.
	5 yrs. or more, less than 10 yrs.	4 wks.	2 wks. if employed 5 yrs. or more
	10 yrs. or more, less than 15 yrs.	6 wks.	
	15 yrs. or more	8 wks.	
Quebec	3 mos. or more, less than 1 yr.	1 wk.	*Civil Code:* Reasonable notice (for employer and employee)
	1 yr. or more, less than 5 yrs.	2 wks.	
	5 yrs. or more, less than 10 yrs.	4 wks.	
	10 yrs. or more	8 wks.	
Saskatchewan	3 mos. or more, but less than 1 yr.	1 wk.	2 wks. notice if employeed at least 13 wks.
	1 yr. or more, less than 3 yrs.	2 wks.	
	3 yrs. or more, less than 5 yrs.	4 wks.	
	5 yrs. or more, less than 10 yrs.	6 wks.	
	10 yrs. or more	8 wks.	

Jurisdiction	Length of Service	Required Notice	Notice by Employee
Proposed Saskatch-ewan legislation	13 wks. or more, but 1 yr. or less	1 wk.	2 wks.
	more than 1 yr., but 3 yrs. or less	2 wks.	
	more than 3 yrs., but 5 yrs. or less	4 wks.	
	more than 5 yrs., but 10 yrs. or less	6 wks.	
	more than 10 yrs.	8 wks.	
Northwest Territories	90 days or more, less than 3 yrs.	2 wks.	none
	3 yrs. or more, less than 4 yrs.	3 wks.	
	4 yrs. or more, less than 5 yrs.	4 wks.	
	5 yrs. or more, less than 6 yrs.	5 wks.	
	6 yrs. or more, less than 7 yrs.	6 wks.	
	7 yrs. or more, less than 8 yrs.	7 wks.	
	8 yrs. or more	8 wks.	
Nunavut	90 days or more, less than 3 yrs.	2 wks.	none
	3 yrs. or more, less than 4 yrs.	3 wks.	
	4 yrs. or more, less than 5 yrs.	4 wks.	
	5 yrs. or more, less than 6 yrs.	5 wks.	
	6 yrs. or more, less than 7 yrs.	6 wks.	
	7 yrs. or more, less than 8 yrs.	7 wks.	
	8 yrs. or more	8 wks.	
Yukon	6 mos. or more, less than 1 yr.	1 wk.	1 wk. if employed less than 2 yrs.
	1 yr. or more, less than 3 yrs.	2 wks.	2 wks. if employed
	3 yrs. of more, less than 4 yrs.	3 wks.	2 yrs. or more, less than 4 yrs.
	4 yrs. or more, less than 5 yrs.	4 wks.	3 wks. if employed
	5 yrs. or more, less than 6 yrs.	5 wks.	4 yrs. or more, less than 6 yrs.
	6 yrs. or more, less than 7 yrs.	6 wks.	4 wks. if employed 6 yrs. or more
	7 yrs. or more, less than 8 yrs.	7 wks.	
	8 yrs. or more	8 wks.	

GROUP TERMINATION NOTICE REQUIREMENTS CHART

Jurisdiction	Notice to Employee	Notice to Minister	Notice to Union
Federal	Same as for individual termination	16 weeks	Yes
Alberta	Same as for individual termination	4 weeks	Not stated
British Columbia	50–100 employees — 8 weeks 101–300 employees — 12 weeks 301+ employees — 16 weeks	Same as for employees	Same as for employees
Manitoba	50–100 employees — 10 weeks 101–299 employees — 14 weeks 300+ employees — 18 weeks	Same as for employees	Same as for employees
New Brunswick	6 weeks	6 weeks	6 weeks
Newfoundland and Labrador	50–199 employees — 8 weeks 200–499 employees — 12 weeks 500+ employees — 16 weeks	Same as for employees	Not stated
Nova Scotia	10–99 employees — 8 weeks 100–299 employees — 12 weeks 300+ employees — 16 weeks	Same as for employees	Not stated
Ontario	50–199 employees — 8 weeks 200–499 employees — 12 weeks 500+ employees — 16 weeks	Same as for employees	Not stated
Prince Edward Island	Same as for individual termination	Not stated	Not stated

Jurisdiction	Notice to Employee	Notice to Minister	Notice to Union
Quebec	Same as for individual termination	10–99 employees — 8 weeks 100–299 employees — 12 weeks 300+ employees — 16 weeks	Not stated
Saskatchewan	10–49 employees — 4 weeks 50–99 employees — 8 weeks 100+ employees — 12 weeks	Same as for employees	Same as for employees
Northwest Territories	Same as for individual termination	25–49 employees — 4 weeks 50–99 employees — 8 weeks 100–299 employees — 12 weeks 300+ employees — 16 weeks	Not stated
Nunavut	Same as for individual termination	25–49 employees — 4 weeks 50–99 employees — 8 weeks 100–299 employees — 12 weeks 300+ employees — 16 weeks	Not stated
Yukon	Same as for individual termination	25–49 employees — 4 weeks 50–99 employees — 8 weeks 100–299 employees — 12 weeks 300+ employees — 16 weeks	Not stated

PAYMENT OF WAGES ON TERMINATION CHART

Jurisdiction	Payment Required
Federal	Within 30 days of termination
Alberta	Within 3 days of termination; 10 days where no notice required; where required notice by employee not provided, 10 days after employee notice period would have expired if proper notice had been given
British Columbia	Within 48 hours of termination by employer; within 6 days of termination by employee
Manitoba	Within 10 working days of termination
New Brunswick	No later than the date the employee would have been paid if employment had continued, but no longer than 21 days after termination
Newfoundland and Labrador	Within 1 week of termination
Nova Scotia	On expiry of termination notice
Ontario	By the later of 7 days after termination and the next payday
Prince Edward Island	Not later than the last day of the next pay period after termination
Quebec	Regular wages by the next scheduled pay period; pay in lieu of notice at the time of termination
Saskatchewan	Within 14 days after the date of termination
Northwest Territories	Within 10 days after termination
Nunavut	Within 10 days after termination
Yukon	Within 7 days after termination

Chapter 11

WRONGFUL DISMISSAL

	Page
INTRODUCTION	170
UNDERSTANDING WRONGFUL DISMISSAL	170
What Is "Wrongful Dismissal"?	170
Isn't Termination of Employment Covered by Employment Standards Laws?	170
When Will an Employee Be Considered To Have Been "Dismissed"?	170
How Can an Employer Avoid a Constructive Dismissal Suit?	172
When Will an Employer Be Considered To Have "Just Cause" for Dismissing an Employee?	173
Can a Single Incident Be Considered Just Cause?	174
What if the Employer Has Overlooked This Type of Behaviour in the Past?	174
How Much Notice of Termination Will Be Considered Reasonable?	174
What if the Employer Does Not Wish To Continue To Employ the Employee During the Notice Period?	175
Are Employees on Probation Entitled To Reasonable Notice?	176
What About Employees on Fixed-Term Contracts?	176
Do Employees Have To Give Reasonable Notice as Well?	177
Can the Amount of Notice Be Limited by an Employment Contract?	177
What Is the Effect of a Collective Agreement?	177
What Kinds of Damages Can an Employee Get in a Wrongful Dismissal Case?	177
What Can an Employer Do To Avoid a Wrongful Dismissal Suit?	179

INTRODUCTION

The following questions and answers provide an introduction to the area of "wrongful dismissal" and the rights and obligations of employers and employees at common law upon the termination of the employment relationship.

UNDERSTANDING WRONGFUL DISMISSAL

Q. What Is "Wrongful Dismissal"?

A. Wrongful dismissal is commonly used to refer to cases before the courts dealing with the termination of employment. At common law, a contract of employment can be terminated if there is just cause for doing so. If just cause does not exist, the employer can terminate the employment relationship if reasonable notice is provided. Wrongful dismissal claims arise where the parties disagree as to whether just cause for the termination of employment existed, or whether the notice of termination provided was reasonable. These concepts are discussed in further detail below.

Q. Isn't Termination of Employment Covered by Employment Standards Laws?

A. Employment standards legislation across the country provides minimum standards for termination of employment, setting out the number of weeks of notice or pay employees who are dismissed should receive, depending on their length of service with the employer. However, the common law requirement for reasonable notice of termination has not been replaced by employment standards legislation. Even though the contract of service between the employer and the employee is terminated in accordance with employment standards legislation, the employee may still seek redress for wrongful dismissal at common law (i.e., damages for breach of contract). In some cases, payment of the employment standards minimum will also be sufficient to discharge the employer's obligations under the common law. In many cases, it will not. The employment standards requirements treat all employees alike without taking into account individual characteristics such as age, position, or pay — all of which are factors considered under the common law in determining reasonable notice.

Q. When Will an Employee Be Considered To Have Been "Dismissed"?

A. In most cases, it is clear when the employer has terminated the employment relationship: the employer decides to end the employment relationship, and informs the employee of that decision. However, it is sometimes the case that an employer has terminated the employment relationship without necessarily intending to, or even being aware of it. For example, if the employer alters a major condition of the employment arrangements between it and the employee, the employer may be considered to have legally ended the employment contract, and it will then be up to the employee to accept continued employment under the new terms, or to resign and claim compensation for termination of employment. This is what is commonly called "constructive dismissal".

There are a number of circumstances in which a constructive dismissal may be considered to have occurred. Some examples are listed below.

It is important to bear in mind that the courts have held that the intention of the employer in making the unilateral and fundamental change to a term and condition of employment is not relevant: *Farber v. Royal Trust Co.* ([1997] 1 S.C.R. 846). Even if the employer wants to retain the employee he or she may quit and sue for damages.

- **Significant change in compensation, job duties or responsibilities, or reporting relationships.** This is a particular cause for concern if the changes could be construed as a demotion. Thus, organizations undergoing restructuring, and changing job descriptions, compensation structures, or the organizational design, should give particular thought to the potential issue of constructive dismissal.

- **Change in location.** An employee may either accept a transfer or allege constructive dismissal. For example, if a manager hired to oversee the sales operation in Calgary is transferred to the Vancouver operation, the manager might treat the transfer as a dismissal and sue for damages for constructive dismissal. The fact that the employer is willing to pay all relocation costs, or that the move may be considered a promotion, will not necessarily matter. To date, Canadian courts have not been particularly sympathetic to employees who are asked to transfer, especially where the move is not accompanied by any adverse changes, the company operates in numerous locations, employees frequently relocate in order to progress, or the individual in question has been transferred previously or was aware of the possibility of future transfers. For a recent example, see the decision of the Alberta Court of Appeal in *Brown v. Pronghorn Controls Ltd.* (2011 ABCA 328), involving a proposed transfer to an equivalent position in another location a two-hour drive away. The Court found no constructive dismissal, noted that the employee had relocated once with the same employer, and also found that the employee had relocated twice before to further his career while employed elsewhere.

- **The "quit or be fired" scenario.** It sometimes occurs that an employee is given to understand, whether implicitly or explicitly, that his or her options are to resign or be dismissed. Where an employee resigns in such circumstances and subsequently alleges constructive dismissal, the resignation will not be considered a voluntary resignation but a constructive dismissal, creating the same obligations for the employer as if the employee had been dismissed outright.

- **Harassment or discriminatory treatment.** Recent cases have found that harassment, bullying, or abusive or unfair treatment of an employee, which causes the employee to quit can give rise to a claim of constructive dismissal.

- **Layoff.** Unpaid temporary periods of layoff, while common in the unionized context, have generally not been recognized at common law and may constitute a constructive dismissal if not accepted by the employee. The law is currently unsettled and it may be possible for a layoff process to form part of the terms and conditions of employment. In a 2013 decision, *Trites v. Renin Corp.* (2013 ONSC 2715), an Ontario court took the position that a layoff which meets the definition of a temporary layoff under the *Employment Standards Act, 2000* (see "Layoffs" on page 156, in Chapter 10) is not a constructive dismissal.

Q. How Can an Employer Avoid a Constructive Dismissal Suit?

A. The doctrine of constructive dismissal may hamper an employer's ability to manage an organization by restricting the employer's right to alter the terms and conditions of employment as necessary for organizational health. However, with proper planning, many constructive dismissal cases can be avoided by the following approaches:

- **Give reasonable notice of major changes to conditions of employment.** The employer can give the employee notice of the new conditions of employment. This period of notice gives the employee an opportunity to decide whether to continue to work under the new conditions of employment. Careful thought must be given to what period of notice is reasonable, particularly where the changes are the result of restructuring and will affect a number of employees, since there may be employees whose age, length of service, and level of responsibility entitle them to lengthy notice periods. The 2008 Ontario Court of Appeal decision in *Wronko v. Western Inventory Service Ltd.* (2008 CLLC ¶210-020; leave to appeal to the Supreme Court of Canada dismissed, October 9, 2008) has thrown the well-established law into some confusion. In that case, the employer gave two years' notice to the employee of the terms of a new employment agreement. The employee refused to accept the terms but continued to work. At the end of the two-year notice period, when the employee still refused to accept the changes, the employer stated that he would not have a job if he refused to accept the new terms. The employee successfully sued for constructive dismissal and was awarded a further two years of pay in lieu of notice because the employer had failed to provide clear notice of dismissal. In light of this development, care must be taken in communicating notice of adverse changes to terms and conditions of employment.

- **A carefully drafted contract of employment.** A carefully drafted contract of employment may provide for additional flexibility by including provisions entitling the employer to transfer employees between corporate locations or to reasonably alter the employee's responsibilities and compensation, bonus, or commission package from time to time.

- **Accompany the change with positive changes.** An employee is more willing to accept a revised package when the overall terms are beneficial or clearly indicate a desire by the employer to retain the employee as a valued member of the organization rather than to "drive the employee out".

Q. When Will an Employer Be Considered To Have "Just Cause" for Dismissing an Employee?

A. As mentioned above, the issue of just cause is important because, if it exists, the employment contract can be terminated without notice or compensation. What will be considered just cause can be determined only in the circumstances of the particular case. However, some grounds for dismissal that the courts have found to constitute just cause include dishonesty, serious and deliberate insubordination, gross incompetence, theft or other violation of the trust relationship between the employer and the employee, conflict of interest, intoxication on the job, and sexual harassment of other employees. Economic pressures on the company, or behaviour off the job will generally not constitute just cause for dismissal.

It must be stressed that the issue of just cause is rarely clear-cut, and the employee's misconduct must be viewed in the context of his or her length of service with the company, performance record, employment history, and the employer's policies and organizational culture. The Supreme Court of Canada requires a "contextual" analysis of the surrounding facts. The Court also applies the principle of proportionality to balance the severity of the misconduct and the sanction imposed by the employer. (*McKinley v. BC Tel*, 2001 CLLC ¶ 210-027.)

Q. Can a Single Incident Be Considered Just Cause?

A. Generally speaking, an employer will not have just cause to dismiss an employee for a single mistake or incident of misconduct, unless it is a very grave one. For example, a single incident of theft or dishonesty may be just cause. A single error in carrying out work responsibilities generally will not be.

Q. What if the Employer Has Overlooked This Type of Behaviour in the Past?

A. Where an employer has condoned employee behaviour, it becomes difficult to rely on the behaviour as just cause for dismissal. Condonation occurs where the employer takes no action for a lengthy period of time after becoming aware of the behaviour in question, or has not responded to similar actions in the past, such that the employee has developed a reasonable expectation that the behaviour in question would not be treated as cause for dismissal. If an employer wishes to treat behaviour that has been condoned in the past as just cause in the future, employees should be explicitly informed of the change in expectations, and of the possible consequences of repeating the behaviour in question.

Q. How Much Notice of Termination Will Be Considered Reasonable?

A. If an employee's employment is terminated without just cause, reasonable notice of the termination must be given. The amount of reasonable notice that is required beyond the legislated minimum depends on a number of variables. The particular circumstances of each case must always be taken into account. The results may vary widely, from a few weeks, to up to two years (or slightly more). For many years there was a presumption that notice periods should not exceed 24 months, but recent court decisions have held that there is no maximum, although 24 months is still considered to be the higher end of the range absent exceptional circumstances. For recent examples, see *DiTomaso v. Crown Metal Packaging Canada LP* (2011 CLLC ¶ 210-038) and *Abrahim et al. v. Albert Sliwin, Avon Sportswear Limited et al.* (2012 ONSC 6295). Some of the factors that the courts take into account in determining the reasonable notice period are listed below.

- **The employee's length of service.** This is one of the more important factors to consider in determining reasonable notice. The longer an employee's record of service with an employer, the greater the employer's obligations to that employee will be deemed to be, and, consequently, the greater the amount of notice that will be required upon the termination of the employment relationship.

- **The position held by the employee:** It has generally been accepted that the greater the level of responsibility held by an employee, the greater the period of notice. This is based on the assumption that, as there are fewer jobs available as employees become more senior and more highly paid, these employees may have more difficulty finding alternative employment. Some court cases have thrown doubt on the appropriateness of considering this factor, and the Supreme Court of Canada responded in 2008, saying that traditional presumptions about the role that a management-level position plays in assessing notice can always be rebutted by the evidence in a case. (*Honda Canada Inc. v. Keays*, 2008 CLLC ¶ 230-025.) We have seen since then a growing number of courts which have confirmed that the character of the plaintiff's employment is "a factor of declining relative importance" aside from very senior positions: *DiTomaso v. Crown Metal Packaging Canada LP, supra.*

- **The availability of similar employment.** Where the possibility of finding similar employment is restricted by geographical location or the nature of the industry, employers may be required to provide their employees with longer notice periods. For example, in single-industry towns, where alternative employment is unavailable, lengthy notice periods may be required.

- **Age.** The greater the age of the employee being discharged, the longer the required notice period will be.

- **Inducement.** If the employee was "lured away" from a prior job and discharged from the second job, the courts may order a longer period of notice than would otherwise be given. While this is a factor to be considered, the weight to be placed on the factor lessens with the passage of time.

This is by no means an exhaustive list of the factors that may be considered in determining appropriate periods of notice. Generally speaking, an employee's work performance does not affect the length of notice.

Q. What if the Employer Does Not Wish To Continue To Employ the Employee During the Notice Period?

A. An employer has the option, where it concludes that it is not appropriate to have an employee working during the period of notice of termination, to substitute pay in lieu of notice. For example, an employer may have determined that three months' notice of termination is appropriate for a particular employee. However, the employer does not want the employee working for three months, because it no longer requires the employee's services. Instead of allowing the employee to work for three months, the employer may provide the employee with three months' pay, in lieu of the period of notice (including total average compensation and benefits), and terminate the employment relationship immediately.

Q. Are Employees on Probation Entitled To Reasonable Notice?

A. Sometimes employment is offered on the basis that the first few months of employment will be a trial period, during which the performance of the new employee will be closely monitored. In order for a probation period to be enforceable, it must be in writing and agreed to by the employee. Otherwise, it will be given little weight by a court. The mere ability to dismiss without notice under employment standards legislation during the first few months of employment does not constitute the existence of a probationary period under the common law or the right at common law to dismiss without notice. The terms of an effective probation clause should be clearly communicated to the new employee at the outset, including the length of the period, the basis on which the assessment will be made, whether the probation period may be extended, and the assistance available to the employee during the probation period. It is open to the parties to stipulate the amount of notice/pay in lieu of notice (if any) to be provided in the case of a dismissal during probation. As well, the employer should ensure that the probationary employee is given a fair chance to succeed. Information about potential performance issues should be passed along regularly and documented. If performance problems are noted, employees should be given a reasonable opportunity to improve, and offered assistance in doing so. Extension of a probation period should only be used in exceptional circumstances: courts tend to look unfavourably upon unilateral extensions of probation periods.

Q. What About Employees on Fixed-Term Contracts?

A. Employees who are employed under a written contract for a fixed and definite period of time have been given notice of termination from the beginning of the contract, so to speak. Therefore, these employees are not entitled to notice of termination or pay in lieu when their contract draws to an end (subject to compliance with employment standards legislation). However, if the employment of the employee is terminated prior to the date fixed in the contract, the employee may be entitled to claim the pay originally promised for the balance of the contract term unless the contract is carefully drafted. On the other hand, if the period of employment is extended beyond the termination date of the contract without a new agreed-upon written termination date, the employee will be entitled to notice of termination when employment is actually terminated because he or she is no longer on a fixed-term contract.

Q. Do Employees Have To Give Reasonable Notice as Well?

A. An employee has duties to an employer under a contract of employment, just as the employer has duties to the employee. Like the employer, if an employee terminates the employment relationship without cause, the employee should give notice of termination. The length of this notice varies with the circumstances, depending mainly on how difficult it will be for the employer to replace the employee.

Although actions by employers against employees for failure to provide reasonable notice are possible, they are rare, as it can be difficult for employers to prove and quantify damages in such cases.

Q. Can the Amount of Notice Be Limited by an Employment Contract?

A. If there is a written and signed agreement between the parties on the terms of the employment relationship, including the conditions for severing that relationship, this will override the common law, so long as the contract is valid. There are certain circumstances in which a contract may not be valid, such as if it is signed under duress, if it violates employment standards laws, if it is signed after employment had commenced, or was not introduced during the hiring process, thereby not becoming a term and condition of employment.

Q. What Is the Effect of a Collective Agreement?

A. A collective agreement is really a type of employment contract, except that the bargaining agent agrees to the conditions on behalf of the group of employees whom it represents. Unionized employees cannot sue in the courts for damages for wrongful dismissal and instead are required to pursue complaints about their dismissal through the grievance and arbitration procedures set out in the collective agreement. Despite a number of court decisions to that effect (including *Weber v. Ontario Hydro*, 95 CLLC ¶ 210-027), unionized employees periodically succeed in commencing wrongful dismissal lawsuits in some jurisdictions, typically because the claim involves some type of claim not addressed in the collective agreement. For example, in *Bugden v. St. John's (City)* (2009 CLLC ¶ 220-003), the Newfoundland and Labrador Supreme Court allowed a unionized employee's lawsuit to proceed where it claimed damages for the manner in which his employer dealt with an assault and subsequent reassignment in the workplace.

Q. What Kinds of Damages Can an Employee Get in a Wrongful Dismissal Case?

A. Damages are awarded based on the amount of wages an employee would have earned had reasonable notice of the termination been given. As an example, if the court determines that six months' notice was reasonable, the employee will receive damages in the amount of six months' salary, incentive compensation, and the value of benefits, less any earnings from self-employment or new employment during the six-month period.

While an employee has a duty to mitigate damages and reduce losses by diligently seeking reasonable alternative employment, the employer has the burden of proving that the employee could reasonably have avoided some part of the loss claimed. A number of trial judges have allowed a dismissed employee a reasonable period of time to get over the sense of shock, to get organized, to do some research and preparation before beginning to apply for new employment: *Systad v. Ray-Mont Logistics Canada Inc.* (2011 BCSC 1202) and *Hussain v. Suzuki Canada Ltd.* ((2011) 100 CCEL (3rd) 295). The Supreme Court of Canada (*Evans v. Teamsters Local Union 31*, 2008 SCC 20) has gone so far as to rule that a 23-year employee failed to fulfill his duty to mitigate his damages stemming from his dismissal when he refused to accept an offer of employment by his employer. This strict approach to mitigation was followed more recently by the Manitoba courts (*Walsten v. Kinonjeoshtegon First Nation*, 2009 MBQB 106), where wrongful dismissal damages were significantly reduced because the dismissed employees rejected an offer of reinstatement under the terms of their original employment contracts made by the employer three months after their termination dates. Similarly, in *Chevalier v. Active Tire & Auto Centre Inc.* (2012 CLLC ¶210-046) the Ontario Superior Court of Justice considered a situation where an employee was provided with written notice of layoff, followed by a letter calling him back to work and stating that the general manager had acted under the mistaken belief that the company could lay him off, followed by an apology. The Court determined that the employee should have returned to work and declined to award any damages for wrongful dismissal.

In *Wallace v. United Grain Growers Limited* (97 CLLC ¶210-029), the Supreme Court of Canada stated that employers are obliged to behave fairly, reasonably, honestly, and forthrightly with employees in the manner of their dismissal, and that if an employer violates these duties of good faith and fair dealing (for example, by publicly alleging just cause where none exists) the employee may be awarded higher damages for reasonable notice.

More recently, the Supreme Court of Canada in *Honda Canada Inc. v. Keays* (2008 CLLC ¶230-025) clarified when employees may be awarded extra damages such as a longer notice period due to the employer's breach of its duty of good faith and fair dealing, aggravated damages, damages for mental distress, and punitive damages. The *Honda* case involved the dismissal of an employee who had been diagnosed as suffering from chronic fatigue syndrome, and who refused to meet with an occupational medicine specialist selected by Honda after his disability benefits had been cut off by the company's insurance carrier. The trial judge had awarded 15 months of reasonable notice of dismissal (for a 14-year non-management employee), had increased this to 24 months in accordance with *Wallace* above, and had ordered an additional $500,000 in punitive damages. The Supreme Court reduced the award to 15 months of pay in lieu of notice only. The Supreme Court stated that extra damages resulting from the manner of dismissal are available only if the employer engages in conduct that is unfair or in bad faith by being, for example, untruthful, misleading, or unduly insensitive. More important, the Court stated that the notice period cannot simply be extended; instead, the total notice period must be compensatory in nature and address actual damages suffered by the employee. The Court provided certain examples of employer misconduct during a dismissal that could result in compensable damages, such as attacking the employee's reputation by declarations made at the time of dismissal, misrepresentation regarding the reason for the decision to terminate, or a dismissal designed to deprive an employee of a pension benefit or some other rights such as permanent status. Damages for mental distress and psychological injury can be awarded, but must be compensatory. Punitive damages, on the other hand, are restricted to intentional wrongful acts that are so malicious and outrageous that they deserve punishment on their own, and are not compensation to the employee. Instead, they are a form of punishment. Conduct meriting punitive damage awards must be "harsh, vindictive, reprehensible and malicious" as well as "extreme in its nature such that by any reasonable standards it is deserving of full condemnation and punishment". Punitive damages will be awarded only in exceptional cases.

Q. What Can an Employer Do To Avoid a Wrongful Dismissal Suit?

A. A wrongful dismissal case can be a time-consuming and expensive experience for any employer. The best way to deal with a wrongful dismissal suit is to avoid it altogether. Some suggestions for preventing wrongful dismissal claims are outlined below.

- **Use of written employment contracts.** An employment contract can be used to specify the types of employee behaviours that the employer may consider just cause for termination of employment without notice or pay in lieu of notice, and the amount of notice that will be considered reasonable if the employee is dismissed without cause. An employment contract, if it has been carefully drafted and properly executed, can be of considerable assistance in increasing the certainty with respect to the consequences of terminating the employment of an employee, and in reducing the possible areas of dispute between the parties if a termination should occur. Any employment contract provisions dealing with termination of the contract of employment should be clear, reasonable, and meet or exceed the minimum requirements under employment standards legislation. An employment agreement may also include an arbitration clause that directs disputes to arbitration rather than to the courts, thus reducing legal costs and providing a speedier conclusion.

- **Use of probation periods.** As discussed above, an employee's rights upon termination of employment are limited during a probation period that is in writing, agreed to, and clearly sets out the consequences of a dismissal. A fair and effective probation period can provide the employer with a good opportunity to assess the suitability of an employee for a position.

- **Use of good human resources management systems.** The effective use of good human resources management systems can be effective, not only in ensuring that personnel problems do not escalate to the point where termination of employment is necessary, but also in helping to ensure that just cause for termination can be supported if the decision to terminate employment is made. In order to ensure that a decision to dismiss an employee for just cause can be supported, an employer's human resources systems must ensure that employees know what the employer's standards for performance and conduct are, that they are given a reasonable opportunity to achieve these standards, and that they are aware of the consequences of failure to meet these standards. This involves the development of effective programs for training and orientation, attendance management, performance appraisal, and progressive discipline. Proper use of human resources management systems will ensure that an employee whose job is in jeopardy is aware of that fact, and is given a reasonable opportunity to correct the problem, and maintain the employment relationship.

- **If an employee must be dismissed, the discharge should be handled as fairly and sensitively as possible.** For example, don't allege just cause or misconduct if it doesn't exist. Try to make the process as easy as possible for the employee (i.e., by providing references and access to outplacement counselling). Try to schedule the termination interview so as avoid a sensitive time in the employee's life and to provide maximum privacy and dignity with respect to the location and time of day. Be discreet and not defamatory in both internal and external communications about the employee's departure.

Chapter 12

DISCRIMINATION IN EMPLOYMENT

                                                                          Page
INTRODUCTION 182
RECOGNIZING DISCRIMINATION... 182
    What Is Discrimination? 182
    Why Should an Employer Be Concerned About Discrimination in Employment? ... 182
    How Are Types of Discrimination Classified? 183
    If Behaviour Is Unintentional, Can It Still Be Considered Discriminatory? 183
    What Are the Prohibited Grounds of Discrimination? 184
    How Are Employees Protected Against Discrimination? 185
DISCRIMINATION IN HIRING AND TERMINATION....................... 185
    When Can Discrimination Occur in the Recruitment and Selection Process? 185
    How Might Discrimination Affect the Conditions of Employment? 187
    How Might Discrimination Occur at the End of the Employment Relationship? 187
DISCRIMINATION IN THE COURSE OF EMPLOYMENT 188
    What if an Employee Is Unable To Perform the Essential Duties of a Particular
        Job? 188
    What Is a BFOR?... 189
    What Is the Process for Determining if a Rule or Standard Is a BFOR? 189
    What Is Accommodation? 189
    What Are Some Examples of Accommodation? 190
    Who Is Responsible for Accommodation?.............................. 190
    How Much Accommodation Does an Employer Need To Provide?.................. 190
    What Is Undue Hardship? 190
EXCEPTIONS.. 191
    Are There Any Exceptions to the Prohibitions on Discrimination in Employment? 191
    What if Customers Prefer Not To Deal with Certain Employees? 192
RESPONSIBILITY OF TRADE UNIONS 192
    What Is the Role of Trade Unions in Ensuring a Discrimination-Free Workplace? 192
    What Are a Union's Obligations with Respect to the Accommodation of
        Employees?... 193
ENFORCEMENT 193
    What Can an Employee Who Has Been Subjected to Discrimination Do?........... 193
    What if an Employee Is Retaliated Against for Filing a Human Rights Complaint? 193

Page

Who Can Be Held Responsible for Discrimination in Employment? 194
How Long Does an Employee Have After the Alleged Discrimination Occurred To
    File a Human Rights Complaint or Application?.................................. 194
What Remedies Can Be Obtained from a Human Rights Tribunal?................... 194
What Should an Employer Do if a Human Rights Complaint Is Filed Against It?... 195
PREVENTION 197
    What Can An Employer Do To Prevent Discrimination in the Workplace? 197
PROHIBITED GROUNDS OF DISCRIMINATION CHART 199
LIMITATION PERIOD FOR FILING A HUMAN RIGHTS COMPLAINT OR
    APPLICATION CHART... 200

INTRODUCTION

As the Canadian workforce becomes increasingly diverse, the issue of workplace discrimination has become more and more important. Tolerance, open-mindedness, and understanding are now more essential than ever in the workplace. The questions and answers below are intended to provide some guidance for recognizing, preventing, and dealing with discrimination in the workplace.

RECOGNIZING DISCRIMINATION

Q. What Is Discrimination?

A. In *Andrews v. Law Society of British Columbia* ([1989] 1 SCR 143), the Supreme Court of Canada defined discrimination as

> ... a distinction, whether intentional or not, but based on grounds relating to personal characteristics of the individual or group, which has the effect of imposing burdens, obligations, or disadvantages on such individual or group not imposed on others, or which withholds or limits access to opportunities, benefits, and advantages available to other members of society.

In other words, not all distinctions are discriminatory. Employers can make distinctions on the basis of legitimate measures of merit or qualifications. Employees are, however, entitled to a workplace that is free from distinctions based on prohibited grounds of discrimination. The prohibited grounds of discrimination in each jurisdiction are set out in the chart on page 199.

Q. Why Should an Employer Be Concerned About Discrimination in Employment?

A. Discrimination is prohibited by law. In the event that an employee believes that he or she is being discriminated against, the employee may file a human rights complaint or application with the appropriate human rights commission or tribunal. In some jurisdictions, human rights claims may also be heard by the courts. If an employee files a complaint or application, an employer may find itself faced with an intrusive and potentially lengthy investigation and/or a hearing. The investigation or hearing may have a negative impact on the employer's public image and the morale of its employees, not to mention the considerable legal costs associated with defending an allegation of discrimination and the potential award against the employer in the event that discrimination is found by a tribunal or a court.

Quite apart from the legal requirement not to discriminate, it is in an employer's own business interest to provide an open and fair work environment where the dignity of all employees is respected. Employers need to recruit, train, and retain the best employees for their organization. In an increasingly competitive market, multicultural society, and global economy, employers must select employees with various backgrounds and talents from the widest possible pool of candidates.

Q. How Are Types of Discrimination Classified?

A. There are three types of discrimination: direct, indirect, and systemic. **Direct discrimination** occurs when a distinction is made expressly by reference to a prohibited ground. This discrimination is overt and can be readily be identified. For example, a job positing may specify that only people of a certain race or gender need apply. **Indirect discrimination** occurs when an apparently neutral rule or policy that is applied to all employees adversely affects members of a group falling within a prohibited ground. An employee's work schedule may, for instance, conflict with the employee's religious observances. Indirect discrimination has come to be recognized as equally unacceptable as compared to direct discrimination and is prohibited in respect of employment. **Systemic discrimination** is a collective version of indirect discrimination. It involves a rule that is neutral on its face, but that adversely affects members of a group in a broad sense.

Q. If Behaviour Is Unintentional, Can It Still Be Considered Discriminatory?

A. Unintentional behaviour can still constitute discrimination. Discrimination is defined by reference to the distinction drawn, and its effect on the employee, not by reference to the motive or intent of the employer or individual drawing the distinction.

Q. What Are the Prohibited Grounds of Discrimination?

A. In all jurisdictions, discrimination based on race, nationality, ethnicity or place of origin, colour, religion or creed, marital status, mental or physical disability, sex, and sexual orientation is prohibited.

Every jurisdiction except **New Brunswick** also expressly prohibits discrimination on the basis of family status. The term "family status" is not defined in **British Columbia, Manitoba**, the **Northwest Territories**, the **Yukon** or the **federal** jurisdiction. In **Alberta** and **Nunavut**, family status is defined as the "status of being related to another person by blood, marriage or adoption", while in **Ontario, Saskatchewan, Nova Scotia, Prince Edward Island**, and **Newfoundland and Labrador**, family status refers to the state of being in a parent–child relationship. The test for determining family status discrimination also varies by jurisdiction. In **British Columbia**, the Court of Appeal ruled in *Health Sciences Association of B.C. v. Campbell River and North Island Transportation Society* (2004 BCCA 260), that the applicant employee must demonstrate that there was a change in a term or condition of employment imposed by the employer which resulted in a serious interference with a substantial parental duty or obligation of the employee. This approach was rejected by the Federal Court of Canada in *Johnstone v. Canada (Border Services Agency)* (2013 FC 113), which defined the test as "whether the employment rule interferes with an employee's ability to fulfill her substantial parental obligations in any realistic way". In the Court's view, "requiring a higher threshold, a serious interference, for the ground of family status is to lessen the protection on that ground as compared with other protected grounds". More recently, the Ontario Human Rights Tribunal has introduced its own test which focuses on whether the employee's caregiving responsibilities are a requirement or simply a matter of choice or personal preference (*Devaney v. ZRV Holdings Limited*, 2012 HRTO 1590). Under this approach, an employer's duty to accommodate will only be triggered where the employee can demonstrate that his or her caregiving responsibilities are legitimately required.

All jurisdictions prohibit discrimination based on age, although the definition of age differs between jurisdictions. Employers are prohibited from discriminating against persons 18 years of age or over in **Alberta, Ontario**, and **Saskatchewan**; and 19 years of age or more in **British Columbia**. A general reference to age exists in **Manitoba, New Brunswick, Newfoundland and Labrador, Nova Scotia, Prince Edward Island, Quebec**, the **Northwest Territories, Nunavut**, the **Yukon**, and the **federal** jurisdiction.

Political belief, conviction, or opinion is a prohibited ground in **British Columbia, Manitoba, New Brunswick, Newfoundland and**

Labrador, **Nova Scotia**, **Prince Edward Island**, **Quebec**, the **Northwest Territories**, and the **Yukon**.

Criminal conviction for which a pardon has been granted is a prohibited ground of discrimination in the **federal** jurisdiction, **Ontario**, **Quebec**, the **Northwest Territories**, and **Nunavut**, as is a criminal conviction for an indictable or summary conviction offence in **British Columbia**, **Newfoundland and Labrador**, **Prince Edward Island**, **Quebec**, and the **Yukon**, unless such charge relates to the occupation or employment of a person.

For details on the prohibited grounds of discrimination by jurisdiction, please refer to the chart on page 199.

Q. How Are Employees Protected Against Discrimination?

A. All jurisdictions have passed laws prohibiting discrimination in employment. Most of these are known as human rights Codes, Acts, or Charters. These statutes set out the sectors in which discrimination is prohibited (such as employment, education, accommodation, access to public services, and contracts), the various prohibited grounds of discrimination, and the mechanisms for filing and enforcing human rights complaints.

The *Canadian Charter of Rights and Freedoms* ("Charter") also protects employees' human rights. Section 15 of the Charter provides for the right to equality before and under the law, and to equal protection and benefit of the law without discrimination. Nonetheless, the Charter only applies to the actions of government, not to private individuals, corporations, or organizations. Thus, it does not directly affect the actions of employers, or provide protection to employees, unless the employers are government bodies.

DISCRIMINATION IN HIRING AND TERMINATION

Q. When Can Discrimination Occur in the Recruitment and Selection Process?

A. Discrimination can occur at every stage of the recruitment and selection process:

- **Advertisements:** Advertisements should be reviewed carefully to ensure that they do not discourage applications from any particular group. For example, gender-neutral job titles should be used. An advertisement for a waitress, for example, is not likely to encourage applications from qualified men. The advertisement should not contain any requirements that may be discriminatory. For instance, employers should not state that applicants should have "Canadian experience". This is rarely a true job requirement, and can have the effect of screening out potential applicants by their place of origin. It is also wise to ensure that advertisements are placed in venues where they will be seen by a wide range of applicants.

- **Employment agencies:** Human rights legislation prohibits agencies from refusing to refer applicants for employment on the basis of a prohibited ground of discrimination. There are cases in which this has occurred, either at the employer's request or because the agency has made assumptions about the kind of applicants that the employer wanted. In order to prevent this from occurring, employers should ensure that the employment agencies they use are aware that they are equal opportunity employers and that they want to see a broad range of applicants.

- **Application forms:** Human rights legislation prohibits employers from making inquiries related to a prohibited ground of discrimination. Employers should therefore carefully review their application forms to ensure that they are not inadvertently soliciting inappropriate information. For example, job application forms should not ask for the marital status of the applicant or request that the applicant provide a photograph. Any questions on the application form should be clearly related to the applicant's ability to perform the job.

Employers should also avoid making assumptions on the basis of group membership. For example, employers may assume that married applicants will be reluctant to relocate, or that applicants with children will have difficulty with business travel. As a result, in some instances, employers will ask discriminatory questions about sex, marital status, or family status. Instead of making assumptions about an applicant, the employer should ask directly whether the applicant is available for business travel or would be willing to relocate.

Employers sometimes wish to ask questions about marital status or family status because such information is required for the administration of benefit plans. However, an employer does not need this information until after an applicant is hired, and it is therefore wise to wait until the applicant is hired to make such inquiries.

- **Hiring criteria:** Since hiring criteria are usually based on the job description, it is important to ensure that the requirements set out in the job description are necessary for the position and not discriminatory.

- **The interview:** Employers should ensure that anyone who conducts employment interviews has been given training on human rights issues. In order to eliminate any bias or perception of bias, it may also be helpful to have more than one person conduct the interview. Interviewers must take care when they meet with the applicant not to consider any characteristics of the applicant that are related to the prohibited grounds of discrimination.

Q. How Might Discrimination Affect the Conditions of Employment?

A. Discrimination may have an impact on all conditions of employment, including compensation systems, benefit programs, access to and delivery of training and development programs, and the overall work environment.

- **Compensation and benefits:** Discrimination may interfere with equal treatment with respect to compensation and benefits, including the right to equal pay for doing the same or similar work. Equal pay provisions for women are included in human rights, employment standards, and pay equity legislation. If women are paid less for doing work that is the same or similar to that which a man is doing, they can file a complaint against the employer. If members of other groups are systematically being paid less for their work than other colleagues doing the same work, they will likely be protected under the general provisions of human rights legislation. Employers should ensure that their compensation systems treat all groups equally, compensating individuals based on merit, and not for membership in a particular group.

- **Training and promotion opportunities:** Discrimination may limit an employee's opportunities for training. Employers are required to carry out their training programs in compliance with the principles of equality and fairness contained in human rights legislation. All employees must have equal access to training opportunities. For example, an employer's failure to provide training to older workers because they might retire in the next few years would constitute discrimination on the basis of age. Another example of discrimination in the context of training would be the failure to develop training programs that could be accessed by an employee with a physical disability.

- **The working environment:** Discriminatory conduct can also occur in day-to-day decisions made by managers or supervisors or in the manner employees are treated by their co-workers. Such discrimination often has a negative impact on employee morale, which will result in lower productivity and issues with employee retention. Workplace harassment is discussed in more detail in Chapter 13, "Harassment at Work".

Q. How Might Discrimination Occur at the End of the Employment Relationship?

A. **Termination of employment:** Discrimination may result in an employer terminating an employee's employment. As with other aspects of employment, the decision to terminate the employment of an employee should be made without reference to membership in a protected group. This is not always as straightforward as it sounds. For example, one issue that many employers grapple with is absenteeism. Chronic absenteeism may be just cause for the termination of employment. However, if the absenteeism is caused by a disability, the issue becomes complex, and prior to termination, the employer must be sure that the employee is not capable of performing the essential duties of the job and that he or she cannot be accommodated without undue hardship to the employer.

Retirement: Mandatory retirement policies are no longer permitted under the human rights legislation in any jurisdiction. Except in very limited circumstances, employers engage in discriminatory conduct if they require employees to retire at a specific age. The majority of the provinces continue to provide an exception permitting mandatory retirement where age is a *bona fide* occupational requirement.

It is important to note that the elimination of mandatory retirement does not mean that employers cannot have voluntary retirement programs based on a certain age. In other words, employers may provide properly structured packages for employees who wish to leave the company prior to or at age 65, so long as the employees are not required to accept the packages.

DISCRIMINATION IN THE COURSE OF EMPLOYMENT

Q. What if an Employee Is Unable To Perform the Essential Duties of a Particular Job?

A. Human rights legislation does not require an employer to hire or retain an employee who is incapable of performing the job. At the same time, if the employee is unable to perform the essential duties of a particular job for reasons directly or indirectly related to a prohibited ground of discrimination, the employer must show that the standard or rule it seeks to rely on is a *bona fide* occupational requirement ("BFOR").

Q. What Is a BFOR?

A. A BFOR is a standard or rule that is integral to carrying out the functions of a specific position. For example, a firefighter must maintain a certain level of physical fitness in order to continue to work in that position.

Q. What Is the Process for Determining if a Rule or Standard Is a BFOR?

A. The Supreme Court of Canada in *Meiorin (British Columbia Public Service Employee Relations Commission) v. B.C.G.S.E.U.* (99 CLLC ¶ 230-028) established a three-step process by which a tribunal or court may determine if an employer's workplace standard or rule is a BFOR. It is the responsibility of the employer to prove each step. If unsuccessful in establishing any of the three steps, the standard or rule will not be a BFOR and the employer will be required to accommodate the employee. If the three-step test is met, the workplace rule is a BFOR and accommodation will not be required.

In the first step, the employer must show that it adopted the standard for a purpose rationally connected to the performance of the job. The second step requires that the employer show that the particular standard or rule was adopted in an honest and good faith belief that it was necessary for the fulfillment of that legitimate work-related purpose. The third and final step requires that the employer show that the rule is reasonably necessary to accomplish the legitimate work-related purpose. To show that it is reasonably necessary, the employer must demonstrate that it is impossible to accommodate the employee without undue hardship.

Q. What Is Accommodation?

A. Accommodation refers to individual adjustments in the workplace that respond to the needs of a specific job applicant or employee. Needs that must be accommodated may result from such factors as disability, family status, religious beliefs, or any other prohibited ground of discrimination.

The key principle of accommodation is that each employee's needs must be considered and assessed individually so that the most appropriate accommodation can be determined for that individual. Appropriate accommodation for one employee will not necessarily be appropriate for another.

Q. What Are Some Examples of Accommodation?

A. Accommodation may take a variety of forms, and may include, but is not restricted to, the following:

- physical assistance such as redesigning a workspace;

- technical aids such as specialized software, magnifiers, or other equipment;

- leave for religious or cultural observances;

- flexible work schedules to meet changing family responsibility needs; or

- use of an employee assistance program.

The employer may also be required to modify the duties, responsibilities, or physical demands of the job. This may involve reassigning duties and responsibilities of the position that an employee cannot complete to other employees.

Q. Who Is Responsible for Accommodation?

A. The onus is on the employee requiring accommodation to make his or her needs known the employer. If the employer is not aware that accommodation is required, the employer will not be liable for failing to provide it.

Once a representative of the employer, whether it is an employee's supervisor, manager, or human resources manager, has been informed by the employee that he or she requires accommodation, it is the employer's responsibility to ensure that appropriate accommodation is provided.

Q. How Much Accommodation Does an Employer Need To Provide?

A. Employers must accommodate employees up to the point of undue hardship.

Q. What Is Undue Hardship?

A. In 1990, the Supreme Court of Canada, in *Central Alberta Dairy Pool v. Alberta (Human Rights Commission)*, listed six factors to be considered in assessing undue hardship: financial cost, safety, size of the employer, employee morale, interchangeability of workplace and facilities, and interruption of a collective agreement. However, in recent cases where accommodation has been examined, employee morale has since been rejected as a key factor and courts have focused on the first two factors: cost and safety.

- **Cost:** In determining whether the cost of accommodating an employee will amount to undue hardship, tribunals or courts will consider the size and financial resources of the employer; whether costs are immediate or can be phased-in over time; and whether costs may be recovered through grants, subsidies, or tax deductions. Overall, the courts will assess whether the cost of the accommodation would alter the nature of the business or affect its viability.

- **Health and safety issues:** In determining whether the health and safety concerns amount to undue hardship, tribunals or courts will consider whether the risk is greater than those normally tolerated on the job, whether the risk will be borne by the employee requiring accommodation, by co-workers, or by the general public, and, if the risk is to be borne by the employee requiring accommodation, the willingness of the employee to assume the risk.

Several provinces also set out the factors to consider in their undue hardship analysis in their human rights legislation. In **Ontario**, for example, the factors to be considered for undue hardship are cost, outside sources of funding (if any), and health and safety requirements (if any). In the **Yukon**, undue hardship will be determined by balancing the factors of safety, disruption to the public, effect on contractual obligations, financial cost, and business efficiency.

EXCEPTIONS

Q. Are There Any Exceptions to the Prohibitions on Discrimination in Employment?

A. Sometimes there are good reasons for distinguishing between employees in making employment decisions. Human rights statutes recognize this, and each of them contains exceptions to the blanket prohibition on discrimination. Some examples of these exceptions are described below, but not all of these exceptions apply in every jurisdiction. If you think an exception applies to your situation, the legislation in your jurisdiction must be carefully reviewed. It is also important to note that these exceptions are interpreted very narrowly in order to avoid undermining the purposes of the human rights legislation. Employers should therefore obtain legal advice about the applicable exemptions in their jurisdiction and invoke the exceptions with great care.

- **Special interest organizations:** It may be legitimate for religious, philanthropic, educational, or other similar organizations which are primarily engaged in serving the interests of a particular group to give preference in employment to members of that group. For example, it may be reasonable for a community centre devoted to the needs of Vietnamese youth to give preference to Vietnamese applicants for counselling positions, or for a religious school to give preference in hiring to teachers who share the religious faith of the school.

- **Affirmative action programs:** Most jurisdictions specifically permit organizations to develop programs or plans to relieve the conditions of disadvantaged individuals or groups. While assistance for disadvantaged groups might not theoretically be considered discriminatory, legislators have thought it necessary to include such provisions to prevent complaints of "reverse discrimination". Employers who wish to implement affirmative action programs may be permitted to do so under these provisions.

- **Medical and personal needs:** When the primary duty of the employee is attending to the individual or personal needs of a person, including an ill child or an aged, infirm, or ill spouse or other relative of a person, an individual may, in some jurisdictions, be able to refuse to hire another based on a prohibited ground.

Q. What if Customers Prefer Not To Deal with Certain Employees?

A. There is no exception from discrimination based on customer preference. Many human rights decisions have dealt with this issue firmly and at length. The preference of customers in a restaurant for being served by people of a similar ethnicity, the preference of strip club patrons for dealing with servers who are not pregnant, and the preference of clients in certain industries for dealing with male sales representatives have all been rejected by human rights bodies as justifications for discrimination. In fact, employers are expected to protect their employees from discriminatory behaviour by their clientele, insofar as this is possible.

RESPONSIBILITY OF TRADE UNIONS

Q. What Is the Role of Trade Unions in Ensuring a Discrimination-Free Workplace?

A. In unionized workplaces, both unions and employers are responsible for ensuring that the provisions of collective agreements are not discriminatory and for removing discriminatory provisions. Where collective agreement provisions must be modified to allow an employee to be accommodated, unions are required to assist employees in this endeavour.

Many unions are active in ensuring a discrimination-free workplace for their members. However, in some cases, unions engage in discriminatory actions. In such cases, employees may file a human rights complaint or grievance against the union and the union may be found liable along with the employer for workplace discrimination.

Q. What Are a Union's Obligations with Respect to the Accommodation of Employees?

A. Unions have a duty to participate in the effort to accommodate an employee. If no action is taken to accommodate the employee, both the union and the employer may be held liable for the discrimination.

ENFORCEMENT

Q. What Can an Employee Who Has Been Subjected to Discrimination Do?

A. An employee who believes that he or she has been subject to discrimination in the workplace has several options depending on the circumstances:

- **Filing a complaint with the employer:** Many employers have anti-discrimination policies and procedures, which may be an effective means for an employee to obtain a resolution of the discrimination.

- **Filing a human rights complaint or application:** Human rights bodies will provide advice and assistance to persons who believe they have been subject to discrimination in employment. If an employee believes that he or she has been subject to discrimination, and has been unable to resolve the issue by dealing with the employer directly, he or she may file a complaint or application with the appropriate body.

- **Filing a grievance:** Most collective agreements contain clauses prohibiting discrimination in the workplace. An employee who is represented by a union may be able to file a grievance under the collective agreement.

- **Filing a civil action:** In some jurisdictions, employees may be able to file a legal action with respect to the discrimination. For example, if an employer terminates an employee's employment for discriminatory reasons, an employee may file a wrongful dismissal claim against the employer which includes a request for damages for the alleged human rights violations.

Q. What if an Employee Is Retaliated Against for Filing a Human Rights Complaint?

A. Retaliation against an employee for raising the issue of discrimination or filing a human rights complaint contravenes human rights legislation. Employers are prohibited from retaliating against employees who in good faith allege their human rights have been violated. Employers are required to protect employees from retaliation by their managers, supervisors, or co-workers. If an employee does experience retaliation, this can be the subject of a human rights complaint and, even if the original complaint is dismissed, an employer may still be found liable for the retaliation.

Q. Who Can Be Held Responsible for Discrimination in Employment?

A. An employer will be held liable for discrimination that occurs in the workplace and that the employer carried out, condoned, or failed to take reasonable steps to prevent. In addition, an employee's supervisor or co-workers can be held personally liable for discriminatory actions that were carried out during the course of their employment. As discussed above, unions can also be held liable for workplace discrimination.

Q. How Long Does an Employee Have After the Alleged Discrimination Occurred To File a Human Rights Complaint or Application?

A. The amount of time that an employee has to file a human rights complaint or application varies by jurisdiction. Generally speaking, the deadline, also known as a limitation period, for submitting a complaint or application is between six and 24 months from the time of the alleged contravention of the human rights legislation. In a situation where there is a pattern or discrimination, the limitation period will typically run from the last incident of discrimination. In **Saskatchewan**, however, the limitation period runs from the time at which the person making the complaint became aware or should have become aware of the discrimination. Please see the chart on page 200 for the specific limitation periods by jurisdiction. It is important to note that in several jurisdictions, the human rights commissions or tribunals retain the discretion to extend the limitation period. The circumstances under which a commission or tribunal may extend the limitation period vary by jurisdiction, but include circumstances in which a commission or tribunal deems it reasonable to grant an extension, it is in the public interest to accept the complaint, or there is no substantial prejudice because of the delay in filing the complaint.

Q. What Remedies Can Be Obtained from a Human Rights Tribunal?

A. The remedies available through a settlement or a tribunal order include:

- monetary damages for losses sustained as a result of the discrimination (for example, if an employee was dismissed or forced to resign from employment because of discrimination, then compensation for loss of wages may be awarded);

- monetary damages for the injury to self-respect and dignity resulting from the discrimination;

- reinstatement if the discrimination resulted in termination of employment (for example, in a recent Ontario case, the Tribunal ordered the reinstatement of an employee with 10 years of back pay (*Fair v. Hamilton-Wentworth District School Board*, 2013 HRTO 440));

- implementation of an anti-discrimination policy, educational workshops for the employees, or other specified changes in the workplace;

- posting copies of human rights laws in the workplace; and/or

- reporting to the human rights body on a regular basis.

Q. What Should an Employer Do if a Human Rights Complaint Is Filed Against It?

A. Employers who find themselves the subject of a complaint should consider the following guidelines:

- **Prevent further discrimination in the workplace.** Employers should be proactive in dealing with human rights issues, and ensure that they respect human rights. This means keeping up-to-date on human rights issues and developments, providing human rights training to management and supervisory personnel, developing anti-discrimination and anti-harassment policies, and implementing appropriate internal complaints processes. Not only will this help to avoid complaints, but it also increases the likelihood that any complaint that is filed will be resolved in the employer's favour.

- **Take the complaint seriously.** A human rights complaint can have a major impact on an organization's finances, employee morale, and public image. Monetary damage awards can be considerable, as are the associated legal costs.

- **Obtain legal advice early on.** Some employers obtain no legal advice until the hearing stage, when the evidence has been gathered and substantial amounts of the employer's time and resources have been consumed. It is more prudent to invest resources at the beginning of the process if there is any possibility of bringing the matter to an early resolution and to ensure that the evidence contained in the employer's response and obtained during investigation portrays the employer in the best possible light.

- **Protect the employee who filed the complaint from retaliation or reprisal.** Ensure that the employee is treated fairly and with respect.

- **Do not imagine that the complaint will go away if it is ignored.** It won't. Because of the heavy caseloads of many human rights bodies, the complaint process can be very lengthy and an employer may not hear from the human rights body for months or, in extreme cases, even years at a time. This does not mean that the complaint has been forgotten or abandoned.

- **Gather all relevant information, and all investigation documentation as soon as the employer is made aware of a complaint.** A written record should be made of the employer's version of events, important documents should be preserved, and a record kept of all conversations with witnesses and human rights staff. Ensure that contact is maintained with important witnesses, so that they can be located if necessary. The human rights body, tribunal, or court will not be overly sympathetic if an employer claims to have misplaced the documents or evidence which would have exonerated it. Generally speaking, the onus is on the respondent (the employer) in a human rights case to preserve the materials necessary for its response.

- **Co-operate with the investigating officer and any other human rights staff.** The role of the investigator is not to find evidence to support the complaint, but simply to find out what happened.

- **Seriously consider settling the complaint.** Some employers have a policy of never settling a human rights complaint. While this is a judgment call on the part of each employer, a settlement is not an admission of fault and can save an employer substantial amounts of time and money and avoid damage to the employer's reputation associated with even an unfounded complaint. In most parts of the country, human rights staff are required to attempt to resolve the matter informally, and it can be to an employer's benefit to take advantage of this.

- **Try to learn from the experience.** Even if a complaint is unfounded, it may indicate other problems within the organization that require attention, such as poor management, lack of supervisory training, lack of communication, poor morale, or unprofessional work atmosphere.

PREVENTION

Q. What Can An Employer Do To Prevent Discrimination in the Workplace?

A. As was noted above, prevention is the best method for dealing with human rights complaints. The following are some suggestions for preventing discrimination in the workplace:

- **Make an organizational commitment to a discrimination-free workplace.** Unless employees see that senior members of the organization are serious about creating a discrimination-free workplace and that it is an organizational priority, they will not take the commitment seriously, and it will be difficult to achieve the goal. Employers should consider formally including the development of a workplace free of discrimination and harassment in the corporation or organization's goals. Demonstrating this commitment can be achieved through having a member of senior management announce the anti-discrimination initiative. At a minimum, senior management must avoid any actions that are or may be perceived to be discriminatory.

- **Develop and implement an anti-discrimination policy.** This is a crucial component of any anti-discrimination initiative. An anti-discrimination policy not only demonstrates organizational commitment to a workplace environment that is free of discrimination, but it also educates employees on types of discrimination, the organization's commitment in dealing with discrimination, and how management will deal with issues of discrimination.

- **Train supervisors and managers to recognize and appropriately handle issues of discrimination.** Supervisors and managers deal with employees on a daily basis. They are the employer representatives who are in the best position to recognize and stop discrimination when it is occurring in the workplace. They are also the employees who are most likely to be named in a discrimination complaint. Without training, supervisors and managers may inadvertently be the source of problems for the employer, or may fail to deal with problems when they arise.

  Training for supervisors and managers should include the importance of ensuring a discrimination-free workplace and the organization's commitment to this; how to recognize discrimination issues when they arise, including detailed examples of unacceptable behaviour; and the organization's procedures for employees to make complaints and for the organization to investigate and resolve them. After the training is completed, supervisors and managers should be kept up-to-date as new issues and developments arise.

- **Provide information to employees.** All employees should be made aware of what discrimination is, what the employer's policy is regarding discrimination, and what employees can and should do when faced with workplace discrimination. The organization's anti-discrimination policy should be distributed to every employee, and should contain a person who can be contacted for further information. Employers should require the employees to sign an acknowledgement that they have read and understood the policy and agree to comply with its terms.

- **Deal promptly with discrimination issues when they arise.** It is no good having an elaborate anti-discrimination policy if it is not effectively implemented. In order for employees to feel comfortable in coming forward with issues of discrimination, they must see that the employer's anti-discrimination policy is applied in a fair, efficient, and consistent manner.

PROHIBITED GROUNDS OF DISCRIMINATION CHART

Jurisdiction[1]	Race/Colour	Ancestry	Place of Origin	National or Ethnic Origin	Nationality/Citizenship	Religion/Creed	Age	Sex/Gender	Pregnancy/Childbirth[6]	Sexual Orientation	Gender Identity	Marital Status	Family Status	Mental or Physical Disability	Criminal Conviction[7]	Political Beliefs	Source of Income	Social Condition	Actual or Presumed Association with a Protected Group
Federal	•			•		•	•	•	•	•	•[10]	•	•	•	•[7]				•
Alberta	•	•	•			•	• (18+)	•	•	•	•[8]	•	•	•			•		•
British Columbia	•	•	•			•	• (19+)	•	•	•	•[8]	•	•	•	•[7]	•			•
Manitoba	•	•		•	•	•	•	•	•	•	•	•	•	•		•[11]	•	•[15]	
New Brunswick	•	•	•	•		•	•	•	•	•	•[8]	•	•	•		•[11]	•[13]	•[13]	
Newfoundland and Labrador[2]	•	•		•	•	•	•	•	•	•	•[8]	•	•	•	•[7]	•	•		•
Nova Scotia[3]	•	•		•		•	•	•	•	•	•[9]	•	•	•		•[11]	•		•
Ontario	•	•	•	•	•	•	• (18+)	•	•	•	•[9]	•	•	•	•[7]				•
Prince Edward Island	•			•	•	•	•	•	•	•	•[8]	•	•	•	•[7]	•	•		•
Quebec[4]	•			•		•	•	•	•	•	•[8]	•[12]	•[12]	•	•[7]	•	•[13]	•	
Saskatchewan	•	•	•		•	•	• (18+)	•	•	•	•[8]	•	•	•			•[14]		
Northwest Territories[5]	•	•		•	•	•	•	•	•	•	•	•	•	•	•[7]	•	•[13]	•[13]	•
Nunavut	•	•		•	•	•	•	•	•	•	•	•	•	•	•[7]	•	•		•
Yukon Territory	•	•		•	•	•	•	•	•	•	•[8]	•	•	•	•[7]	•[11]	•		•

[1] Harassment is banned on all proscribed grounds of discrimination in all jurisdictions, except in New Brunswick which only refers to sexual harassment.

[2] Newfoundland and Labrador also prohibits discrimination on the basis of disfigurement and on the basis of social origin.

[3] Nova Scotia also prohibits discrimination on the basis of irrational fear of contracting illness or disease.

[4] Quebec also prohibits discrimination on the basis of language.

[5] The Northwest Territories also prohibits discrimination on the basis of family affiliation.

[6] Pregnancy is a separate ground of discrimination in Quebec and Nunavut. In all other jurisdictions, discrimination of the basis of pregnancy is included in discrimination on the basis of sex/gender.

[7] Ontario, Quebec, the Northwest Territories, Nunavut, and the federal jurisdiction prohibit discrimination on the basis of a pardoned conviction. British Columbia, Newfoundland and Labrador, Prince Edward Island, Quebec, and Yukon Territory prohibit discrimination on the basis of a conviction which is unrelated to a person's employment.

[8] In Alberta, British Columbia, New Brunswick, Newfoundland and Labrador, Prince Edward Island, Quebec, Saskatchewan, and the Yukon, discrimination on the basis of gender identity is included in discrimination on the b[asis...]

[9] Nova Scotia and Ontario prohibit discrimination on the basis of both gender identity and gender expression.

[10] Under proposed legislation, the *Canadian Human Rights Act* is to be amended to include gender identity as a prohibited ground of discrimination.

[11] In Manitoba, New Brunswick, Nova Scotia, and Yukon Territory, political activity is a prohibited ground of discrimination as well as political beliefs.

[12] Quebec uses the term "civil status" instead of marital/family status.

[13] In New Brunswick, Quebec, and Northwest Territories, discrimination on the basis of source of income is included within discrimination on the basis of social condition.

[14] Saskatchewan prohibits discrimination only on the basis of receipt of public assistance.

[15] Manitoba uses the term "social disadvantage".

LIMITATION PERIOD FOR FILING A HUMAN RIGHTS COMPLAINT OR APPLICATION CHART

Jurisdiction	Limitation Period
Federal	12 months
Alberta	12 months
British Columbia	6 months
Manitoba	6 months
New Brunswick	12 months
Newfoundland and Labrador	12 months
Nova Scotia	12 months
Ontario	12 months
Prince Edward Island	12 months
Quebec	24 months
Saskatchewan	12 months
Northwest Territories	24 months
Nunavut	24 months
Yukon	6 months

Chapter 13

HARASSMENT AT WORK

Page

INTRODUCTION 202

RECOGNIZING HARASSMENT 202

Does the Law Protect Employees Against Harassment? 202

What Is Harassment? 202

Is It Harassment if the Person Is Not a Superior? 203

What Kinds of Behaviours Can Be Considered Harassment? 203

What if the Behaviour Was Not Intended To Offend or Upset Anyone? 203

Can a Joke Really Be Harassment? 203

Does the Rule Against Workplace Harassment Extend Beyond the Work Site
Itself and Regular Working Hours? 204

Can One Upsetting Incident Be Considered Harassment? 204

SEXUAL HARASSMENT 204

What Is Sexual Harassment? 204

What Kinds of Behaviours Can Be Considered Sexually Harassing? 204

What Is the Difference Between Sexual Harassment and an Office Romance or
Innocent Flirtation? 205

WORKPLACE HARASSMENT AND VIOLENCE 205

What Is Psychological Harassment? 205

How Are Employees Protected from Violence in the Workplace? 206

EMPLOYER RESPONSIBILITY TO PREVENT HARASSMENT 206

What Responsibility Does an Employer Have for Harassment Occurring in the
Workplace? 206

What Can an Employer Do To Prevent Harassment from Occurring in the
Workplace? 206

CHECKLIST: CREATING A HARASSMENT-FREE WORKPLACE 207

What Should an Anti-Harassment Policy Contain? 207

CHECKLIST: DEVELOPING AN EFFECTIVE HARASSMENT POLICY 208

DEALING WITH HARASSMENT 208

What Should an Employee Do Who Finds Himself or Herself Being Harassed? 208

CHECKLIST: DEALING WITH HARASSMENT 209

If the Employer Will Not Help, What Other Options Are Available? 209

Page

What Should an Employer Do if a Complaint of Harassment Arises in the
Workplace? 210

What Should an Employer Do if Harassment Is Found To Have Occurred in the
Workplace? 210

What if Someone at Work Tries To Retaliate for the Filing of a Complaint about
Harassment? 210

THE ROLE OF HUMAN RIGHTS BODIES 210

What Can a Human Rights Body Do To Help? 210

What Kinds of Remedies Can Be Obtained from a Human Rights Tribunal? 211

INTRODUCTION

All employees have the right to be treated with dignity and respect in the workplace. This overview provides both employees and employers with guidance in recognizing, preventing, and dealing with workplace harassment when it occurs.

RECOGNIZING HARASSMENT

Q. Does the Law Protect Employees Against Harassment?

A. All employees have a right to work in an environment where their dignity is respected and they are free from harassment. All jurisdictions prohibit harassment based on the prohibited grounds of discrimination. Some jurisdictions, such as **British Columbia**, **Manitoba**, **Ontario**, **Quebec**, and **Saskatchewan**, prohibit harassment in the workplace, whether or not the harassment is based on a prohibited ground of discrimination. While only **Ontario**, **New Brunswick**, **Nova Scotia**, and **Prince Edward Island** specifically mention sexual harassment in their respective legislation, sexual harassment is typically covered under the general prohibition on harassment in the **federal** jurisdiction and in other provinces and territories.

Q. What Is Harassment?

A. Generally speaking, harassment can be defined as engaging in a course of comment or conduct that is known or ought reasonably to be known to be unwelcome. Even if the comments or conduct are not directed at one person, another individual may still experience discrimination and harassment as a member of the group targeted by the comments or conduct. For example, the Canadian Human Rights Commission has defined harassment as "any unwanted physical or verbal conduct that offends or humiliates you". Likewise, the Manitoba Human Rights Commission defines harassment as "a course of abusive and unwelcome conduct or comment that is directed at individuals because of the group to which they belong or appear to belong". Harassment causes some employees to experience a work environment that is stressful, degrading, disrespectful of their fundamental human dignity, and, in some cases, even unsafe. Harassment can result in unfair disadvantage in terms of work opportunities and benefits. For instance, if an employee is the target of racial slurs and jokes, he or she may be unable to concentrate on the job in order to be productive and promoted by the employer.

Q. Is It Harassment if the Person Is Not a Superior?

A. When people think of workplace harassment, they often think of it as being inflicted by an employee's supervisor or superior. Nonetheless, harassment can also be carried out by co-workers, customers, clients, business associates, or anyone connected with the workplace.

Q. What Kinds of Behaviours Can Be Considered Harassment?

A. There is no complete list of the behaviours which can be considered harassment. As stated previously, any demeaning or offensive behaviour based on membership or perceived membership in a protected group can constitute harassment. The following list gives some examples of behaviours that have in the past been found to be harassing: unwelcome remarks or jokes about subjects like race, religion, disability, or age, display or electronic distribution of offensive pictures or posters, or verbal threats, intimidation, or abuse.

Q. What if the Behaviour Was Not Intended To Offend or Upset Anyone?

A. Some behaviour is so obviously intended to cause stress and humiliation to the recipient that it is clearly harassment. With other behaviour, it may be less clear. What one person may consider to be lighthearted teasing or fun may cause someone else stress, anxiety, and unhappiness. Whether something is harassing depends on the effect it has on the person who is its target, rather than on the intent of the harasser.

Q. Can a Joke Really Be Harassment?

A. While some joking around can have a very positive effect on the workplace, certain types of jokes degrade or insult other employees and is harassing. For example, "blonde" jokes or ethnic jokes can send the message that some members of the workforce are less valuable than others, and do not really belong in the workplace. If a joke could offend a member of a protected group and make an employee feel uncomfortable, excluded, or humiliated, it may be harassing.

Q. Does the Rule Against Workplace Harassment Extend Beyond the Work Site Itself and Regular Working Hours?

A. Workplace harassment can occur outside the physical work site and can occur before, during, and after working hours. For example, workplace harassment could occur at other locations associated with the work of the organization, such as company social gatherings, conferences, training sessions, business travel, or customer calls. These need not fall during work hours. Moreover, harassment includes harassing or bullying conduct via email or the Internet (e.g., on social networking sites or blogs). In a recent **Ontario** case, the Human Rights Tribunal decided that a statement made by an employee on her Facebook page about a workplace incident involving one of her colleagues amounted to harassment in employment (*Perez-Moreno v. Kulczycki*, 2013 HRTO 1074).

Q. Can One Upsetting Incident Be Considered Harassment?

A. Although harassment typically involves a series of incidents, a single incident, if sufficiently serious, can be enough to constitute harassment. For example, if the supervisor of an employee who is a member of a certain race was overheard making comments about members of that racial group being unwelcome in the workplace, this could taint an employee's entire working experience.

SEXUAL HARASSMENT

Q. What Is Sexual Harassment?

A. Sexual harassment is a subset of workplace harassment involving sex discrimination. Sexual harassment is any unwelcome conduct or comment of a sexual nature that is likely to cause offence or humiliation to an employee, or that might be perceived as placing a condition of a sexual nature on employment or on any employment opportunity.

Q. What Kinds of Behaviours Can Be Considered Sexually Harassing?

A. Any sexual conduct in the workplace can potentially constitute sexual harassment. Actions which have been found to constitute sexual harassment include:

- jokes or comments about sex, sexual preferences, and sexual matters;

- inquiries about an employee's sex life;

- use of derogatory language that is gender biased;

- standing or getting too close to someone;

- unfair evaluations or reprimands, reduced working hours, over-work, dismissals, discipline, or refusals to hire when they are in retaliation for refusal to submit to sexual advances;

- sexually suggestive remarks or gestures;

- leering or whistling;

- unwelcome physical contact, such as pinching, hugging, touching, patting, or brushing up against someone; and

- sexual assault.

Q. What Is the Difference Between Sexual Harassment and an Office Romance or Innocent Flirtation?

A. Office flirtations and romances are *not* considered to be sexual harassment as the conduct is not unwelcome — it is mutual. Sexual harassment is behaviour that is unwanted and coercive by one of the parties and is often an attempt by one person to exercise power over another. However, this is not to say that employers should not be wary of office flirtations or romances, as there is the potential for them to develop into unwanted conduct and the danger that they may result in a conflict of interest if the employees work together or are in a direct reporting relationship to one another.

WORKPLACE HARASSMENT AND VIOLENCE

Q. What Is Psychological Harassment?

A. In 2004, **Quebec** legislated a right for employees to work in an environment free from psychological harassment. Psychological harassment is defined as any vexatious behaviour in the form of repeated and hostile or unwanted conduct, verbal comments, actions, or gestures that affect an employee's dignity or psychological or physical integrity and that results in a harmful work environment for the employee. Psychological harassment may also consist of a single serious incidence that has a lasting, harmful effect on an employee. Maliciousness or intent to harm are not required and are not determining factors. There must be some form of disagreement with the conduct expressed, although it need not be stated expressly. This definition is sufficiently broad to include harassment under any of the prohibited grounds, or even harassment that is not based on a prohibited ground.

While neither **British Columbia**, **Manitoba**, **Ontario**, nor **Saskatchewan** use the term "psychological harassment", all three have introduced legislation which expands the definition of "harassment" such that the harassment need not be based on a prohibited ground in order for it to be unlawful.

Q. How Are Employees Protected from Violence in the Workplace?

A. **Alberta**, **British Columbia**, **Manitoba**, **Newfoundland and Labrador**, **Nova Scotia**, **Ontario**, **Prince Edward Island**, and **Saskatchewan** all have legislation or regulations that expressly impose obligations on employers to protect employees from violence in the workplace. Violence is defined in various ways, but typically includes threatening statements and conduct that gives the employer reasonable cause to believe that the employee is at risk of physical injury. The obligations typically require that employers conduct workplace risk or hazard assessments, which consider the risk of violence in their workplaces, create workplace harassment and violence policies, and provide training to employees on such policies.

Although the other jurisdictions do not have specific legislation on point, employers have a general duty under occupational health and safety legislation to ensure the safety of their employees.

EMPLOYER RESPONSIBILITY TO PREVENT HARASSMENT

Q. What Responsibility Does an Employer Have for Harassment Occurring in the Workplace?

A. Employers are responsible for providing their employees with a work environment that is free from harassment. Employers are, therefore, required by law to take steps to prevent and deal with harassment in the workplace.

Q. What Can an Employer Do To Prevent Harassment from Occurring in the Workplace?

A. In order to prevent harassment, employers should consider developing anti-harassment policies. Although this is a recommended practice in all jurisdictions, **Alberta**, **Manitoba**, **Ontario**, **Prince Edward Island**, **Saskatchewan**, and the **federal** jurisdiction require employers to have anti-harassment policies in their legislation or in their respective Human Rights Commission policy documents. Once these policies are introduced, employers must provide training on them to all of their supervisors and employees.

In addition to the applicable legal requirements, the Canadian Standards Association, the Bureau de normalisation du Québec, and the Mental Health Commission of Canada have together released a national voluntary standard for workplace mental health and safety. The "National Standard on Psychological Health and Safety in the

Workplace" is intended to help employers promote good mental health and prevent psychological harm for every employee. The standard includes guidance on policy statements that can be amended to reflect the employer's unique circumstances as well as recommendations regarding implementation.

To assist employers, we have provided the following checklist to assist employers in meeting their obligation to provide a harassment-free workplace.

CHECKLIST: CREATING A HARASSMENT-FREE WORKPLACE

❑ Have you made it clear that yours is a workplace where harassment will not be tolerated?

❑ Have you developed an anti-harassment policy?

❑ Have you communicated that policy to all employees?

❑ Have you ensured that all managers and supervisors understand their responsibility to provide a harassment-free work environment?

❑ Have you made sure that all employees understand the company policy and procedures for dealing with harassment?

❑ Do you promptly investigate and deal with all complaints of harassment?

❑ Do you appropriately discipline employees who are found to have harassed other employees?

❑ Do you provide protection and support for employees subject to harassment?

❑ Have you taken action to eliminate discriminatory jokes, posters, graffiti, and photos at the work site?

Q. What Should an Anti-Harassment Policy Contain?

A. Developing an anti-harassment policy can be a complex undertaking, and employers who are doing so should ensure that their legal counsel reviews their policy. As a starting point, however, **British Columbia**, **Manitoba**, **Ontario**, **Prince Edward Island**, and **Saskatchewan**, as well as the **federal** government, have set out the statements that anti-harassment policies must contain in their respective jurisdictions.

Many human right bodies also have helpful guidelines and policy statements to assist employers drafting notices to ensure that they comply with their obligations. For example, **Alberta**'s Human Rights Commission has developed a sample sexual harassment policy, the purpose of which is to demonstrate the employer's commitment to a workplace free of harassment and to educate employees on the nature of harassment and how to deal with the issue. The checklist below lists some of the items which should be included in an anti-harassment policy.

CHECKLIST: DEVELOPING AN EFFECTIVE HARASSMENT POLICY

A policy on workplace harassment should include:

❏ the definition of "harassment" applicable under the human rights and/or occupational health and safety legislation of that jurisdiction;

❏ a statement that every employee is entitled to a work environment free of harassment;

❏ a commitment by the employer to make every reasonable effort to ensure that no employee is subject to harassment;

❏ an explanation of how harassment complaints may be brought to the employer's attention;

❏ a detailed description of the procedures for investigating and resolving a complaint;

❏ a commitment to protect the identity of the parties wherever possible;

❏ a commitment to take disciplinary measures against employees who harass other employees, and a description of the types of discipline that may be imposed; and

❏ an explanation of the employee's right to file a complaint under human rights or occupational health and safety law.

DEALING WITH HARASSMENT

Q. What Should an Employee Do Who Finds Himself or Herself Being Harassed?

A. The first thing an employee who is being harassed should do is to tell the harasser to stop. It is essential that the employee make it clear that the behaviour is unwelcome and objectionable.

If the employee feels unable to approach the harasser, the employee should approach a member of management with whom he or she feels comfortable for help in communicating the problem to the harasser. If the behaviour does not stop, the employee should follow the reporting protocol in the employer's anti-harassment policy (if applicable) or contact any member of management with whom the employee feels comfortable, and report the harassment. We have provided a checklist below to assist employees who find themselves subject to harassment.

CHECKLIST: DEALING WITH HARASSMENT

An employee faced with harassment should consider taking the following steps:

❑ Let the harasser know that the behaviour is unwelcome. Make it clear that the behaviour must stop, whether by approaching the harasser in person or through an intermediary.

❑ Document the incidents related to the harassment and maintain a written record that includes the who, where, when, and how of the harassment, and the names of any witnesses.

❑ If the harassment does not stop, bring it to the attention of the employer, either through the procedure set out in the company harassment policy (if one exists), or by contacting a member of management.

❑ If these steps do not get appropriate results, depending on the circumstances, the employee should consider other courses of action, such as filing a grievance, contacting the police, filing a complaint or application to the appropriate human rights body, or filing a civil suit.

Q. If the Employer Will Not Help, What Other Options Are Available?

A. There are a number of avenues of assistance open to an employee if the employer is unwilling to provide assistance:

• An employee who is a member of a union may approach a union representative. The union may be able to intervene or file a grievance on the employee's behalf.

• If the employee has been subject to physical or sexual assault in the course of employment, the employee should contact the police.

• An employee may contact the local human rights commission or tribunal or the appropriate employment or labour standards branch (if applicable), which can provide advice and assistance. If appropriate, a complaint may be filed.

- The employee may be able to file a civil action in the courts and may contact legal counsel in order to assess the merits of his or her claim.

Q. What Should an Employer Do if a Complaint of Harassment Arises in the Workplace?

A. Complaints should be investigated promptly and in a manner that is fair and represents the rights of both the complainant and the alleged harasser. A thorough investigation will include interviews with the complainant, witnesses, and the alleged harasser to obtain all of the relevant facts, preparation of a written report of the investigation, and providing a timely report to the complainant of the results of the investigation.

Q. What Should an Employer Do if Harassment Is Found To Have Occurred in the Workplace?

A. If a complaint of harassment is found to be substantiated, the employer must assess what discipline is appropriate for the employee engaging in the harassment. The discipline may include a verbal or written reprimand, mandatory human rights training or counselling, suspension, or termination of employment with or without cause.

Q. What if Someone at Work Tries To Retaliate for the Filing of a Complaint about Harassment?

A. Retaliation against an employee for filing a complaint is prohibited under human rights or occupational health and safety legislation. If an employee does experience retaliation, this retaliation can be the subject of a further complaint, for which an alleged harasser or employer could be found liable.

THE ROLE OF HUMAN RIGHTS BODIES

Q. What Can a Human Rights Body Do To Help?

A. In all jurisdictions, once a complaint has been filed, the human rights body will contact the employer. With the exception of **British Columbia**, **Ontario**, and **Nunavut**, the human rights body will then investigate the complaint and, if possible, attempt to achieve a settlement. If no settlement is reached and there is sufficient evidence, the case will be referred to a tribunal for a hearing. At the hearing, both the employee and the alleged harasser will have the chance to tell their stories. The human rights body can assist the employee in presenting his or her case. If the employee's case is proven, the tribunal will make an order to redress the wrong done.

British Columbia, **Ontario**, and **Nunavut** have all introduced direct access models to their human rights systems. This means that, instead of a human rights commission investigating the complaint, the matter is referred directly to a hearing by the tribunal.

Q. What Kinds of Remedies Can Be Obtained from a Human Rights Tribunal?

A. The remedies available through a settlement or a tribunal order include:

- monetary damages for losses sustained as a result of the harassment. For example, if an employee was dismissed or forced to resign from employment because of harassment, compensation for loss of wages may be awarded;

- monetary damages for the injury to self-respect and the loss of dignity resulting from the harassment;

- reinstatement to the position if the harassment resulted in termination of employment or resignation;

- implementation of an anti-harassment policy, educational workshops for the employees, or other changes to the workplace;

- posting copies of human rights laws in the workplace; and

- reporting to the human rights body on a regular basis.

Chapter 14

EQUAL PAY AND PAY EQUITY

	Page
INTRODUCTION	214
EQUAL PAY	214
What Is "Equal Pay"?	214
Is Equal Pay Mandatory?	214
What Is "Similar or Substantially Similar Work"?	214
Are There Any Exceptions To Equal Pay Requirements?	215
Can Men's Rates of Pay Be Reduced To Ensure Equal Pay?	215
How Is Equal Pay Enforced?	215
Can Men File Equal Pay Complaints?	215
PAY EQUITY	215
What Is Pay Equity?	216
How Is Pay Equity Different from Equal Pay?	216
Is Pay Equity Mandatory?	216
Are All Employers in These Jurisdictions Required To Complete the Pay Equity Process?	217
What Are the Steps in Achieving Pay Equity?	217
How Is a Job Class Defined?	218
How Does One Determine Whether a Job Class Is "Female-Dominated" or "Male-Dominated"?	218
How Is the Value of a Job Determined?	219
How Is the Compensation for a Job Calculated?	219
How Are Male and Female Jobs Compared?	220
Are There Any Circumstances Where a Pay Disparity Is Acceptable?	220
What Must a Pay Equity Plan Contain?	221
What if Circumstances Change after a Pay Equity Plan Is Developed?	221
Can Compensation Be Reduced in Order To Achieve Pay Equity?	222
How Quickly Must a Pay Equity Plan Be Established or Adjustments in Compensation Determined?	222
How Quickly Must Pay Adjustments Be Made?	222
Are Employees Involved in the Pay Equity Process?	223
How Is Pay Equity Enforced?	223
PAY EQUITY AT A GLANCE CHART	224

INTRODUCTION

Equal pay and pay equity laws are legislative attempts to address the wage gap that persists between pay for male and female workers. Equal pay laws predate pay equity laws and are more widespread: they deal with the portion of the wage gap that is due to direct discrimination, where men and women performing the same or similar work are paid differently for it. Pay equity laws are more complex and controversial; they are described as addressing the effects of occupational segregation and the historical undervaluation of work done by women by requiring that female-dominated jobs be compensated in the same way as male-dominated jobs of the same value.

EQUAL PAY

Q. What Is "Equal Pay"?

A. The principle of equal pay requires that men and women be paid the same when they do the same work, or do work that is substantially similar. For example, under equal pay legislation, the pay of female nurses' aides has been compared to that of male hospital orderlies, and that of male janitors to female cleaners.

Proposed **Saskatchewan** employment standards legislation provides that an employer may not pay an employee a different rate of pay on the basis of any prohibited ground in *The Saskatchewan Human Rights Code*, unless permitted in the Code. **Quebec** equal pay legislation is also broader in scope than addressing only gender discrimination.

Q. Is Equal Pay Mandatory?

A. Every government in Canada has enacted legislation prohibiting employers from paying to employees of one sex wages on a scale different from that on which wages are paid to employees of the other sex in the same establishment, where the work performed by employees of each sex is the same or substantially the same.

Q. What Is "Similar or Substantially Similar Work"?

A. In assessing whether work is the same or substantially the same, one must determine whether the work requires substantially the same

- skill;
- effort;
- responsibility; and
- working conditions.

Work need not be "identical" in order to be considered to be "the same or substantially similar". Lack of intent to discriminate on the part of the employer is irrelevant.

Q. Are There Any Exceptions To Equal Pay Requirements?

A. Pay differences between men and women performing the same or substantially similar work will be justified if they are due to

- a seniority system or experience (depending on the jurisdiction);

- a merit system;

- (in most jurisdictions) quantity or quality of production; or

- (in some jurisdictions) a differential based on any factor other than sex.

Q. Can Men's Rates of Pay Be Reduced To Ensure Equal Pay?

A. No. Employers are prohibited from reducing an employee's wages to comply with equal pay requirements.

Q. How Is Equal Pay Enforced?

A. In some jurisdictions, the right to equal pay is protected under employment standards legislation; in others it is protected under human rights laws. In either case, employees who believe that their right to equal pay has been violated can file a complaint with either the employment standards or the human rights body, whichever is appropriate. The complaint will be investigated, and an order may be made to remedy any violation.

Q. Can Men File Equal Pay Complaints?

A. While it is more common for women to be paid less, when men and women are performing similar work, equal pay legislation applies equally to both sexes. If a man believes that he is being paid less than a woman for performing the same or substantially similar work, he can file a complaint, and his right to equal pay will be enforced.

PAY EQUITY

Because pay equity legislation is highly technical and detailed, and varies from jurisdiction to jurisdiction, the following questions and answers can provide only a general overview of, and introduction to, the subject matter.

Q. What Is Pay Equity?

A. The purpose of pay equity legislation is to ensure that employees who work in jobs that have historically been dominated by female workers, and therefore undervalued, receive compensation determined by the value of their work. The Ontario Pay Equity Hearings Tribunal describes the legislation as designed to address systemic gender discrimination by fairly compensating female workers for the value of their work. Pay equity requires employers to take proactive steps to compare the value of female-dominated jobs with that of male-dominated jobs and address any disparities in pay that become apparent.

Q. How Is Pay Equity Different from Equal Pay?

A. Pay equity legislation differs from equal pay legislation in two key respects:

- Equal pay legislation deals with pay inequality between employees who are performing the same or similar work. Pay equity legislation deals with pay inequality between employees who are performing *work of equal value* even where the work is dissimilar. Pay equity addresses the fact that women historically have been, and continue to be, concentrated in a few occupations, such as caregiving, service, and clerical and administrative work. Because women usually perform work that is different from that of men, equal pay legislation tends to have limited application. Pay equity has a much broader effect on gender-based discrimination in compensation.

- Pay equity legislation is *proactive*, rather than complaints-based. Under pay equity legislation, employers are obliged to take active steps to seek out and remove gender discrimination in compensation, rather than simply remedying problems that become apparent through complaints, as is the case with equal pay legislation. The Ontario Pay Equity Hearings Tribunal has stated that implementing pay equity is a highly specialized and integrative undertaking blending aspects of labour relations, compensation practices, employment law, and human rights.

Q. Is Pay Equity Mandatory?

A. In the public sector, pay equity is legislatively mandated in nine jurisdictions: **Manitoba**, **New Brunswick**, **Nova Scotia**, **Ontario**, **Prince Edward Island**, **Quebec**, the **Northwest Territories**, the **Yukon**, and the **federal** jurisdiction. As well, **British Columbia** and **Newfoundland and Labrador** have implemented administrative pay equity programs for their public services.

In the private sector, only the **federal** jurisdiction, **Ontario**, and **Quebec** have passed legislation requiring private sector employers to implement pay equity. The **federal** legislation differs from that in **Ontario** and **Quebec** in that it is complaints-based. This chapter addresses only the private sector legislation.

Q. Are All Employers in These Jurisdictions Required To Complete the Pay Equity Process?

A. The **federal** legislation applies to all **federally regulated** employers. However, in **Ontario**, the *Pay Equity Act* does not apply to private sector employers with fewer than 10 employees. As well, private sector employers with more than nine but fewer than 100 employees have different and less onerous pay equity obligations than do larger, private sector employers. Specifically, while they are still required to achieve pay equity, they are not required to prepare and post pay equity plans. As well, their mandatory schedules for payment of compensation adjustments are different. Similarly, in **Quebec**, employers with fewer than 10 employees are exempted from the requirements of the legislation — although they may still be required to file a report on pay equity if they employ at least six employees. Employers with more than 49 but fewer than 100 employees, are exempted from the requirement to set up a pay equity committee. Employers with at least 10 but fewer than 50 employees, are not required to establish a pay equity plan, although they are still required to determine and make the adjustments to compensation necessary to achieve pay equity.

Q. What Are the Steps in Achieving Pay Equity?

A. The pay equity process is detailed, technical, and complex, and varies somewhat between jurisdictions. However, the steps outlined below are the basic components of a pay equity process.

- **Identify the unit for which the pay equity plan will be developed.** In some cases this will be self-evident. However, where the employer is large and geographically scattered, or where there is a mix of unionized and non-union employees, this issue becomes more complex. It is an important issue, however, as it determines the types of comparisons that can be made to achieve pay equity.

- **Identify the job classes.** Positions within an organization must be divided into job classes, to determine the units for comparison purposes.

- **Identify female and male job classes.** A variety of criteria may be used to determine whether a job class is "female" or "male" for comparison purposes.

- **Assess the value of jobs.** The value of each of the job classes identified must be assessed using a gender-neutral job evaluation system and the criteria set out in the legislation.

- **Compare male and female job classes.** Various methods of comparison are set out in different jurisdictions, including the job-to-job approach, the wage-line approach and proxy comparisons.

- **Identify where compensation adjustments are required.** The comparison between male and female job classes will indicate where there are disparities in compensation. Not all of these disparities will violate pay equity legislation. The employer must determine where disparities exist that must be corrected.

- **Develop a pay equity plan when required by law.** The pay equity plan sets out how unjustified differences in compensation that were discovered through the pay equity process will be remedied.

- **Make compensation increases.** Generally employers are permitted to make the necessary compensation adjustments over a period of years.

Q. How Is a Job Class Defined?

A. In **Ontario**, a job class consists of those positions within an organization that have similar duties and responsibilities, have similar qualifications, are filled by similar recruiting procedures, and have the same compensation schedule, salary grade, or range of salary grades. A job class may consist of a single position, or a single person doing a job. The definition in **Quebec** is the same, except that it does not include consideration of recruitment procedures. Under the **federal** legislation, jobs or occupational groups may be compared.

Q. How Does One Determine Whether a Job Class Is "Female-Dominated" or "Male-Dominated"?

A. The legislation sets out various criteria for whether a job class is a male or female one:

- **Gender predominance.** Perhaps the most obvious criterion is the percentage of employees of each gender in the job class. In **Quebec**, if 60% or more of the positions in the job class are held by employees of the same sex, that will generally be the gender of the job class. In **Ontario**, if 60% of the job class is female, it will be considered female-dominated, but a job class will only be considered male-dominated if 70% of the members are male. In the **federal** jurisdiction, the gender predominance test is 70% for both female and male job classes if the occupational group has fewer than 100 members, 60% if the occupational group has from 100 to 500 members, and 55% if the occupational group has more than 500 members.

- **Historical incumbency.** This factor may be used to determine the gender of a job class in **Ontario** and **Quebec**.

- **Gender stereotypes.** This factor may be used to determine the gender of a job class in **Ontario** and **Quebec**.

- **Comparison to the total workforce.** This factor is only permitted in **Quebec**. In applying this factor, one considers the difference between the rate of representation of women or men in the job class and their rate of representation in the total workforce.

Q. How Is the Value of a Job Determined?

A. The criteria that must be used for assessing the value of a job are:

- **Skill**, including intellectual and physical qualifications acquired by experience, training, education, or natural ability.

- **Effort**, including both physical and intellectual effort.

- **Responsibility**, for example, for technical, financial, or human resources.

- **Working conditions**, which could include both physical and psychological conditions, such as noise, temperature, isolation, physical danger, health hazards, and stress.

The system used for assessing these criteria for the various job classes must be gender neutral.

Q. How Is the Compensation for a Job Calculated?

A. Although the definition of the pay rate for a job class differs between jurisdictions, in calculating the wages for a job class for the purpose of making a comparison, the following should be considered:

- salaries, commissions, vacation pay, and bonuses;

- flexible pay, including merit and performance pay, and income from gain-sharing schemes;

- reasonable value for board, rent, housing, and lodging;

- employer contributions to pension funds or plans, long-term disability plans, and all forms of health insurance plans;

- benefits that are not equally available to all job classes subject to comparison; and

- any other remuneration received directly or indirectly from an individual's employer.

Q. How Are Male and Female Jobs Compared?

A. There are a number of methods of comparing male and female job classes. Each of the jurisdictions requires different methods of comparison.

- **Job-to-job.** This is the most common type of comparison. In it, each female job class is compared with a male job class of equal or comparable value. This method of comparison is used in **Ontario**, **Quebec** (also called an individual comparison), and the **federal** jurisdiction.

- **Wage line (proportional value).** This method requires employers to look at the relationship between the value of the work performed and the pay received by male job classes and apply the same relationship to setting pay for female job classes. One may draw a male wage line and compare female jobs to the line or use regression analysis. This method of comparison is used in **Ontario**, **Quebec** (also called an overall comparison), and the **federal** jurisdiction. The proportional value method of comparison is required of employers in **Ontario** that have female job classes with no appropriate male comparators under the job-to-job system. The **federal** jurisdiction requires the use of a wage curve to compare occupational groups.

- **Proxy.** This method of comparison, required only of **Ontario's** broader public sector and only where it has been determined that pay equity cannot be achieved through either job-to-job or proportional value comparisons (typically due to a lack of male-dominated job classes), requires female job classes in public sector workplaces to be compared with similar female job classes in another public sector establishment.

Q. Are There Any Circumstances Where a Pay Disparity Is Acceptable?

A. Not all disparities between compensation for male and female job classes can be attributed to systemic gender discrimination, and pay equity legislation sets out permissible differences in compensation.

- seniority (in **Ontario**, **Quebec**, and the **federal** jurisdiction);

- performance ratings (in **Ontario** and the **federal** jurisdiction);

- red circling (in **Ontario**, **Quebec**, and the **federal** jurisdiction);

- rehabilitation assignments (in the **federal** jurisdiction) or special arrangements for a handicapped person (in **Quebec**);

- demotion pay or phased-in reduction of pay (in the **federal** jurisdiction);

- temporary training assignments (in the **federal** jurisdiction, **Ontario**, and **Quebec**);

- skills shortage (in **Ontario** and **Quebec**) or an internal labour shortage (the **federal** jurisdiction);

- regional rates (in **Quebec** and the **federal** jurisdiction); and

- temporary, casual, or seasonal nature of a position (**Quebec** and **Ontario**).

Q. What Must a Pay Equity Plan Contain?

A. The pay equity plan sets out how differences in compensation that violate pay equity legislation will be remedied. Only **Ontario** and **Quebec** provide detailed requirements for the contents of a pay equity plan. Generally speaking, a pay equity plan should contain:

- a description of the establishment for which the pay equity plan has been developed;

- an identification of all of the job classes that formed the basis of comparisons, including which were female and which were male;

- a description of the gender-neutral system used to evaluate job classes and the development of a value determination procedure;

- the determination of the value of the job classes, the results of the comparisons between them and the valuation of differences in compensation;

- an identification of those job classes where permissible differences in compensation existed;

- for those job classes where differences in compensation exist which are not permissible, a description of how the compensation will be increased to achieve pay equity; and

- a schedule for the payout of compensation increases.

Q. What if Circumstances Change after a Pay Equity Plan Is Developed?

A. Employers are required to maintain as well as implement pay equity. Thus, where there are significant changes in circumstances, employers must update or revise their pay equity programs. Events that should trigger an update of the pay equity plan include the creation or elimination of job classes, changes to the value of job classes, changes in the gender predominance of job classes, or changes to job comparison systems. Large-scale revisions to the plan may become necessary when a business is sold, or there are other important changes in circumstances. In **Quebec**, the sale or transfer of an enterprise has no effect upon obligations relative to adjustments in compensation, a pay equity plan, or a pay equity audit, which are binding on the new employer. Under the **Ontario** legislation, a buyer of a business is required to pay the compensation increases that were to be made under the seller's pay equity plan on the payment dates set out in the plan. If, because of the sale, either the seller's or buyer's pay equity plan is no longer appropriate, a new pay equity plan must be prepared.

Q. Can Compensation Be Reduced in Order To Achieve Pay Equity?

A. No. Employers are strictly prohibited from reducing the compensation payable to any employee, or the rate of compensation for any position, in order to achieve pay equity.

Q. How Quickly Must a Pay Equity Plan Be Established or Adjustments in Compensation Determined?

A. In **Quebec**, employers will generally have to determine the adjustments in compensation or the pay equity plan within four years after becoming subject to pay equity legislation, i.e., when they first employ 10 or more employees. **Ontario** employers in existence when the legislation was passed had a phase-in period for making the required pay increases. Employers which hired their tenth employee after 1988 must come into immediate compliance.

Q. How Quickly Must Pay Adjustments Be Made?

A. In order to reduce the financial burden on employers of making compensation increases, employers are permitted to phase in adjustments over a period of years. In **Quebec**, employers must make the first compensation adjustments by the date on which the plan was completed, or the date on which adjustments in compensation were determined, and will generally have a period of four years after that date to complete the payments. However, for employers to which pay equity legislation applied on March 12, 2009 and who had to determine the adjustments in compensation no later than December 31, 2010, the payment of the adjustments in compensation could not be spread over a period of time, subject to certain exceptions. In **Ontario**, employers in existence on January 1, 1988 were required to set aside at least 1% of their total **Ontario** payroll for the previous year for making pay equity adjustments. New employers have no phase-in period and must have pay equity in place when the tenth employee is hired in the province.

Q. Are Employees Involved in the Pay Equity Process?

A. Where employees are unionized in **Ontario**, they are entitled to participate in the pay equity process through their bargaining agents. In **Quebec**, participation of a bargaining agent in the process depends on the size of the workforce. Non-union employees in **Ontario** have an opportunity to review and submit comments on a pay equity plan before it is deemed approved. As well, if employees submit a complaint regarding the contents of the plan to the Pay Equity Commission within 30 days after the end of the review period, the plan will not be deemed approved until the complaint has been investigated and resolved.

Quebec has made extensive provision in its legislation for the involvement of employees in the development of pay equity. Where an employer has 100 or more employees, a pay equity committee representative of employees must be established, and this pay equity committee is entitled to participate in the establishment of a pay equity plan. After the posting requirements have been fulfilled, employees will also be given the opportunity to request additional information from or make observations to the pay equity committee or the employer with respect to the pay equity plan or the adjustments in compensation regardless of the size of the workforce.

Q. How Is Pay Equity Enforced?

A. In the **federal** jurisdiction, pay equity is enforced through the Canadian Human Rights Commission. In **Ontario** and **Quebec**, pay equity is enforced through special pay equity bodies. Generally speaking, where pay equity legislation is not being complied with, a complaint may be filed with the appropriate government body, and an officer will investigate the matter. Where a failure to comply is found, an order may be issued. In **Ontario**, this may include the imposition of a pay equity plan. **Ontario** also has a Monitoring Program under which employers are proactively contacted by the Pay Equity Commission to determine their pay equity compliance. The Monitoring Program initially focused on various industry sectors and geographic territories. However, it is currently focusing on employers who are flagged as part of the Wage Gap Program. The Wage Gap Program, launched in 2011, is designed to determine whether gender-based wage gaps have decreased. The Pay Equity Commission is planning to contact all Ontario employers with at least 10 employees. The pilot project canvassed employers with 500 or more employees. Phase 2 looked at employers with 250 to 499 employees, and in late 2013, the goal is to contact employers with 100 to 249 employees. The Pay Equity Commission is excluding unionized employee data. If an employer does not respond by the deadline, or the wage data indicates the presence of a gender-based wage gap, the employer is referred to a Review Officer.

PAY EQUITY AT A GLANCE CHART

	Federal	Manitoba	New Brunswick	Nova Scotia	Ontario	Prince Edward Island	Quebec	Yukon
Legislation	*Canadian Human Rights Act* (1978)	*Pay Equity Act* (1984)	*Pay Equity Act, 2009*	*Pay Equity Act* (1988)	*Pay Equity Act* (1987)	*Pay Equity Act* (1988)	*Pay Equity Act* (1996)	*Human Rights Act* (1987)
Model	Complaint-based	Proactive	Proactive	Proactive	Proactive	Proactive	Proactive	Complaint-based
Coverage	Federal Public Sector, Crown Corporations, Federally Regulated Industries	Public & Broader Public Sectors (except municipalities, school boards)	Public & Broader Public Sector	Government, Crown corporations, hospitals & school boards, universities, municipalities & other Broader Public Sector	Public & Broader Public Sector, Private Sector	Public & Broader Public Sectors	Public & Private Sectors	Public Sector
Approach	Wage Line/Job-to-Job	Wage Line	Wage Line	Job-to-Job	Wage Line/Job-to-Job/Proxy comparison in broader public sector	Job-to-Job	Wage Line/Job-to-Job	Job-to-Job
Gender Predominance	Staggered percentages, equally applicable to female & male	70% female/male	60% female/male (historical incumbency)	60% female/male	60% female, 70% male (historical incumbency, gender stereotypes)	60% female/male (historical incumbency, gender stereotypes)	60% female/male (historical incumbency, gender stereotypes, total workforce)	Not defined

	Federal	Manitoba	New Brunswick	Nova Scotia	Ontario	Prince Edward Island	Quebec	Yukon
Establishment	Common personnel and wage policy	N/A	N/A	N/A	Geographic	N/A	Not specified	Not specified
Incumbency Rule	No	10 employees in a job class	10 employees in a job classification	10 employees in a job class	No	No	No	N/A
Exceptions	Performance ratings, seniority, red circling, rehabilitation assignments, demotion procedure, training assignments, internal labour shortage, regional wage rates	Factors justifying pay differences may be negotiated	Seniority, temporary training, merit pay plan, red-circling, temp skills shortage	Seniority, temporary training, merit pay, skills shortage	Seniority, red circling, temp training, skills shortage, merit pay	Performance appraisal, seniority, skills shortage	Seniority, temp training, regional rates, skills shortage, red circling, temp/casual work, special arrangement for a handicapped person	Not specified
Agency	Canadian Human Rights Commission	Pay Equity Bureau	Pay Equity Bureau	Pay Equity Commission	Pay Equity Commission	Pay Equity Bureau	Commission de l'équité salariale	Yukon Human Rights Commission

Chapter 15

EMPLOYMENT EQUITY

Page

INTRODUCTION 227
UNDERSTANDING EMPLOYMENT EQUITY 228
    What Is Employment Equity? 228
    How Is Employment Equity Different from Human Rights Legislation? 228
    Doesn't Employment Equity Violate Human Rights Laws? 228
    Is Employment Equity Mandatory? 229
IMPLEMENTING EMPLOYMENT EQUITY 230
    What Must an Employer Do To Implement Employment Equity? 230
    How Is an Employment Equity Survey Carried Out? 231
    What Must Be Reviewed in an Employment Systems Review? 232
    What Criteria Are Used To Evaluate Employment Systems? 233
    What Must an Employment Equity Plan Contain? 233
    What Is a Numerical Goal? 233
    How Long Does an Employment Equity Plan Last? 234
    How Is Employment Equity Enforced? 234

INTRODUCTION

Employment equity is a response to the employment issues that face designated groups or others disadvantaged in employment. Generally, in Canada, the designated groups are women, members of visible minorities, Aboriginals, and people with disabilities. Although anti-discrimination legislation has been in place for decades, the Royal Commission on Equality in Employment found that these four groups in particular continue to face higher rates of unemployment, underemployment, and employment discrimination, including systemic discrimination. This has been identified as a labour force issue, as members of these groups will make up an increasing proportion of the labour force as time goes on. Mandatory or voluntary employment equity initiatives are one response to these labour force issues.

UNDERSTANDING EMPLOYMENT EQUITY

Q. What Is Employment Equity?

A. Employment equity is both a process and a result. In a workplace where employment equity has been achieved, ideally all barriers to equal participation and treatment of employees will have been removed, with the result that the internal composition of the workplace will eventually mirror the makeup of the population from which the organization recruits, and the organization's policies, procedures and practices will work equally well for all employees, including those from the four designated groups: women, members of visible minorities, Aboriginal people, and people with disabilities. Employment equity is this state of equality of opportunity, as well as the process by which it is achieved. The Royal Commission described employment equity as a strategy designed to obliterate the present and residual effects of competition for employment opportunities to those arbitrarily excluded. It is otherwise known as affirmative action.

Q. How Is Employment Equity Different from Human Rights Legislation?

A. The enforcement of human rights legislation is complaints-based. Employment equity requires employers to take positive, proactive measures to remove barriers to equality, rather than simply respond to instances of discrimination when they become apparent. Employment equity requires employers to make adjustments to their employment systems to ensure that systemic discrimination does not occur. To some degree, employment equity has evolved as a response to the types of subtle, complex discrimination that were difficult to tackle through human rights legislation.

Q. Doesn't Employment Equity Violate Human Rights Laws?

A. While the creation of a level playing field is not controversial, employment equity goes a lot further. It also requires special programs to be put into place to deal with issues specific to members of the four designated groups and to set numerical goals to improve the representation of these groups. These are not quotas imposed by governmental agencies. Instead, they are essentially quotas established by employers, based on external labour force data and internal opportunities. As a result, it is sometimes perceived that employment equity discriminates against persons who are not members of the designated groups, and violates the anti-discrimination provisions of human rights laws.

In fact, human rights legislation across the country specifically permits employers to undertake special programs to remedy conditions of disadvantage experienced by particular groups. The intent of employment equity-type programs is in harmony with the purpose of Canadian and provincial human rights legislation. In fact, the *Canadian Charter of Rights and Freedoms* (subsection 15(2)) specifically permits special programs for disadvantaged individuals or groups, including those disadvantaged because of race, national, or ethnic origin, colour, religion, sex, age, or disability.

Q. Is Employment Equity Mandatory?

A. Although employment equity programs are permissible across the country, they are mandatory in only a few limited circumstances described below.

Federally regulated employers are required to implement employment equity under the *Employment Equity Act*, which was passed in 1986 and has been substantially revised since. Employees covered by the federal *Employment Equity Act* include not only persons in the federal public service, but those in industries regulated by the federal government, such as banking, aerospace, nuclear power, and telecommunications.

Quebec's *Charter of Human Rights and Freedoms* (section 86 *et seq.*) also specifically permits special programs for disadvantaged individuals or groups. The *Act respecting equal access to employment in public bodies* came into effect on April 1, 2001. This Act legislates employment equity for certain groups, namely: women, those with handicaps, Aboriginal peoples, persons who are members of visible minorities because of their race or the colour of their skin, and persons whose mother tongue is neither French nor English and who belong to a group other than the Aboriginal peoples group or the visible minorities group. The legislation applies to public bodies if they employ more than 100 employees for a continuous period of six months in each of two consecutive years, bodies where a majority of the members or directors are appointed by the Quebec government or whose capital stock forms part of the domain of the State, the educational sector and related institutions, health and social services institutions, the Sûreté du Québec, and municipal and related bodies. The Act does not apply to private sector corporations.

As well, two contractors programs exist which make employment equity mandatory for suppliers of goods and services.

Under the Federal Contractors Program, contractors who employ 100 or more employees, and who wish to bid on goods or services contracts, standing offers, or a supply arrangement for the **federal** government worth $1 million or more, must sign an Agreement To Implement Employment Equity. The requirements under the Federal Contractors Program are similar to those under the **federal**

Employment Equity Act, including the same four designated groups. While the Federal Contractors Program is not legislated, it is mandatory for companies wishing to do a certain value in business with the federal government. Until 2012, the **federal** *Employment Equity Act* required the Federal Contractors Program requirements to be equivalent to the **federal** Act. However, this requirement was repealed and, in June 2013, a streamlined Federal Contractors Program was announced. The redesigned Program sets out four requirements the contractor must fulfill:

- collect workforce information through a self-identification questionnaire and employee survey with an 80% response rate;

- complete a workforce analysis at least once every three years that compares internal workforce representation against external census data;

- establish short-term goals (which cover a period of one to three years) and long-term goals; and

- make reasonable progress and reasonable efforts.

The **Quebec** government has a similar contract compliance program, applying to both contractors and subcontractors that have more than 100 employees and bid on provincial government grants or contracts worth at least $100,000. Employers who fall under the program are required to identify and eliminate discrimination for the four target groups: women, visible minorities, Aboriginal peoples, and people with disabilities.

Finally, it should also be noted that human rights tribunals have the power to order employment equity-type measures as a remedy in cases where it seems necessary to combat pervasive systemic discrimination. Although this is rare, it has occurred in a few high-profile cases.

IMPLEMENTING EMPLOYMENT EQUITY

Q. What Must an Employer Do To Implement Employment Equity?

A. Generally speaking, the implementation of an employment equity program involves the following steps:

- **Commit:** Organizations undertaking employment equity must obtain and demonstrate senior-level commitment to the process.

- **Consult:** Employment equity is intended to be a process of organizational change, in which employees fully participate. As a result, employers are required to consult with employee representatives regarding the communication, preparation, implementation and maintenance of employment equity. Where the workforce is unionized, this process of consultation needs to include the union as the employee representative.

- **Communicate:** Employers must provide information to their employees explaining the purpose of employment equity and keeping employees informed about the measures which have been taken or will be taken to implement employment equity.

- **Survey:** Every employer must collect information on, and conduct an analysis of its workforce, in order to determine the degree of under-representation of persons in designated groups in each occupational group in the workforce. This information must be obtained by a confidential workforce survey.

- **Review:** Employers must conduct a review of all of their employment systems, policies, and practices, in order to identify employment barriers against persons in designated groups. The systems, policies, and practices reviewed must include those relating to recruitment, selection and hiring of employees, development and training, promotion, retention and termination of employees, and reasonable accommodation of the special needs of members of the designated groups.

- **Plan:** Based on the information collected from the workforce survey and the employment systems review, each employer must develop an employment equity plan indicating how the employer will remove barriers, institute positive policies and practices to correct the effects of past discrimination, and set goals for correcting under-representation of designated groups in the workforce.

- **Monitor:** The implementation of employment equity must be monitored.

- **Update:** The employment equity plan must be updated on a regular basis, to ensure continued progress towards an equitable workplace.

Q. How Is an Employment Equity Survey Carried Out?

A. Statistical information on the makeup of an employer's workforce is essential to an employment equity initiative. This information allows the employer to identify the equity issues that are most pressing. For instance, if the data reveals that members of the designated groups are well-represented in the organization, but concentrated in low-paying, low-prestige positions, the types of initiatives that are necessary will be different from those required where the issue is one of low representation. As well, quantitative information allows employers to measure the success of their initiatives, and determine whether progress is being made towards the achievement of employment equity.

Statistical information on the makeup of an employer's workforce is gathered through a confidential, organization-wide survey of all employees. The **federal** *Employment Equity Act* sets out the precise form of questions to be used. Basically, employees must be asked if they are members of any of the four designated groups. While the employer must ensure that all employees have the opportunity to complete a questionnaire, self-identification must be voluntary. If employees do not wish to complete a questionnaire, they may not be compelled to do so and the employer is not permitted to provide the data. Confidentiality of the responses to the questionnaire must be stringently protected.

Once the questionnaires have been completed and compiled, the employer must compare the internal workforce composition against the available external workforce. Information on the representation of members of designated groups in various sectors of the labour market is obtained from the **federal** government. Employers must compare internal and external availability for each of a number of occupational groups. **Federal** legislation also requires employers to track the salary ranges for employees and the degree of representation of designated group members in each range.

Q. What Must Be Reviewed in an Employment Systems Review?

A. The employment systems review should provide insight into the reasons for the representation patterns indicated by the workforce survey and analysis. Employers are required to review all policies, practices and procedures relating to employment systems, whether these are written or unwritten, formal or informal. The systems reviewed should include those for:

- recruiting, selecting, and hiring employees;

- promotion and the movement of employees between occupational groups;

- training and development;

- termination of employment, including dismissals, resignations, and retirement; and

- accommodation of the special needs of members of the designated groups.

Q. What Criteria Are Used To Evaluate Employment Systems?

A. The **federal** government has developed the following criteria for evaluating each of the employment systems listed above:

- Is it legal? For example, does it comply with human rights, employment standards, and health and safety legislation?

- Does it have an adverse impact? Does the employment policy or practice affect some employees more than others for non-job-related reasons?

- Is it job-related? Is the policy or practice reasonable and related to the job? Does a test accurately predict performance on the job? Are selection criteria based upon *bona fide* occupational requirements?

- Is it applied consistently? Do all employees, whether from the four designated groups or not, receive consistent treatment?

- Can an accommodation be made if the policy or practice is otherwise valid but tends to exclude designated group members?

Q. What Must an Employment Equity Plan Contain?

A. The employment equity plan must contain the following components:

- the measures that will be taken to remove the barriers identified in the employment systems review, together with a timetable for completion;

- a description of the positive policies and practices that the employer will institute for the hiring, training, promotion, and retention of members of the designated groups, in order to correct the under-representation identified by the workforce survey, with a timetable for the implementation of these policies and practices; and

- where the workforce survey has shown under-representation, short-term numerical goals for the hiring and promotion of members of the designated groups, in order to increase their representation, and longer term goals for improving representation.

The employment equity plan must constitute reasonable progress towards the implementation of employment equity.

Q. What Is a Numerical Goal?

A. Numerical goals are designed to make the employer's workforce more representative of the community from which it draws its employees. A numerical goal is the proportion of job openings in each occupational group that are targeted for the members of a particular designated group. Job openings may include new hires, promotions, and transfers from other occupational groups within the company. These goals are set by the employer, not by the government. In setting numerical goals, employers consider:

- the degree to which members of each designated group are under-represented in each occupational group within the organization;

- the availability of qualified members of the designated groups within the employer's workforce and in the Canadian workforce;

- the anticipated growth or reduction of the employer's workforce during the period in question; and

- the anticipated turnover of employees within the employer's workforce during the period in question.

Q. How Long Does an Employment Equity Plan Last?

A. For **federally** regulated employers, an employment equity plan may last from one to three years. The plan must be periodically reviewed and revised.

Q. How Is Employment Equity Enforced?

A. The obligations of **federally** regulated employers under the *Employment Equity Act* are enforced by the Canadian Human Rights Commission. Compliance officers have the power to conduct audits of employers, and for that purpose, have powers of search and entry. Where an employer is not in compliance, the officer will first attempt to ensure compliance through negotiation and written undertakings. Where this approach fails, the officer may issue a written direction to an employer. Where an employer fails to comply with a direction, the direction may be confirmed by the Human Rights Tribunal and the Tribunal may issue an order. Violations of the Act are an offence and may lead to financial penalties.

The government's annual summary report, the annual reports filed by employers under the Act, and the ratings given to each employer are published annually and posted on the government website at **www.labour.gc.ca/eng/standards_equity/eq/emp/tools/index. shtml#ar**.

The obligations of **Quebec** public sector employers, under the **Quebec** *Act respecting equal access to employment in public bodies*, are enforced by the Quebec Human Rights Commission.

The **Quebec** contractors program is enforced by the Quebec Human Rights Commission. Employers are required to submit regular reports to the Quebec Human Rights Commission and those which fail to comply with the program may lose the certificate needed to bid on **Quebec** government contracts.

The Federal Contractors Program is administered by Human Resources and Skills Development Canada ("HRSDC"). A compliance assessment will be conducted by Labour Program Officers after a contractor has been in the program for one year. The employer will be asked to provide its self-identification questionnaire, survey response and return rates, workforce analysis, and a completed goal-setting template for short- and long-term goals. A third-year compliance assessment requires the employer to submit an updated workforce analysis, updated goals, and an achievement table. A non-compliant contractor is placed on the Federal Contractors Program Limited Eligibility To Bid List and loses the right to bid on **federal** government goods and services contracts, standing offers, and supply arrangements of any value. A contractor that chooses to withdraw from the program is treated in the same way. All companies that have signed up for the program are publicly listed on the HRSDC website at **www.labour.gc.ca/eng/standards_equity/eq/emp/fcp/index.shtml**.

Chapter 16

ENFORCEMENT OF EMPLOYMENT STANDARDS

Page

INTRODUCTION 237

How Are Employment Standards Enforced? 238

THE EMPLOYMENT STANDARDS COMPLAINT PROCESS 238

What Is the Process for Filing a Complaint to the Government? 238

What Are the Powers of the Investigating Officer? 239

What Defences Are Available to the Employer? 239

What Happens if the Complaint Is Not Resolved Through the Investigation
    Process? 239

How Do the Courts Get Involved in Employment Standards Complaints? 240

CLASS ACTION 241

What Is a Class Action? 241

INDIVIDUAL LIABILITY 242

Can Individuals Be Held Liable for Employment Standards Amounts? 242

EMPLOYER COMPLIANCE 242

What Can an Employer Do To Ensure That It Is Compliant with the Employment
    Standards Legislation? 242

STATUTORY ENFORCEMENT SCHEMES CHART 244

INTRODUCTION

Employers in Canada are expected to comply with the applicable employment standards legislation on what is, in a sense, a voluntary basis. In other words, there is no requirement to certify to the government that one is complying; there are no reports required and no regular pattern of government inspections. However, there is also a wide array of enforcement mechanisms available to deal with cases of suspected non-compliance.

Q. How Are Employment Standards Enforced?

A. Employment standards legislation can be enforced through a number of different approaches. The most common is the filing of a complaint by an employee, former employee, or group of employees to the ministry responsible for employment standards in that jurisdiction, typically the Ministry of Labour. From time-to-time, various government agencies may also conduct payroll audits of employers, depending on government resources and government direction and policy.

Employment standards complaints can end up in the court system as well, either as part of an individual lawsuit or a class action. While this is relatively rare, employers can also be prosecuted criminally in the courts for a failure to comply with employment standards legislation. The reason this is fairly rare is that employment standards legislation is described as *remedial legislation*, designed to ensure that employees are treated fairly and in accordance with the law, rather than seeking to punish the employer. Remedial legislation is given a broad interpretation by tribunals, and exclusions and exemptions will be read very narrowly. Having said that, some provinces, such as **British Columbia**, **Manitoba**, and **Ontario**, have administrative penalties, much like fines, that increase if the employer has previously breached the legislation.

In a unionized workplace, while this varies from jurisdiction to jurisdiction, a failure to comply with employment standards legislation may also end up as part of a grievance that goes through the arbitration process.

THE EMPLOYMENT STANDARDS COMPLAINT PROCESS

Q. What Is the Process for Filing a Complaint to the Government?

A. An employee, former employee, or a group of employees may contact or visit the applicable government office and file a complaint, which may trigger an investigation by the Ministry. The process varies from jurisdiction to jurisdiction, and within a jurisdiction the process and resources will vary over time, depending on the particular government currently in office. An official, generally known as an officer or an inspector, will usually investigate the complaint to determine whether it is well-founded. At times, the review of one individual complaint can lead to a broader investigation by the Ministry if a problem is viewed as a company-wide issue.

Q. What Are the Powers of the Investigating Officer?

A. In general, the inspector, investigator, or Employment Standards Officer has the power to enter the workplace, inspect records, interview individuals, and make copies of records. At the end of the investigation, the officer generally has the power to make a payment order against the employer where the complaint is well-founded.

It is important to bear in mind that under most employment standards legislation it is a breach of the *Employment Standards Act* or even an offence to refuse to co-operate with the officer or refuse to assist him or her.

Q. What Defences Are Available to the Employer?

A. Where the legislation has been breached, it is not a defence for an employer to establish that the violation of the law was inadvertent or unintentional. As noted above, this is remedial legislation and the intention of the employer is not relevant.

There may be certain technical defences available to an employer, however. There are generally time limits for the filing of an employment standards complaint, and there are often limitations on the amount of money that can be recovered. **Ontario**, for example, has an unusual provision in its legislation that limits a wage order by an Employment Standards Officer to $10,000 per employee. Where an officer issues an order to pay in **Ontario**, there is also a fee for administrative costs equal to the greater of $100 or 10% of the compensation being ordered.

While the limitation period covering the period for which wages may be recovered is typically six to 12 months, in the case of vacation pay, the period is often 22 to 36 months because vacation pay is earned in one year and taken in the following year.

Q. What Happens if the Complaint Is Not Resolved Through the Investigation Process?

A. At the end of the investigation, if the officer feels that the complaint is well-founded, the officer can issue an order of compensation or, in some cases, an order of reinstatement (for example, where someone is dismissed during maternity leave). If the employer or employee objects to the resolution by the officer, either party can pursue an administrative appeal process. This varies from province to province, but many jurisdictions have a referee hearing (*Canada Labour Code*), or a standing Employment Standards Tribunal (for example, **British Columbia**). At this point, the process becomes more formalized and evidence is entered through documentation and witnesses.

While the parties may wish to have legal representation, it is not always necessary.

Q. How Do the Courts Get Involved in Employment Standards Complaints?

A. First, if an order from the administrative process described above is not complied with, it is generally possible to file the order with a court to have it enforced as if it were a decision of the court.

Second, employees sometimes claim for employment standards amounts during lawsuits, usually a wrongful dismissal or constructive dismissal case. For example, an employee suing for damages for wrongful dismissal may include a claim for statutory termination pay, or statutory severance pay and statutory vacation pay. The **Ontario** *Employment Standards Act, 2000* provides that, where an employee commences a civil proceeding against the employer under the Act, notice of the proceeding must be served on the Director of Employment Standards on or before the date that the matter is set down for trial. However, the **Ontario** legislation precludes an employee from filing an employment standards complaint if the employee has commenced a court proceeding with respect to a failure to pay wages, for wrongful dismissal, or a failure to comply with the benefit plan provisions of the Act. Similarly, an employee who has commenced a court action for wrongful dismissal is precluded from filing an employment standards complaint alleging an entitlement to termination pay or severance pay if the complaint relates to the same termination or severance of employment.

In a decision issued in 2008, the British Columbia Court of Appeal in *Macaraeg v. E. Care Contact Centers Ltd.* (2008 CLLC ¶ 210-021), held that the minimum standards provided in the *Employment Standards Act* cannot be considered implied terms of an employment contract. Therefore, an employee is not entitled to commence a civil action for an amount such as statutory vacation pay. The Court held that the Act lays out a comprehensive scheme which an employee can pursue to receive an appropriate remedy. In *Macaraeg*, the employment agreement did not address overtime pay. The plaintiff sought to sue for overtime pay, saying that the minimum standards of the employment standards legislation must be implied to be part of her employment agreement. The Court held that the only appropriate way to enforce rights provided under the *Employment Standards Act* of **British Columbia** is the administrative scheme set out in the Act itself. (Leave to appeal was denied, Supreme Court of Canada, October 2008.) Similarly, the issue of whether entitlements established under the employment standards legislation are enforceable at common law has not yet been decided definitively in **Nova Scotia**. In many other provinces, there is a presumption that employment standards rights are an implied term of every employment agreement.

An employment standards complaint can also come before the criminal courts should the Ministry of Labour choose to prosecute the employer for an offence under the Act. In such a case, the offence is generally punishable by a fine and, at times, directors, officers, or employees who directed the corporation in committing the offence may also be fined personally.

Finally, there have also been class action lawsuits by employees seeking to enforce compliance with the employment standards legislation.

CLASS ACTION

Q. What Is a Class Action?

A. A class action is a lawsuit which may span more than one jurisdiction, commenced on behalf of an identifiable group of individuals who have similar claims against the same party. For example, a class action could be commenced by all former employees of a particular employer for failure to pay vacation pay correctly. In such a case, there is a representative plaintiff who commences the action and the action generally needs to be certified by the court as being appropriate for the class action process — i.e., the claims have commonality in that they raise common issues and the class action is the preferred procedure. A class action is sometimes known as a representative action. It is often described as being the most expeditious manner in which a large number of individuals can litigate relatively small claims. Claims based on employment standards are not always certified because the legislation sets out a quick and cost-effective complaint resolution procedure. The representative action has been used with some frequency in the United States, typically with respect to payment of wages and overtime claims. Starting around 2006, we have seen a significant increase in class actions by employees and former employees against employers in Canada. Many of these cases have been with respect to unpaid overtime pay or retiree benefits. A proposed class action must first be certified by a court. The **Ontario** courts have refused to certify a class action based on misclassification of front-line supervisors (non-exempt) as managerial (exempt) employees because of lack of commonality — i.e., there was a wide disparity in job functions among the proposed class members, depending on their job title, work location, size of workplace, and reporting relationship. The Court found that a judge would not be able to determine whether a front-line supervisor is managerial or non-managerial without hearing evidence of individual employees (*McCracken v. Canadian National Railway Company*, 2012 CLLC

¶210-041). On the other hand, more recently a "misclassification" case has been certified, involving over 1,600 investment advisors ("IAs") employed by an investment dealer in the province of Ontario. The employer has argued that the IAs are exempt from Ontario's overtime laws because their work is of a managerial character and because an IA's autonomy and potential for high earnings provides a greater right or benefit than the statutory overtime rules. The Court determined that the job functions of IAs are very similar across the province (*Rosen v. BMO Nesbitt Burns Inc.*, 2013 ONSC 2144). Two other high profile class actions claiming unpaid overtime pay have been certified where the claims were not based on misclassification. Instead, the claims were based on alleged breaches of contractual and statutory obligations to pay for overtime work that was allegedly required or permitted on a routine basis. The employer's overtime policies, which required managerial pre-approval, were also alleged to create barriers to claiming and receiving overtime pay: *Fresco v. Canadian Imperial Bank of Commerce* (2012 CLLC ¶210-040), involving 31,000 customer service staff claiming $600 million; *Fulawka v. Bank of Nova Scotia* (2012 CLLC ¶210-009), involving 5,000 front-line staff claiming $350 million. Leave to appeal was denied in both cases by the Supreme Court of Canada, March 2013.

INDIVIDUAL LIABILITY

Q. Can Individuals Be Held Liable for Employment Standards Amounts?

A. As noted above, a director, officer, or employee who directs a corporation to breach legislation may be found guilty of an offence and be punished by a fine. However, an individual would not normally be held personally liable for any amounts owing. The exception is in the case of directors on the board of directors of the corporation. Where recovery is not possible against the corporation (for example, due to insolvency), most legislation allows the government agency to pursue an action for recovery of wages and vacation pay (typically up to six months of pay) against the directors personally.

EMPLOYER COMPLIANCE

Q. What Can an Employer Do To Ensure That It Is Compliant with the Employment Standards Legislation?

A. The best thing to do is to periodically conduct a self-audit of the organization's payroll practices. Particular attention should be paid to compliance with the record-keeping requirements of the legislation, as the employment standards agencies often focus on compliance with record-keeping rules and, under some legislation, there are more significant penalties for failure to comply with the record-keeping requirements. For example, under the *Canada Labour Code*, where an employer breaches the requirement to maintain payroll records for 36 months, a fine of up to $100 per day may be levied.

In addition, do not ignore a complaint relating to employment standards by an employee. If an incorrect practice was applied to that employee, it was probably applied to a number of employees. It is far better to correct the situation than to wait for a complaint or lawsuit.

An employment standards audit should focus initially on the following hot spots which are frequently areas of non-compliance and risk for employers:

- accurate and complete records;

- written agreements, where required, for excess hours, compressed workweeks, averaging of hours;

- exemptions of job classifications from overtime pay requirements;

- compliance with overtime lieu time rules;

- rules for approval of overtime work;

- calculation of holiday pay where employees work on the day;

- proof of payment of vacation pay;

- calculation of vacation pay;

- use it or lose it (forfeiture) vacation policies should not conflict with legislation;

- use of US-style paid time off policies, which lead to issues because the breakdown for vacation and public holidays does not get accurately recorded; and

- drafting of employment agreements with severance provisions that inadvertently breach the legislation by calculating termination pay on the wrong basis such as on base wage only or (in certain jurisdictions) omissions of benefits or vacation pay.

The chart on the following page sets out key features of the statutory enforcement schemes.

STATUTORY ENFORCEMENT SCHEMES CHART

Jurisdiction	Orders To Pay by Officer/Inspector Following Investigation	Administrative Penalties	Prosecution (Fines Payable upon Conviction)
Federal	√	X	*Pending amendments included in parentheses.* Generally a fine of up to $5,000 (up to $50,000 for 1st offence/$100,000 for 2nd offence/$250,000 for subsequent offences). (Individuals may be fined up to $50,000.) Breach of group termination provisions fine of up to $100,000 ($250,000). Breach of record-keeping requirements or refusal to make records available, fine of $100 per day ($1,000 per day).
Alberta	√	Greater of $100 or 10% of the amount in the order to pay per employee.	Fine of up to $100,000. Fine of up to $50,000 for an individual.
British Columbia	√	Generally, a $500 fine. $2,500 fine for recurrence within 3 years. $10,000 fine for further recurrence within 3 years.	Prosecution provided for; penalty not prescribed. (Proposed legislation increases maximum fine to $50,000.)

Jurisdiction	Orders To Pay by Officer/Inspector Following Investigation	Administrative Penalties	Prosecution (Fines Payable upon Conviction)
Manitoba	√	Order to pay plus greater of $100 or 10% of the amount ordered, not exceeding $1,000. $500 administrative penalties prescribed for specific breaches of Act. $1,000 administrative penalty for breach of youth age limit restrictions.	Fine of up to $25,000. Fine of up to $5,000 for an individual. Additional fines for subsequent offences and/or imprisonment up to 3 months.
New Brunswick	√	Labour and Employment Board can order penalties of up to $1,000 per day in case of continuing refusal to comply with an order.	Fine of $240 to $10,200 per day.
Newfoundland and Labrador	√	X (can be ordered to pay expenses, which are not stipulated).	General offence for breach of Act, fine of $100 to $2,000, and imprisonment up to 3 months if payment is not made. Specific and additional fines for acts of reprisal or failure to comply with an order.
Nova Scotia	√	X	Fine of up to $25,000. Fine of up to $5,000 for an individual. Additional fines for subsequent offences or imprisonment up to 3 months.

Jurisdiction	Orders To Pay by Officer/Inspector Following Investigation	Administrative Penalties	Prosecution (Fines Payable upon Conviction)
Ontario	√	Greater of $100 or 10% of the wages owing under the order. Also prescribed penalties for breaches of specific sections of Act, ranging from $250 for a first offence to $1,000 for subsequent offences per employee.	Fine of up to $100,000; up to $500,000 for subsequent contraventions. Fine of up to $50,000 for an individual and/or imprisonment of up to 12 months. Fines of $4,000 per day where failure to comply with order in connection with reprisal complaints ($2,000 per day for individuals).
Prince Edward Island	√	X	Fine of $200 to $10,000.
Quebec	√	Where Commission pays out wages owing to an employee due to delay by employer can charge 20% penalty.	Fines of $600 to $1,200; fines for subsequent offences up to $6,000. Fine of $1,500 per week for failure to provide collective dismissal notice to Minister.
Saskatchewan	√	Fee of 10% of amount of wages assessed to a maximum of $500, with a minimum fee of $100.	*Pending amendments included in parentheses.* Fine of up to $2,000 ($10,000). Fine of up to $10,000 ($50,000) for subsequent offences.
Northwest Territories	√	X	Fine of up to $100,000. Fine up to $50,000 and/or imprisonment up to 1 year for individual.

Jurisdiction	Orders To Pay by Officer/Inspector Following Investigation	Administrative Penalties	Prosecution (Fines Payable upon Conviction)
Nunavut	√	X	Fine of up to $10,000 and/or imprisonment up to 1 year.
Yukon	√	$500 penalty for breach of certain record-keeping requirements.	Fine of up to $10,000.

Fine of up to $10,000 and/or imprisonment for up to 3 months for individual.

Penalty of 10% of wages owing in event of conviction. |

GOVERNMENT ADDRESSES AND INTERNET SITES

EMPLOYMENT STANDARDS OFFICES

NOTE: Regional Offices (if any) are listed on the websites.

Human Resources and Skills Development Canada
290 Dupuis Street, 4th Floor
Ottawa, Ontario
K1A 0J2
Phone: 1-800-641-4049
Fax: (613) 946-2827
www.hrsdc.gc.ca/eng/labour/index.shtml

Alberta Employment Immigration and Industry
Sterling Place, Main Floor
9940 – 106 Street
Edmonton, Alberta
T5K 2N2
Phone: (780) 427-3731 (Edmonton)
Toll-free: 1-877-427-3731
www.humanservices.alberta.ca/working-in-alberta/1224.html

British Columbia Ministry of Labour and Citizens' Services
P.O. Box 9570, Stn Prov Govt
Victoria, British Columbia
V8W 9K1
Phone: (250) 612-4100
Toll-free: 1-800-663-3316 (in British Columbia)
Fax: (250) 356-1886
www.labour.gov.bc.ca/esb

Manitoba Labour and Immigration
401 York Avenue, Room 604
Winnipeg, Manitoba
R3C 0P8
Phone: (204) 945-3352
Toll-free: 1-800-821-4307
Fax: (204) 948-3046
www.gov.mb.ca/labour/standards

New Brunswick Department of Post-Secondary Education, Training and Labour
470 York Street
P.O. Box 6000
Fredericton, New Brunswick
E3B 5H1
Phone: (506) 453-2725
Toll-free: 1-888-452-2687
Fax: (506) 453-3806
www2.gnb.ca/content/gnb/en/departments/post-secondary_education_training_and_labour.html

Newfoundland and Labrador Labour Standards Division
Labour Standards Division
Beothuck Building, 3rd Floor
20 Crosbie Place
P.O. Box 8700
St. John's, Newfoundland
A1B 4J6
Phone: (709) 729-2715
Toll-free: 1-877-563-1063
Fax: (709) 729-3528
www.gov.nl.ca/lra/agency/contact.html

Nova Scotia Department of Labour and Advanced Education
Labour and Advanced Education
Duke Tower
5151 Duke Street, 8th Floor
Halifax, Nova Scotia
B3J 1P3
Phone: (902) 424-6991
Toll-Free: 1-877-223-0888
Fax: (902) 424-2037
www.gov.ns.ca/lwd/employmentworkplaces/

Ontario Ministry of Labour
400 University Avenue, 9th Floor
Toronto, Ontario
M7A 1T7
Phone: (416) 326-7160
Toll-free: 1-800-531-5551 (Canada-wide)
Fax: (416) 326-7061
www.labour.gov.on.ca/english/es/

Prince Edward Island Department of Environment, Labour and Justice
Jones Building, 2nd Floor
11 Kent Street
P.O. Box 2000
Charlottetown, Prince Edward Island
C1A 7N8
Phone: (902) 620-3777
Toll-free: 1-800-237-5021 (in Prince Edward Island)
Fax: (902) 368-5476
www.gov.pe.ca/labour/index.php3?number=1004723&lang=E

Quebec Commission des normes du travail
Hall Est, 7e étage
400, boulevard Jean Lesage
Quebec, Quebec
G1K 8W1
Phone: (418) 644-0817
Toll-free: 1-800-265-1414
Fax: (418) 643-5132
www.cnt.gouv.qc.ca

Saskatchewan Labour Standards
1870 Albert Street, 3rd Floor
Regina, Saskatchewan
S4P 4W1
Phone: (306) 787-2438
Toll-free: 1-800-667-1783
Fax: (306) 787-4780
www.lrws.gov.sk.ca/labour-standards

Northwest Territories Education,
Department of Education, Culture and Employment
Nova Plaza, 1st Floor
5019 – 52nd Street
P.O. Box 1320
Yellowknife, Northwest Territories
X1A 2L9
Phone: (867) 873-7486
Toll-free: 1-888-700-5707 (Canada-wide)
Fax: (867) 873-0483
www.ece.gov.nt.ca/advanced-education/employment-standards

Nunavut Labour Standards Board
Labour Standards Compliance Office
P.O. Box 1269
Iqaluit, Nunavut
X0A 0H0
Phone: (867) 975-6159
Fax: (867) 975-6376
www.justice.gov.nu.ca/apps/authoring/dspPage.aspx?page=boards

Yukon Department of Community Service
Box 2703 (C-7)
Whitehorse, Yukon
Y1A 2C6
Phone: (867) 667-5944
Toll-free: 1-800-661-0408, ext. 5944 (in Yukon)
Fax: (867) 393-6317
www.community.gov.yk.ca/les.html;

HUMAN RIGHTS OFFICES

Canadian Human Rights Commission
344 Slater Street, 8th Floor
Ottawa, Ontario
K1A 1E1
Phone: (613) 995-1151
Toll-free: 1-888-214-1090
TTY: 1-888-643-3304
Fax: (613) 996-9661
www.chrc-ccdp.ca

Alberta Human Rights and Citizenship Commission
Northern Regional Office
800 Standard Life Centre
10405 Jasper Avenue
Edmonton, Alberta
T5J 4R7
Phone: (780) 427-7661
Fax: (780) 427-6013
Southern Regional Office
200 J.J. Bowlen Building, Main Floor
620 – 7 Avenue SW
Calgary, Alberta
T2P 0Y8
Phone: (403) 297-6571
Fax: (403) 297-6567
www.albertahumanrights.ab.ca

British Columbia Human Rights Tribunal
1170 – 605 Robson Street
Vancouver, British Columbia
V6B 5J3
Phone: (604) 775-2000
Toll-free: 1-888-440-8844 (in British Columbia)
TTY: (604) 775-2021
Fax: (604) 775-2020
www.bchrt.bc.ca/

Manitoba Human Rights Commission
700 – 175 Hargrave Street
Winnipeg, Manitoba
R3C 3R8
Phone: (204) 945-3007
Toll-free: 1-888-884-8681
TTY: 1-888-897-2811
Fax: (204) 945-1292
www.gov.mb.ca/hrc/

New Brunswick Human Rights Commission
Barry House
P.O. Box 6000
Fredericton, New Brunswick
E3B 5H1
Phone: (506) 453-2301
Fax: (506) 453-2653
TTY: (506) 453-2911
www.gnb.ca/hrc-cdp/index-e.asp

Newfoundland and Labrador Human Rights Commission
The Beothuk Building
21 Crosbie Place
P.O. Box 8700
St. John's, Newfoundland
A1B 4J6
Phone: (709) 729-2709
Toll-free: 1-800-563-5808
Fax: (709) 729-0790
www.justice.gov.nl.ca/hrc/index.html

Nova Scotia Human Rights Commission
Joseph Howe Building, 6th Floor
1690 Hollis Street
P.O. Box 2221
Halifax, Nova Scotia
B3J 3C4
Phone: (902) 424-4111
Toll-free: 1-877-269-7699 (in Nova Scotia)
Fax: (902) 424-0596
http://humanrights.gov.ns.ca/

Ontario Human Rights Commission
180 Dundas Street West, Suite 900
Toronto, Ontario
M7A 2R9
Phone: (416) 326-9511
Toll-free: 1-800-387-9080
TTY (local): (416) 326-0603
TTY (toll-free): 1-800-308-5561
www.ohrc.on.ca/en

Prince Edward Island Human Rights Commission
P.O. Box 2000
Charlottetown, Prince Edward Island
C1A 7N8
Phone: (902) 368-4180
Toll-free: 1-800-237-5031 (in Prince Edward Island)
Fax: (902) 368-4236
www.gov.pe.ca/humanrights

Quebec Commission des droits de la personne et des droits de la jeunesse
360 Saint-Jacques Street, 2nd Floor
Montreal, Quebec
H2Y 1P5
Phone: (514) 873-5146
Toll-free: 1-800-361-6477
TTY: (514) 873-2648
Fax: (514) 873-6032
www2.cdpdj.qc.ca

Saskatchewan Human Rights Commission
1942 Hamilton Street
Suite 301
Regina, Saskatchewan
S4P 2C5
Phone: (306) 787-2530
Fax: (306) 787-0454
Toll-free: 1-800-667-8577
www.shrc.gov.sk.ca/

Northwest Territories Human Rights Commission
P.O. Box 1860
Yellowknife, Northwest Territories
X1A 2P4
Phone: (867) 669-5575
Toll-free: 1-888-669-5575
Fax: (867) 873-0357
www.nwthumanrights.ca/

Nunavut Human Rights Tribunal
P.O. Box 15
Coral Harbour, Nunavut
X0C 0C0
Phone: (867) 925-8447
Toll-free: 1-866-413-6478
Fax: 1-888-220-1011
www.nhrt.ca/splash.html

Yukon Human Rights Commission
101 – 9010 Quartz Road
Whitehorse, Yukon
Y1A 2Z5
Phone: (867) 667-6226
Toll-free: 1-800-661-0535
Fax: (867) 667-2662
www.yhrc.yk.ca/

TOPICAL INDEX

Page

A

Accommodation
. defined....................................189
. examples..................................190
. how much must employer provide...... 190
. responsibility for..........................190
. undue hardship...........................190

Addresses
. government offices and Internet
   sites......................................249

Adoption leave
. benefits, eligibility.......................101
. parental leave.............................78

Affirmative action programs
. legislative provisions.....................192

B

Bereavement leave
. length of time.............................83
. requirements..............................83

Bona fide occupational requirement (BFOR)
. definition..................................189
. determination.............................189

Breaks — see Rest periods

C

Call-in pay
. cancellation of work.......................24
. circumstances beyond employer
   control...................................24
. coverage...................................22
. definition..................................22
. entitlement...............................23
. exemptions................................22
. exemptions from protection..............24
. rate.......................................23

Charts
. compassionate care leave benefits...... 107
. employment standards
   enforcement schemes....................244

Page

Charts — continued
. hours of work.............................39
. human rights
. . limitation period for filing
   complaint................................200
. . prohibited grounds of
   discrimination..........................199
. maternity/parental leave.................111
. minimum age
. . jurisdictions............................15
. . requirements and restrictions
   under minimum..........................16
. minimum wage
. . age-based and experience-based........26
. . regular rates............................25
. overtime pay..............................41
. pay equity at a glance....................224
. payment of wages.........................125
. personnel records........................133
. reservist leave............................99
. statement of wages.......................127
. statutory holidays
. . by jurisdiction...........................51
. . entitlement..............................52
. termination of employment
. . group termination requirements........165
. . individual termination notice
   requirements............................162
. . payment of wages.......................167
. vacationable earnings inclusion..........68
. vacations
. . entitlement..............................65
. . pay requirements........................65

Checklist
. employee/independent contractor
   status...................................11
. harassment
. . creating harassment-free
   workplace................................207
. . dealing with.............................209
. . establishing policy.....................208
. maternity leave...........................110

Page

Child care leave — see Parental leave

Citizenship ceremony, unpaid leave
. Manitoba......95
. Nova Scotia......95
. Saskatchewan......96

Civic holiday — see Statutory holidays

Class action
. defined......241

Collective agreements
. effect on reasonable notice......177
. effect on termination
. . Alberta......160
. . British Columbia......160
. . federal......160
. . Manitoba......161
. . New Brunswick......161
. . Newfoundland and Labrador......161
. . Nova Scotia......161
. . Ontario......161
. . Prince Edward Island......161
. . Quebec......161
. . Yukon......161
. relationship with employment
standards laws......10

Collective dismissals — see Layoffs;
Termination of employment

Common law
. employment relationship......9
. redress for wrongful dismissal at......170

Compassionate care leave
. benefits
. . care for a family member after
receiving maternity/parental/sick
benefits......108
. . defined......106
. . family member chart......107
. . family member described......106
. . maximum benefit......106
. entitlement......97

Compressed work week
. hours of work......31

Contractor
. determination......11

Crime-related death or disappearance of
child leave
. Employment Insurance benefits......108
. federal......89
. Manitoba......90
. Nova Scotia......91
. Ontario......92

Page

Crime-related death or disappearance of
child leave — continued
. Quebec......93
. Yukon......94

Criminal offence
. eligibility for leave for injury
resulting from, in Quebec......90

Critical illness of child leave
. Employment Insurance
benefits......104; 108
. federal......89
. Manitoba......90
. Nova Scotia......91
. Ontario......92
. Yukon......94

D

Days of rest
. employer to accommodate
employees' religious beliefs......35

Deductions from pay
. employee consent......113
. legal deductions......121
. room and board......22
. uniforms and special clothing......23

Definitions
. annual wage......61
. *bona fide* occupational
requirement......189
. class action......241
. contractor......11
. discrimination......181
. employees......3
. employment equity......228
. equal pay......214
. group termination......153
. harassment......202
. job class, pay equity......218
. labour jurisdictions......5
. maternity leave......73
. overtime......35
. pay equity......216
. severance pay......149
. sexual harassment......204
. statutory holidays......44
. undue hardship......190
. work week......29

Directors' liability
. payment of wages......123

Disappearance of a minor — see Leaves
of absence

Page

Discrimination — see also Harassment; Human rights
. accommodation
. . employer's responsibility...................... 190
. . examples... 190
. *bona fide* occupational
requirement.. 189
. charts
. . limitation period for filing
complaint... 200
. . prohibited grounds.............................. 199
. compensation and benefits.................. 187
. complaint
. . employer's response............................ 195
. consequences... 181
. definition... 181
. employees
. . protected from..................................... 185
. . unable to perform essential
duties of job..................................... 188
. enforcement
. . complaints.. 193
. . liability.. 194
. . remedies.. 194
. . reprisal... 193
. exceptions
. . affirmative action programs.............. 192
. . customer preference........................... 192
. . exemptions... 191
. . medical and personal needs.............. 192
. . special-interest organizations............. 191
. hostile work environment...................... 187
. mandatory retirement............................ 188
. prevention.. 197
. prohibited grounds................................. 184
. recruitment and selection
. . advertisements................................... 185
. . application forms................................. 185
. . employment agencies......................... 186
. . hiring criteria....................................... 186
. . interviews... 186
. responsibility for..................................... 194
. termination of employment.................. 188
. time limit for complaint......................... 194
. trade unions
. . accommodation................................... 193
. . party to discriminatory practices....... 192
. . role of.. 192
. training and promotion
opportunities.................................... 187
. types classified....................................... 183

Page

Discrimination — continued
. undue hardship
. . cost... 191
. . definition.. 190
. . health and safety issues..................... 191
. unintentional... 183

Dismissal — see Termination of employment; Wrongful dismissal

E

Elections — see Voting, time off

Emergency leave
. time off.. 88

Employees
. definition... 3
. exemptions... 10
. fourfold test.. 3; 11
. giving notice for terminating
employment
. . minimum notice.................................. 150
. . reasonable... 177
. . requirements....................................... 150
. involvement with pay equity................. 223
. minimum wage — see Minimum wage
. obligation to provide reasonable
notice.. 177
. part-time, entitlement to statutory
holidays.. 45
. pregnant, health threatened
by work.. 82
. protection of privacy............................. 129
. provision of information to.................... 132
. volunteers and interns.............................. 5

Employers
. accommodation of employees
with disabilities
. . defined.. 190
. . examples... 190
. . exceptions... 191
. . how much must employer
provide.. 191
. . responsibility for................................. 190
. . undue hardship................................... 190
. compliance with employment
standards legislation......................... 242
. defence against employment
standards violation............................ 239
. discrimination
. . prevention.. 197
. . response.. 195

Page

Employment
. beyond fixed term..................................147
. company mergers, acquisitions..............10
. contractor, defined...............................11
. hostile work environment.....................189
. minimum age.......................................13
. relationship
. . defined...2
. . laws governing...................................8
. severance of....................................149

Employment contracts
. conflict with employment law
    requirements...10
. definition...9
. fixed-term contracts, notice of
    termination...176
. relationship with employment
    standards law...9

Employment equity
. definition...228
. employment equity plan
. . contents...233
. . numerical goal....................................233
. employment systems
. . evaluation...233
. . review..232
. enforcement...234
. . federal...229
. . Quebec..229
. implementing.......................................230
. introduction...227
. legislative requirements........................229
. relation to human rights
    legislation...228
. survey..231
. time limit for plan................................234

Employment Insurance
. benefits during leave of absence
. . entitlement..104
. . working while collecting.....................109
. chart, maternity/parental leave............111
. child care benefits
. . eligibility..105
. . hospitalization of child........................105
. . length..105
. . maximum benefits..............................105
. crime-related death or
    disappearance of child
. . benefits...108
. critical illness of child benefits............108
. how to apply for benefits.....................109

Page

Employment Insurance — continued
. maternity/parental benefits
. . chart...111
. . eligibility...105
. . sick benefits, combined......................106

Employment standards
. employer compliance............................232
. enforcement...238
. . overview...244

Employment Standards Branches
. government offices and Internet
    sites...245

Employment standards violation
. class action...241
. complaint
. . defences available to employer..........239
. . involvement of the courts..................240
. . powers of investigating officer..........239
. . process..238
. . where not resolved through
    investigation.......................................239
. individual liability..................................242

Equal pay — see also Pay equity
. complaints by men................................215
. definition...214
. differing from pay equity......................216
. enforcement...215
. exceptions..215
. mandatory..214
. reductions in pay rates prohibited........215
. relation to pay equity............................216
. similar or substantially
    similar work..214

G

General holidays — see Statutory
    holidays

Group termination — see Termination of
    employment

H

Harassment — see also Discrimination;
    Human rights
. anti-harassment policy
. . checklist for creating policy...............208
. . checklist for harassment-free
    workplace...207
. . employers' obligation.........................206
. . what it should contain.......................208
. co-workers..203

Page

Harassment — continued
. dealing with
. . complaints..................................210
. . investigation............................210
. . reprisal.....................................210
. . request to stop......................... 208
. definition......................................202
. developing anti-harassment
    policy checklist........................ 208
. employer responsibilities......................206
. human rights bodies, role.................. 210
. jokes.. 203
. liability..206
. off-site.. 204
. options when employer won't help......209
. prevention....................................206
. prohibited grounds............................203
. psychological....................................205
. remedies....................................... 211
. sexual harassment
. . definition.................................. 204
. . office romance........................... 205
. . types of behaviour.......................204
. single incident............................. 196
. types of behaviour............................ 203
. unintentional................................ 203
. violence in the workplace.................... 206

Health and safety benefits for pregnant
    employees
. health threatened by work...................... 82
. time off for medical exams.................... 82

Hours of work
. averaging...................................... 30
. chart... 39
. communication of...............................32
. compressed work week.......................... 31
. emergency work................................ 30
. enforcement....................................32
. exceeding...................................... 29
. exemptions.................................... 30
. limits on...................................... 28
. maximum hours........................28; 39
. overtime.............................28; 32
. permits.. 31
. rest periods — see Rest periods
. shift work...................................... 34
. split shifts.....................................34
. standard hours
. . application..................................29
. . limits......................................28
. statutory holidays, effect of.................... 31

Page

Hours of work — continued
. waiting for work to be assigned.............28
. work week...................................... 30
. young workers................................14

Human rights — see also Discrimination;
    Harassment
. coverage.. 9
. human rights bodies, remedies............ 194
. protection against discrimination........ 185
. relation to employment equity............ 228

Human Rights Commissions
. government offices and Internet
    sites.. 252

I

Interns
. as employees.................................... 5

J

Jurisdiction
. application..................................6; 7
. defined..5

Jury duty
. employer to grant time off..................... 96

L

Labour relations
. avoiding possible disputes........................ 4

Layoffs — see also Severance pay;
    Termination of employment
. Alberta....................................... 157
. British Columbia.............................. 158
. federal....................................... 157
. introduction.................................. 156
. Manitoba......................................158
. New Brunswick............................... 158
. Newfoundland and Labrador............... 158
. Northwest Territories......................... 160
. Nova Scotia................................... 159
. Nunavut...................................... 160
. Ontario...................................... 159
. Prince Edward Island.......................... 159
. Quebec..159
. Saskatchewan................................. 159
. Yukon...................................160; 161

Leave to care for dying family member —
    see Compassionate care leave;
    Leaves of absence

Leaves of absence
. bereavement..................................... 83–86

Page

Leaves of absence — continued
. citizenship ceremony
. . Manitoba... 95
. . Nova Scotia... 95
. . Saskatchewan....................................... 96
. criminal injuries
. . Quebec.. 93
. crime-related death or
    disappearance of child leave
. . federal... 89
. . Manitoba... 90
. . Nova Scotia... 91
. . Ontario.. 92
. . Quebec.. 93
. . Saskatchewan....................................... 93
. . Yukon.. 94
. critical illness of child leave
. . federal... 89
. . Manitoba... 90
. . Nova Scotia... 91
. . Ontario.. 92
. . Quebec.. 93
. . Saskatchewan....................................... 93
. . Yukon.. 94
. emergency leave..................................... 88
. Employment Insurance
. . benefits entitlement............................ 104
. . working while collecting..................... 109
. family responsibility................................ 89
. illness or injury....................................... 87
. jury duty
. . employer to grant time off................... 96
. maternity.. 73
. organ donation
. . Manitoba... 94
. . Ontario.. 94
. . Quebec.. 94
. . Saskatchewan....................................... 94
. parental.. 77
. service in Canadian Forces
. . entitlement... 98
. . reservist leave chart............................. 99
. special occasions, Quebec...................... 93
. suicide of family member, Quebec......... 93
. voting
. . federal election..................................... 96
. . municipal election................................. 96
. . provincial election................................. 96
. . territorial election................................. 96

Page

M

Maternity leave — see also **Parental
    leave**
. benefits
. . accrual of.. 81
. . chart, Employment Insurance
      benefits... 111
. checklist.. 110
. defined... 73
. eligibility.. 74
. employer discontinuing business
    while employee away........................... 82
. employer's refusal to grant.................... 82
. Employment Insurance
. . entitlement to benefits........................ 105
. . parental benefits also available......... 106
. extensions.. 76
. involuntary.. 76
. job security.. 81
. length of.. 75
. miscarriage.. 75
. notice requirements................................ 74
. parental leave prohibited........................ 78
. part-time employees............................... 74
. qualifying period..................................... 74
. reprisal for requesting............................ 82
. return to work... 77
. seniority... 81
. timing... 75; 76
. vacation entitlement, effect of.........60; 81

Minimum age
. chart
. . jurisdictions.. 15
. . requirements and restrictions
      under minimum.................................... 16
. exceptions.. 14
. legal requirements.................................. 14
. restrictions.. 13; 14

Minimum wage
. calculation.. 21
. chart
. . age-based and experience-based........ 26
. . regular rates... 25
. coverage... 20
. exceptions.. 22
. inexperienced workers............................ 20
. introduction.. 19
. non-entitlement...................................... 22
. non-hourly workers................................. 20
. room and board...................................... 22
. students... 20

Page

Minimum wage — continued
. tips and gratuities....................21
. uniforms and special clothing.................21

O

Organ donation leave of absence
. Manitoba......................94
. Ontario......................94
. Quebec......................94
. Saskatchewan...................94

Overtime
. averaging of hours, effect.................31; 35
. calculating pay in lieu of notice...........143
. chart......................41
. definition......................35
. exemptions.....................36
. rate......................35; 41
. requirement to work...................36
. statutory holidays, effect on
    calculation......................32
. time off in lieu......................36

P

Paid holidays — see Statutory holidays

Parental leave — see also Maternity leave
. adoption......................78
. benefits, accrual of....................81
. chart, Employment Insurance.............111
. definition......................77
. employer discontinuing business
    while employee away.................82
. employer's refusal to grant.................82
. Employment Insurance benefits
. . available to both parents..................106
. . qualifying for........................105
. entitlement......................77; 78
. extensions......................80
. hospitalized child......................79
. job security......................81
. length......................78
. notice requirements.................81
. reprisal......................82
. seniority......................81
. timing......................81
. vacation entitlement, effect of.........60; 81
. when maternity leave already taken......79

Part-time work
. general coverage......................9
. maternity leave......................74

Page

Part-time work — continued
. statutory holidays......................45
. vacations......................56

Pay equity — see also Equal pay
. chart......................224
. comparison methods
. . job to job......................220
. . proportional......................220
. . proxy......................220
. compensation calculation..................219
. compensation not to be reduced........222
. definition......................216
. differing from equal pay.....................216
. employee involvement......................223
. employers required to complete
    process......................217
. enforcement......................223
. gender predominance...................218
. job class
. . defined......................218
. . how value determined......................219
. job value......................219
. mandatory......................216
. pay equity process......................217
. phasing in adjustments......................222
. relation to equal pay......................216
. steps in achieving......................217
. where pay disparity acceptable...........220

Pay equity plan
. change in circumstances.....................221
. contents......................221
. maintaining......................221

Pay statements — see Statement of wages

Payment of wages
. absent employees......................120
. chart......................125
. deductions......................121
. directors' liability......................123
. enforcement
. . complaints......................122
. . limits on recovery......................124
. . powers of Director......................122
. frequency......................120
. introduction......................119
. methods of payment......................120
. pay periods......................121
. priority, compared to other
    creditors......................124
. upon termination......................121; 145

Page

Personnel records
. access to
. . employees.....................................132
. . government..................................130
. . third parties................................131
. chart..133
. electronic pay statements.................. 132
. information provided to employees..... 132
. length of retention........................ 130
. location of...................................130
. protection of privacy......................... 131
. required records............................ 129

Pregnancy leave — see Maternity leave

Pregnant employee
. health threatened by work.................... 83

Privacy legislation
. federal.. 131
. provincial.................................... 131

Psychological harassment
. legislation, other provinces................. 205
. Quebec legislation..........................205

Public holidays — see Statutory holidays

R

Reservist leave
. chart.. 99
. entitlement....................................98

Resignation
. coercion by employer........................153
. employer termination following...........152

Rest periods
. chart.. 39
. meal breaks
. . entitlement................................ 33
. . exceptions................................. 34
. . length......................................33
. . payment.................................... 34
. . work during............................... 34
. Sunday closings............................ 34
. weekly....................................... 32

S

Sale of business
. effect on employee rights..............10; 148

Severance pay
. calculation...................................149
. definition....................................149
. entitlement
. . federal...................................149

Page

Severance pay
. entitlement — continued
. . Ontario.................................... 149
. severance of employment................... 149

Sick leave benefits
. Employment Insurance
. . benefits....................................106
. . combined with parental and
      maternity benefits........................ 106
. entitlement to time off......................... 87
. family responsibility......................... 88

Statement of wages
. chart..127
. electronic.....................................132
. methods of provision..........................122
. requirements..................................121

Statutory holidays
. affecting standard hours of work...........31
. chart
. . entitlement................................ 52
. . jurisdiction.................................51
. civic holidays
. . jurisdictions having August 1
      holiday....................................45
. . not a statutory holiday.......................44
. continuous operations, special
      industries.................................49
. definition.....................................44
. entitlement
. . chart..52
. . employee................................... 45
. . part-time employee.......................... 45
. exemptions................................... 45
. falling during vacation time.................. 47
. jurisdiction
. . chart..51
. . having August 1 holiday...................... 45
. non-working days............................46
. part-time employees......................... 45
. payment for
. . calculation of..............................48
. . exceptions................................. 47
. . qualifying period.......................... 47
. . rate.. 48
. requirement to work..........................45
. substitution................................46; 51
. termination of employment................... 50
. third Monday in February,
      jurisdictions having............................45
. vacations, effect on.............................47

Page

Suicide
. family member, eligibility for
  leave, Quebec..93

Sunday closings — see Days of rest

T

**Termination of employment — see also
Wrongful dismissal**
. by employee
. . coercion by employer..........................153
. . employer termination following.........152
. . minimum notice not required............151
. . notice requirements............................150
. calculation of "normal" hours..............143
. calculation of vacation pay owing..........63
. charts
. . group termination requirements........165
. . individual termination notice
   requirements...................................162
. . payment of wages on
   termination......................................167
. collective agreements............................161
. employment after date of
  termination...146
. group termination
. . chart..165
. . definition...154
. . employees giving notice.....................156
. . employer planning committees.........156
. . exclusion from provisions..................156
. . notice requirements............................155
. . provinces having no provisions.........154
. . what constitutes..................................154
. introduction..138
. layoffs
. . Alberta..158
. . British Columbia..................................158
. . federal...157
. . Manitoba...158
. . New Brunswick....................................158
. . Newfoundland and Labrador..............158
. . Northwest Territories..........................160
. . Nova Scotia..159
. . Nunavut..160
. . Ontario..159
. . Prince Edward Island..........................159
. . Quebec..159
. . Saskatchewan......................................159
. . Yukon.. 160; 161
. notice
. . conditions of employment
   changed...144

Page

Termination of employment
. notice — continued
. . continuation of benefits......................144
. . entitlement to.......................................140
. . exclusion from......................................141
. . interruptions in employment,
   effect on..146
. . method of notification.........................143
. . minimum requirements.......................140
. . pay in lieu of................................. 140; 143
. overtime in calculation of pay in
  lieu of notice.......................................143
. payment of vacation pay.........................63
. payment of wages.........................121; 145
. sale of business, effect of.....................149
. severance pay
. . calculation...149
. . definition...149
. . federal...149
. . Ontario..149
. vacation
. . during notice period............................144
. . payment of outstanding
   vacation pay............................. 62; 145
. vacation not part of notice......................64

U

Undue hardship
. cost...191
. definition..190
. health and safety issues.........................191

**Unjust dismissal — see Wrongful
dismissal**

V

Vacation
. chart
. . entitlement...65
. . pay requirements...................................66
. . vacation able earnings..........................68
. division of..58
. exceptions...56
. length..56
. maternity and parental leave,
  effect of..60
. not part of termination notice................64
. notice of..58
. part-time employees.................................56
. postponement...59
. qualifying period.......................................57
. requirement to take..................................59

Page

Vacation — continued
. statutory holidays, effect of.............. 47; 60
. timing of..57

Vacation pay
. annual wage, definition........................... 61
. calculation...61
. inclusion...61
. salary deductions....................................62
. termination of employment
. . calculation of pay.................................. 62
. . outstanding pay....................................145
. . when to be paid..................................... 63
. time of payment.................................61; 62

Violence in the workplace
. protection of employees...................... 206

Volunteers
. as employees... 5

Voting, time off
. federal election...96
. municipal election....................................96
. provincial election....................................96
. territorial election.....................................96

W
Wage statements — see Statement of wages

Page

Work week
. compressed.. 31
. definition.. 29
. shortened... 35

Wrongful dismissal
. avoiding wrongful dismissal suit..........179
. common law..170
. constructive dismissal
. . avoiding suit.. 172
. . definition.. 172
. damages..177
. definition..170
. employees' rights.................................. 139
. just cause
. . condoning behaviour.......................... 173
. . grounds for dismissal.........................173
. . single incident...................................... 173
. reasonable notice
. . collective agreement, effect of..........177
. . employee obligations..........................177
. . factors in determining........................ 174
. . fixed-term contract employees..........176
. . pay in lieu..174
. . probationary employees....................176